The Night the Referee Hit Back

Also by Mike Silver

The Arc of Boxing: The Rise and Decline of the Sweet Science
Stars in the Ring: Jewish Champions in the Golden Age of Boxing

PRAISE FOR *THE NIGHT THE REFEREE HIT BACK*

"Mike Silver is the Sugar Ray Robinson of boxing writers—smooth, smart, powerful, and tough to beat. The good news is that you can step in the ring with him and not get hurt. Read this book. It's a gem."—**Jonathan Eig, author of** *Ali: A Life*

"Mike Silver is among the most knowledgeable boxing historians in the world. His interviews and observations in *The Night the Referee Hit Back* are both compelling and stimulating. Boxing has always given us plenty to write about, and Silver is right on it."—**Steve Farhood, boxing analyst for Showtime and member of the International Boxing Hall of Fame**

"For decades, boxing was an art. It was filled with great practitioners and an array of rogues. In this collection of essays by Mike Silver, the reader is given a rare insight to what made boxing such a popular sport while at the same time pointing out its many flaws. Like the great art critics throughout the ages, Silver has that rare ability to look at something he loves while remaining honest about its flaws. If you want to truly understand what made boxing great and why it no longer is, you can have no better guide than Mike Silver."—**Bobby Franklin, editor, BoxingOverBroadway.com**

"Mike Silver takes us on a journey through the history of boxing. He brings us inside places that no longer exist, and through his writing they suddenly come back to life. You can hear the rhythm of the speed bag and the thud, thud, thud of a heavybag. He gives a voice to the great fighters of yesteryear and compares them with the stars of today. Silver is unparalleled as a boxing historian, and his work on these pages illustrates exactly why."—**Bobby Cassidy,** *Newsday*

"Brilliant! Mike Silver's collection of essays and interviews in *The Night the Referee Hit Back* is informative and ceaselessly entertaining. He has the ear of a masterful writer, the keen eye of a critic, and the heart of an avid boxing fan. Silver might be the most perceptive and skillful sportswriter of our generation."—**Colleen Aycock, author of** *The Magnificent Max Baer: The Life of the Heavyweight Champion and Film Star*

"Anyone who comes to me with a boxing question, I reflexively redirect to Mike Silver, who to my mind is, pound for pound, the greatest authority on the subject. (And no one who's taken my advice has ever asked for a second suggestion!) This book is only further evidence of his expertise."—**David Margolick, author of** *Beyond Glory: Joe Louis vs. Max Schmeling, and a World on the Brink*

"This new book by Mike Silver does an amazing thing—at least it did to me. It brought a tear to my eye, a lump in the pit of my stomach, and a smile in my heart. This book has so much going for it—insight, knowledge, and wit are found on every page. Silver explores fighters and the colorful lives they lead. No one writes so thoroughly and accurately about boxing than Mike Silver."—**Peter Wood, member of the New Jersey Boxing Hall of Fame and author of** *A Clenched Fist: The Making of a Golden Gloves Champion*

"There was a time boxing was the biggest sport in this country, bigger than baseball. The great historian Mike Silver reminds us why in his latest book, *The Night the Referee Hit Back.* His stories punch, bob, weave and bang the body—but this time in a way that can touch your heart without cracking a rib."—**Teddy Atlas, Hall of Fame trainer and ESPN boxing analyst**

"Mike Silver's knowledge of boxing history is unparalleled, but what makes him so valuable to read is the insight he brings to the subject— whether he's demythologizing the Thrilla in Manila, putting Floyd Mayweather's achievements into critical perspective, or chronicling boxing's bygone golden age. Collecting some of his finest work over the years, *The Night the Referee Hit Back* is a Silver primer for the uninitiated and a treasure trove for the connoisseur. Opinionated but fair, unsentimental but compassionate, and restless in its desire to improve understanding of a misunderstood sport, Silver's work is essential for serious students of the fight game."—**Paul Beston, author** *of The Boxing Kings: When American Heavyweights Ruled the Ring*

"Mike Silver, perhaps boxing's most revered historian, carries cotton swabs and smelling salts. *The Night the Referee Hit Back,* a survey of his best writing, is a head-clearing reminder that boxing wasn't always such a mess, that it has the capability to be more than it is, that it should aspire to be more like it was. In this era of franchise champions and fading skill sets, Silver is here to stop the bleeding."—**Springs Toledo, author and essayist**

The Night the Referee Hit Back

Memorable Moments from the World of Boxing

Mike Silver

Rowman & Littlefield
Lanham • Boulder • New York • London

Published by Rowman & Littlefield
An imprint of The Rowman & Littlefield Publishing Group, Inc.
4501 Forbes Boulevard, Suite 200, Lanham, Maryland 20706
www.rowman.com

6 Tinworth Street, London SE11 5AL, United Kingdom

Grateful acknowledgment is made for permission to reprint the following:

Excerpt from *The Arc of Boxing: The Rise and Decline of the Sweet Science* by Mike Silver:
    pp. 156, 158–64. Copyright 2014 (2008) Mike Silver. Reprinted by permission of
    McFarland & Company, Inc., Box 611, Jefferson NC 28640 (www.mcfarlandbooks.
    com).
"'I Coulda Been a Contender'—Roger Donoghue: The Man Who Taught Brando How
    to Box," *The Ring*, August 1994.
"No Heart Shaped Boxes on This Valentine's Day," ESPN.com, February 14, 2003.
"Where Were You on the Night of March 8, 1971?" ESPN.com, March 8, 2003.

British Library Cataloguing in Publication Information Available

Library of Congress Cataloging-in-Publication Data

Names: Silver, Mike, author. | Rowman and Littlefield, Inc.
Title: The night the referee hit back : memorable moments from the world of
    boxing / Mike Silver ; [foreword by Teddy Atlas].
Other titles: Selections | Memorable moments from the world of boxing
Description: Lanham : Rowman & Littlefield Publishing Group, 2020. |
    Includes bibliographical references and index. | Summary: "This book is
    a collection of twenty-eight of the best articles on boxing by renowned
    boxing historian Mike Silver, looking back at some of the sport's most
    iconic moments. The essays are a colorful mix of hard-hitting exposés
    and light-hearted stories featuring legendary boxers Sugar Ray Robinson,
    Rocky Marciano, Muhammad Ali, and more"— Provided by publisher.
Identifiers: LCCN 2019041325 (print) | LCCN 2019041326 (ebook) | ISBN
    9781538136904 (Cloth : acid-free paper) | ISBN 9781538136911 (ePub)
Subjects: LCSH: Boxing—History. | Boxing—Social aspects—History. |
    Boxers (Sports)—Interviews. | Silver, Mike
Classification: LCC GV1121 .S55 2020 (print) | LCC GV1121 (ebook) | DDC
    796.83—dc23
LC record available at https://lccn.loc.gov/2019041325
LC ebook record available at https://lccn.loc.gov/2019041326

∞™ The paper used in this publication meets the minimum requirements of
American National Standard for Information Sciences—Permanence of Paper
for Printed Library Materials, ANSI/NISO Z39.48-1992.

For Penni and Bennett

CONTENTS

CONTENTS

FOREWORD
Teddy Atlas

Tom Cruise, Woody Allen, Denzel Washington, Jack Nicholson, Tom Brady, Michael Jordan. You might think I'm describing stars on the Oscars' red carpet. This scene is of celebrities attending a fight night at the Garden or Vegas. The geography is not the draw. The stars and nonstars in the audience have come, answering their own private siren to arms, and they will sit and watch, hoping to learn and perhaps be touched by what they see.

The boxing ring has been referred to as a chamber of truth, a giant CAT scan, that instead of showing torn cartilage, examines one's soul. To see what a man does when "the devil" knocks at the door. When the temptation comes to abandon what is noble, in exchange for what is easy. To be weak, or to be strong.

The business of boxing has these magical shows that take place in squared circles all across the country. And while the setting can change and the weight classes of the boxers vary, the goals are the same. To climb those three steps into the ring, and to always keep climbing. Whether in the large venues of New York or Vegas, or the small towns of the South and Midwest, where the crowds' attire is more casual, but the dreams and hopes of the combatants are the same. In the backwater towns where the purses are small, but the chance for redemption is still large.

So come and see, feel and hear their stories, of how they became, of where they started, of who they are. It is all here. Boxing historian Mike Silver has painted a picture, a montage of broken noses and scarred eyebrows, a kaleidoscope of what is good and special about these hard men and why the boxing business has existed for so long and why it must continue, so that we can always know that there are champions in this world.

PREFACE

During my teenage years, at the very beginning of my obsession with boxing, I trained in New York's fabled Stillman's Gym alongside established professionals. My old-school trainer drilled me in the proper way to throw a jab, how to stay balanced, and how to hit and avoid being hit. I learned to jump rope and punch the speed bag like a pro. But that was as far as I took it. A bad headache after one sparring session helped to convince me that becoming a professional boxer would not be a wise career choice. Nevertheless, I continued to train (sans sparring) and I never regretted the experience, because it helped me to better understand the people and the world I would eventually write about.

I also acquired a profound respect for what it takes to be successful in the toughest professional sport. From a purely athletic standpoint, boxing is unique in that it contains elements of every other sport. A world-class boxer must possess the stamina of a marathon runner, hand-eye coordination of a basketball player, accuracy of a pitcher, toughness of a football lineman, speed of a hockey player, balance of a dancer, and split-second timing of a bullfighter. And he must put all these attributes to work while his opponent is trying to hit him in the face and body with two glove-encased fists.

There is yet one more ingredient that every truly great boxer must possess. It can even make up for deficiencies in some of the above categories. Athletes in other professional sports who may or may not possess it can still achieve greatness without it—but not in boxing. No boxer can ascend to the mantle of greatness without possessing this quality. I am referring here to the *character* of the athlete, or as it is called in the boxing vernacular, "heart." One of the best definitions of "heart" as it applies to the boxer was written by journalist Pete Hamill in 1996: "We are not speaking here of simple courage. Any man who ties on the gloves and walks into the ring has a degree of courage. To say that a man had heart was a more complicated matter. The fighter with heart was willing to endure pain in order to inflict it. The fighter with heart accepted the cruel rules of the sport. He must not—could not—quit. He might be outclassed and outgunned but he never looked for an exit."[1]

Reading that definition, the first image that came to mind was former heavyweight champion Rocky Marciano and his dramatic title-winning effort against Jersey Joe Walcott in 1952. Marciano's persistent drive to stay the course despite fighting under extreme conditions is described in this book (chapter 13, "Foul Play in Philly"). That story is one of 28 (chosen from nearly 100) that I selected for this tome. Taken together, they are as varied, colorful, and multidimensional as the sport itself. The stories are a mix of old and new, happy and sad, dramatic and comedic, glamorous and absurd, spectacular and seamy. If that doesn't describe boxing's fascinating and exciting history in a nutshell, I don't know what does.

Here you will find chapter and verse glorifying and romanticizing boxing's legendary champions and iconic contests, while others expose the sport for its corruption, shoddy regulation, erosion of boxing skills, and the tragic physical toll it exacts from too many of its athletes.

For the purists among us, what is most alarming, from a safety standpoint, is the lack of defensive skills exhibited by the vast majority of today's boxers—that and the pervasive incompetence of referees, trainers, ringside physicians, and boxing officials. Such conditions contribute to making a dangerous contact sport even more dangerous (see chapters 17 and 18).

Unfortunately, there are only a handful of trainers today who are capable of teaching the finer points of boxing technique. Scores of qualified teacher-trainers left the sport in the 1950s and 1960s when hundreds of neighborhood arenas (boxing's farm system for developing new talent) were forced out of business, unable to compete with free televised fights airing almost every night of the week. With the number of arenas and gyms drastically reduced, and fewer young men becoming boxers, the ranks of quality trainers, many of whom had been active since the 1920s, continued to decline. Unable to earn a decent living, they were forced to leave the sport or retire. As a result, a decades-old oral tradition of trainers passing knowledge to a new generation became disrupted. In their absence, mistakes went uncorrected, important lessons were never taught, and valuable information was lost. Eventually the level of skills declined as mediocre fighters became mediocre trainers.

Bearing witness to all of the above are revealing and insightful interviews with five great boxers (four in the Hall of Fame and one who should be) whose combined careers total 630 professional fights from the 1930s to the 1970s (see chapters 19 to 23).

There used to be a television commercial in the mid-1980s advertising an automobile with the words "This is not your father's Oldsmobile." For those fans approaching middle age, the statement can apply to boxing as well, but with one caveat: This is not your *grandfather's* sport.

Boxing has changed in many ways from the time I saw my first professional bout in 1959, when it was still an important part of American popular culture. From the 1920s to the 1950s (a golden age for the sport) it rivaled baseball in popularity. Boxing still retains the power to attract international attention to an important contest, but those instances are few and far between.

A big part of the problem is boxing's confusing and chaotic title situation. At present there are about 100 world champions recognized by an assortment of competing self-appointed and self-serving "sanctioning organizations." Unlike other professional sports, boxing has never had a national commissioner. Yet for more than 60 years the industry was able to maintain a semblance of self-imposed regulation with regard to the orderly succession of champions. Even during periods of mob infestation that aspect of the sport was not disturbed, and especially as concerned the heavyweight championship. There were eight world champions for the eight traditional weight divisions and, fan or not, everyone knew the name of the one and only heavyweight champion of the world.

That began to change in the late 1970s when boxing's traditional infrastructure responsible for recognizing world champions and rating the "top ten" title challengers for each weight division was compromised.[2] Rising to powerful positions within the sport was an insidious cartel of rival promoters and an alphabet soup of quasi-official "sanctioning organizations" (WBC, WBA, IBF, WBO) that took it upon themselves to consolidate their authority by naming their own set of world champions and title contenders. Each group formed a symbiotic relationship with one of the major promoters, thereby solidifying their power within the sport but ending the ability to maintain an independent rating system free of a promoter's influence and his wallet. It soon became apparent that what was best for boxing and the boxers took a backseat to greed, stupidity, and arrogance. The boxing cartels were quick to add seven new (and unnecessary) weight divisions. They also created superfluous satellite titles (Super, Interim, Diamond, Emeritus, Franchise) all with the purpose of forcing the boxers to pay huge "sanctioning fees" every time they fought for an organization's title. Author Jim Brady puts the title situation in historical context: "In the 1950s, there were approximately 5,000 fighters worldwide. There were generally eight weight divisions, with one champion in each. That breaks down to one champ for every 625 boxers. Today, with just the major sanctioning bodies and not counting the whackos, you have about one 'world champion' for every sixty-nine pros. It's ridiculous."[3]

Entrenched within the sport for decades, it is highly improbable the sanctioning organizations will ever be removed or replaced. One is headquartered in Mexico (and ruled by the same family for more than 40 years); another is located in Panama. Professional football, baseball, basketball, and hockey would never tolerate the type of anarchy and confusion that is emblematic of the professional boxing scene today.

Since most of the champions are unknown even to hard-core fans, what drives interest in the sport today are the few marquee names that have established a following and can bring in the big dollars. The biggest draws are Floyd Mayweather Jr., Manny Pacquiao, and Canelo Alvarez. Back in the 1980s it was Roberto Duran, Sugar Ray Leonard, Marvin Hagler, Tommy Hearns, Alexis Arguello, Aaron Pryor, Salvatore Sanchez, and Julio Cesar Chavez. In the 1990s and early 2000s it was Oscar De La Hoya, Shane Mosley, Bernard Hopkins, Roy Jones Jr., Evander Holyfield, Lennox Lewis, and, of course, Mike Tyson.

But with the continuing Balkanization of the sport—and more alphabet champions and top contenders preferring to meet inferior opponents in order to avoid a loss—the most desirable matches are rarely made. There is no responsible centralized authority to force the best to meet the best in order to unify the titles and determine the one true champion. That is why it's doubtful the most desirable fight in 2019, a matchup between the two best welterweight champions—Errol Spence Jr. and Terence Crawford—will likely never take place while they are still in their prime, if at all.

For many older fans who remember a time before cable TV, when major contests featuring the best fighting the best were regularly broadcast over network television, their interest in the sport has become problematic. Having grown up in the Cassius Clay/Muhammad Ali era (1960s and 1970s), we watched with alarm the subsequent deterioration of the most famous athlete the world has ever known. Ali's condition made us all too aware of the terrible consequences of taking too many punches to the head (see chapter 3).

Watching today's boxers take so much unnecessary punishment provokes a measure of guilt and frustration on the rare occasion when I tune into a contemporary match, as if my merely observing it makes me complicit in the travesty. I think part of the pleasure I get from watching videos of classic fights from the 1910s to the 1970s is knowing these boxers will not have to take any more punishment. Budd Schulberg, who wrote the screenplay to *On the Waterfront* and authored one of the best books on boxing, *The Harder They Fall*, spoke for many fans to whom boxing has an obsessive appeal when he penned the following words in 1985:

> As much as I love boxing, I hate it, and as much as I hate it, I love it. Every sensitive aficionado of the sport must bring to it this ambivalence. For make no mistake about it, at its worst, professional boxing is a cruel sport, just as at its best, it is exhilarating, artistic and, yes, ennobling. A natural rivalry for the championship of the world between two gifted professionals, tuned to perfection, is in this opinion, a sporting event surpassing all others, from Super Bowls to Kentucky Derbies. . . . Two men parrying each other's blows and trying to box, think and will their way to victory make an exhilarating contest. One man beating on a defenseless opponent round after round makes it brutal and boring.
>
> Those who abhor the fight game see it as a brawl between two mindless brutes trying to bash in each other's skulls. And it is sadly true that a fight between two stiffs who are all muscle and no talent illustrates just what is base and heartless about boxing in general and maybe the human race.[4]

Love it, or hate it, the fact is that throughout its long history boxing has appealed to many people from all walks of life. Pugilism even drew the attention of the ancient world's greatest thinkers and philosophers. As their writings indicate, Plato, Socrates, and Aristotle considered the subject a worthy topic for discussion and analysis. Written accounts of Greek boxing matches that took place more than 2,000 years ago describe fighters ducking and slipping blows, and being "light of foot." In the following comment Plato's teacher, Socrates (ca. 470–399 BCE), muses about the superior fighting qualities of a properly trained boxer and asks, "Do you not suppose that a single boxer who is perfect in his art would easily be a match for two or more well-to-do gentlemen who are not boxers?"[5]

Notice that Socrates uses the word "art." He obviously had an appreciation for the finer points of the sweet science. Boxing would not

Face of a 2,000-year-old Hellenistic Greek sculpture of a boxer. The dented nose, facial injuries, and cauliflower ear reveal a veteran of many ring wars. *Photograph by Sol Korby*

have engaged the Greek philosophers and artists unless it also appealed to their intellect.

Then, as now, individual boxers have transcended the world of sport to impact the social and artistic culture from whence they came. As demonstrated by former heavyweight champions John L. Sullivan, Jack Johnson, Jack Dempsey, Joe Louis, and Muhammad Ali, boxing's capacity to simultaneously address issues involving history, ideology, violence, politics, gender, and race was possible as long as the sport remained a relevant part of the social fabric. No other sport can make that claim (see chapters 5 and 14).

Even people who have no interest in ever going to a boxing match have been intrigued by the sport's social history and the unusual lives of its participants. Is it any wonder that boxing has attracted a diverse range of artists, authors, sculptors, playwrights, and poets going back to the first written description of a boxing match in *The Iliad*, an epic poem written nearly 3,000 years ago and traditionally attributed to Homer?

In every era and in every country where it thrived, boxing has inspired artists, writers, and performers. Two recent examples are Marlon Brando and Woody Allen, whose connection to boxing makes an appearance in this book (see chapters 24 and 25, respectively). The movie industry has been particularly prolific. More than 500 boxing films have been made. That is more than all baseball, football, and basketball films combined.[6]

There have been hundreds of books written on the subject by some of the world's greatest authors, and the output of boxing literature has not diminished. In fact, there seems to be more books written about boxing than ever before. From Homer and Hemingway to Joyce Carol Oates, from Socrates and Scorsese to Sylvester Stallone, this ancient and primal mano a mano contest will always attract the artist and writer. The reasons for this are as eternal as the sport itself. For no matter the caliber of present and future talent as compared with the past, boxing's potential for pulse-stirring excitement, drama, pathos, and humor will always remain. And if there is nothing in the current scene to inspire the creative juices—not to worry. One can always revisit boxing's colorful and vibrant history for ideas and inspiration for a story or a book.

Speaking of stories, I've got a few of my own I'd like to share with you. . . .

ACKNOWLEDGMENTS

I am very grateful to my independent editor and agent Bonny V. Fetterman. Her expertise, guidance, and friendship were instrumental in bringing this book to fruition. I also want to thank Christen Karniski, acquisitions editor at Rowman & Littlefield, for her enthusiasm and belief in my project.

No matter how much you think you know about boxing, its history, and its science, there is always more to learn and discover. That is why I have always sought out the most knowledgeable experts in the field to augment the research and enhance the quality and integrity of my work. In that regard I have been very fortunate and thankful for the people that, over the years, I have met and come to know.

To Chuck Hasson, boxing historian and researcher extraordinaire, for his generosity and especially for sharing with me his voluminous archives on Jewish boxers, which helped me so much on my last book, *Stars in the Ring*. To Ray Arcel, Bill Goodman, Mike Capriano Jr., Tony Arnold, Willie Grunes, Vic Zimet, and Teddy Atlas—seven superb connoisseurs of the finer points of the sweet science whose wisdom and opinions are infused throughout this book. To my fellow boxing aficionados: Dan Cuoco, Bobby Franklin, Leroy Hassler, Erik Arnold, Terry Matzner, Mike Hunnicut, Ted Lidsky, J. J. Johnston, Tony Gee, Phil Guarneri, Paul Beston, Mitch Levin, Ken Burke, and Mike Wolf. May we continue to enjoy discussing, analyzing, and questioning the many and varied aspects of our shared passion.

ACKNOWLEDGMENTS

To Archie Moore, Emile Griffith, Carlos Ortiz, Ted Lowry, Curtis Cokes, and Roger Donoghue for consenting to be interviewed.

To Sol Korby, Steve Lott, Toby Weston Cone, Patrick Scholz, Dave Bergin, Herb Cohen, Jim Houlihan, the Dr. Theodore Atlas Foundation, and the Houghton Library, Harvard University, for their contribution of photos. To Laurent Duguet, grandnephew of Benny Valgar, for providing additional information on his uncle's life and career.

To Barry Young, Don Harwood, Iris Topel, Betty Gittman, Fran Radin, Karen Barth, and Sallie Kraus, whose sole interest in my project was to offer encouragement and see me succeed.

To Boxrec.com for the accurate records provided by that amazing website.

To BoxingOverBroadway.com and Boxing.com for publishing many of my articles, and to my fellow members of the International Boxing Research Organization who are always ready to help with a research question.

Finally, to my family. To Penni, Gail and Bennett, Stephanie and Doug, Carrie and Scott, Pamela and Michael, and Greg. Thanks to all of you for your love, support, and encouragement.

Part I

THE WAY IT WAS

I
BOXING IN OLDE NEW YORK: UNFORGETTABLE STILLMAN'S GYM

Once in a while, when a nostalgic mood strikes me, I walk over to the west side of New York's Eighth Avenue between 54th and 55th Streets and stare wistfully at the space now occupied by an apartment building. Perhaps you are thinking I am reminiscing about some long ago love affair. Well, in a sense I am. You see, for many years I was in love with the sport of boxing, and one of the major objects of my affection stood on this very site. I can still remember the address: 919 Eighth Avenue.

If you wanted to see some of the best professional boxers in the world up close and personal, Stillman's was the place to go. If you wanted to understand firsthand the attraction that boxing held for so many of us, you would get more than a taste of it at Stillman's. Whether you were a boxing fan or not the place made an indelible impression. The gym had an international reputation.

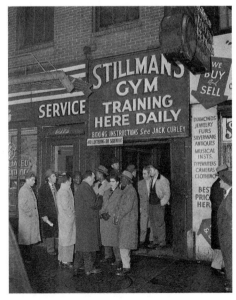

Entrance to Stillman's Gym, 1954. _The Stanley Weston Archive_

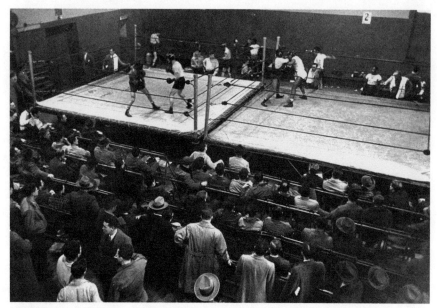

Main floor of Stillman's Gym, 1948. Getty/The Life Images Collection/Leonard McComb

Many tourists to the city considered it as important an attraction as the Empire State Building, Radio City Music Hall, or the Statue of Liberty. But don't bother trying to find anything like it today because you will search in vain. The unique confluence of circumstances that created and nurtured Stillman's Gym from the 1920s to the 1950s—a veritable golden age for the sport—no longer exists.

Background

For some 40 years, from 1921 to 1961, Stillman's Gym was an iconic presence in New York City. It is no coincidence that the life span of the world's most famous gymnasium coincided with boxing's golden age of talent and activity. Stillman's history, like that of New York City, was a product of the seismic social and economic changes that occurred when millions of mostly poor and uneducated immigrants from eastern and southern Europe came to America between 1881 and 1924.

At the turn of the last century, rapidly industrializing American cities presented the best opportunity for employment, so that is where a majority of the immigrants and their families settled. Of immediate concern was the need to find work. Although menial, low-paying jobs were available, having one was no guarantee of financial security. Four of every ten immigrant workers did not earn enough to support a family. By 1914 at least half the populations of major cities in the United States lived in poverty. Not surprisingly, the majority of these people were immigrants.[1]

There weren't many alternatives to working in a sweatshop or behind a pushcart. One alternative was to enter the world of show business. The flourishing vaudeville circuit employed thousands of people, many of whom were first- or second-generation immigrants. Another thriving industry with close ties to show business was professional boxing. Both show business and boxing were open to anyone regardless of race, religion, or ethnicity.

The first great wave of immigration (some 3 million strong) came to America from Ireland between 1846 and 1870. The Irish brought with them an athletic tradition that included boxing. They dominated the sport in America from the latter half of the 19th century to the 1910s.

Nudging and eventually replacing the Irish American boxers from their dominant position were Jewish and Italian boxers who derived from the second and much larger wave of 24 million immigrants mentioned earlier (a figure that included 4 million Italians and 2 million Jews).[2] This change in boxing's hierarchy was due not only to increased competition but also to improving employment opportunities for Irish American youth. As noted by historian Steven A. Riess, "The ethnic succession in the ring reflected the changing racial and ethnic complexion of the inner city as older ethnic groups who were doing better economically moved out and were replaced by the new urban poor."[3]

At the time there were only three professional sports of any significance in America—baseball, boxing, and horse racing. For the aspiring athlete, boxing was not only the most accessible professional sport, but it also offered the best opportunity to earn quick money. As a result, thousands of young men hardened by poverty and possessing street smarts and physical strength were motivated to test their mettle in the prize ring.

It was common knowledge that successful boxers were the highest-paid athletes in the world. In the 1920s, superstar boxers Mickey Walker, Benny Leonard, and Harry Greb were each taking in well over $100,000 in annual income—the equivalent of several million dollars in today's currency. In 1924 the highest-paid African American boxer in the sport was the popular heavyweight Harry Wills, who received $150,000 for his bout against the Argentine contender Luis Angel Firpo. The $80,000 annual salary paid to baseball great Babe Ruth in 1927 paled in comparison to the $1 million heavyweight champion Gene Tunney received for his title bout with Jack Dempsey that same year. Of course, not everyone could be a world champion or top contender, but even an ordinary preliminary boxer could make more money in one four-round bout than a sweatshop laborer made for an entire week.[4]

Yet the benefits to both the boxers and the ghetto communities that spawned them went beyond monetary rewards. Champions and title contenders, virtually all of whom came from ethnic minorities, were heroes in poor urban neighborhoods. They were a source of inspiration, pride, and hope to a population struggling to break free of poverty and gain acceptance into the social and economic mainstream. More than any other sport or activity, boxing became a symbol of the immigrants' struggle for status, assimilation, and a path to Americanization.

In the 1920s New York City, along with being the hub for commerce, communications, media, and theater, was also the world capital of boxing. Other cities could boast of great fighters and bustling competition, but New York had more of everything: fighters, trainers, promoters, managers, arenas, gymnasiums. It was not only home to the sport's most famous gymnasium, but it was also home to boxing's holy of holies—Madison Square Garden.

Boxing activity in New York State reached record levels during the Roaring Twenties. In 1925 the New York State Athletic Commission's annual report stated that 1,890 licensed professional boxers resided in the state—up from 1,654 the year before. Two years later, in 1927, that number had climbed to 2,000 licensed professionals with over half the boxers either Italian or Jewish.[5] (In 2016, only 107 licensed professional boxers resided in the state.)

It was into this environment that Stillman's Gym was born. Prior to its existence, the most widely known training facility in the city was Grupp's Gymnasium and Athletic Club, located at 116th Street and Eighth Avenue. An ex-fighter named Billy Grupp started the gym in 1915. Most of the city's top professional boxers trained there, including the great Jewish lightweight champion Benny Leonard.

Unfortunately, Billy Grupp had a drinking problem and when plastered would often launch into an anti-Semitic tirade blaming the Jews for World War I. This was not exactly good for business as many of the boxers who worked out in his gym happened to be Jewish. Fed up with the lush's behavior, Benny Leonard led a mass exodus of all the Jewish fighters to a new gym located a few blocks away that was operated by the Marshall Stillman movement. Two millionaire philanthropists had established the movement in 1919 to rehabilitate juvenile delinquents. The gymnasium was managed by a 32-year-old former police officer named Louis Ingber who was thrilled to have a famous world champion training in his facility. The fighters agreed to work out in the evenings (the juvenile delinquents used the gym in the afternoons).

When word got out that Benny Leonard was no longer training at Grupp's, the new gymnasium became a magnet for other boxers and trainers. Fans of Leonard began crowding into the gym to watch him train. Ingber saw a business opportunity and began charging admission to the spectators. But the small gym would only accommodate a limited number of people. So, two years later, in 1921, the owners moved the gym to much larger quarters at 919 Eighth Avenue. Lou Ingber continued to manage the new facility for the Marshall Stillman movement.

The new facility would be for the exclusive use of professional and amateur boxers. Unlike the previous location, they would be able to use it in the afternoons. The patrons at the new gym continued to call the manager "Mr. Stillman," thinking that was his name. Lou Ingber eventually tired of correcting everyone so he had his name legally changed to Lou Stillman.[6]

The Eighth Avenue location was perfect. It was in an exciting part of the city, near the Broadway theater district, and only four blocks north of Madison Square Garden. Of course Stillman's was not the only boxing gym in the city. The Pioneer Gym on West 44th Street was competitive with Stillman's for a time, but it closed its doors in 1942. Gleason's Gym opened in the Bronx in 1935. It was a fine facility, but most of its membership was confined to fighters who lived in that borough. Uptown, Grupp's was still around, but it had neither the charm nor charisma of Stillman's. There were other gyms as well, such as the Seward Gym on Hester Street, the St. Nicholas in midtown, and Beecher's in Brooklyn.

In addition to its great location, a big part of Stillman's appeal was the size and layout of the gym. It occupied the entire second and third floors of a three-story building. The main floor of the gym was two stories high and measured 140 by 65 feet. It was dominated by two elevated boxing rings placed side by side. In front of the rings were eight rows of wooden folding chairs meant for spectators. In a corner of the gym, near the entrance, was a small lunch counter (operated by Lou Stillman's brother, Larry Ingber) where sandwiches, coffee, tea, and snacks were sold. Boxing equipment was also for sale as was the sport's most important trade publication—*The Ring* magazine. The wall adjacent to the lunch counter featured dozens of framed photos of famous fighters.

On the far side of the rings, against the back wall, there was a narrow space where fighters sat on benches while they waited for their turn to spar. Against the opposite wall stood a row of four phone booths. A few feet from the phones a metal stairway led to a large balcony area that overlooked the floor below. This is where the speed bags and heavy punching bags were located. There was also plenty of room for shadowboxing and floor exercises. (For many years a third boxing ring was located on this floor, but it was removed in the 1950s.)

The space underneath the balcony housed the lockers and showers, in addition to 20 wooden cubicles that were big enough for each to contain a locker and massage table. These private dressing rooms were reserved for champions and top contenders.

In an open area between the last row of spectators' chairs and the wall that separated the main floor from the dressing rooms, matchmakers, managers, promoters, and kibitzers mixed and mingled as they conducted business and exchanged gossip.

Posted on a second-floor window, in large letters visible from the street, was the name of a champion or contender who was training that day. At any time one might see both active and former ring greats either training or just in for a visit. Some of the regulars included such legendary fighters as Jack Johnson, Jack Dempsey, Benny Leonard, Johnny Dundee, Tony Canzoneri, Henry Armstrong, Beau Jack, Kid Gavilan, Sandy Saddler, and Rocky Graziano.

Stillman's was open seven days a week. The busiest hours were from noon to 4:00 p.m. when the gym became a beehive of activity as an assortment of fighters of every size and ability, ranging from green amateurs to world champions, went through their training routines. During the 1940s gym dues were $5 per month. Admission for spectators was 15 cents in the 1920s and 1930s, 25 cents in the 1940s, and then 50 cents in the 1950s. Sometimes as many as 200 people would crowd into the gym to watch a famous fighter work out.

The Best Show in Town

During boxing's heyday, an afternoon at Stillman's provided one of the greatest shows in town. For little more than the price of a cup of coffee a fan could watch some of the world's best boxers prepare for an upcoming bout. There was also the chance to converse with a past ring great who might stop by to take in the action, evaluate the latest rising star, or simply reconnect to the fight crowd.

People of every background and economic stratum went to the fights. They also went to Stillman's. It was not unusual for spectators to rub shoulders with businessmen and blue-collar workers, writers and actors, gangsters and cabdrivers. Boxing writers for New York's ten daily newspapers were often in attendance, as were professional gamblers who were there to study the boxers training for a Garden main event and hoping to see something that might give them an edge. (For decades Stillman's was a place where rival elements of the underworld could meet under a flag of truce.)

According to Lou Stillman, the most popular attractions in the history of the gym were heavyweight champion Jack Dempsey and Georges Carpentier, the debonair Frenchman who fought the "Manassa Mauler," as Dempsey was known, for the title in 1921. But the fighter who drew the largest crowd was Primo Carnera, the six-foot-six, 270-pound Italian giant who was heavyweight champion from 1933 to 1934.[7]

"I had 1,800 people in here when Primo Carnera first came over from Italy," Stillman said. "The place is only supposed to hold 290 people. I took out all the seats and had them standing all over the place. Primo was ugly but he drew the women in."[8]

"When Carpentier was in training, the place was always crowded with Broadway chorus girls. When Carnera trained the gallery was packed with Italian women carrying their babies. I liked them better than the chorus girls, so I always let the babies in for free."[9]

Of course the world's most famous boxing gym, located in the world's greatest city, all but guaranteed that a host of "Runyonesque" characters would be on display including, not infrequently, Damon Runyon himself. One of those characters was the ever-present Lou Stillman, who had bought out the owners in the late twenties and became sole owner of the gym. Lou, a quintessential New Yorker, was right out of central casting.

Described as a "big, gruff, sour-dispositioned autocrat," Lou Stillman kept everyone in line by running his gym like a drill sergeant.[10] Perched on a high stool under a big clock located near one of the rings, Stillman would announce over the loudspeaker in his raspy voice which fighters were about to spar. In between announcements, or whenever he chose to, Stillman had the nasty habit of spitting on the floor of the gym.

A lot of the trainers, managers, and boxers who experienced Stillman's wrath would have liked to belt him, but they took his verbal abuse only because he held the key that opened the door to boxing's busiest and best training site. For example, the right kind of sparring is essential to a boxer's development. Due to the sheer number of boxers who regularly trained at Stillman's, a variety of sparring partners were readily available.

Although he'd never admit it, Stillman, on rare occasions, displayed a softer side. "Sure he was loud, but his heart was as big as his mouth," recalled George Palazzo, a fair lightweight boxer back in the 1920s.[11]

"Many's the time he let me wait a couple of months to pay my locker fee. He could tell when a guy had the shorts. A couple of times he slipped me a deuce when I needed it bad.

"I seen him do other things that showed he had a heart," added Palazzo. "Like with washed up fighters—some of them a little punchy. They'd come in and tell Lou they wanted to make a comeback. They'd ask if they could work out.

"Lou didn't throw them out. He'd tell them to start shadow boxing and skipping rope to get in shape. But he never let them get in the ring. Lou let them down as easy as he could."

In 1967, six years after the gym closed, and two years before his death at the age of 82, Stillman was interviewed by *The Ring* magazine's Ted Carroll, who expressed surprise that Lou still wore his famous grim facial expression. "How can you change something that's been part of you for forty years?" Stillman replied. "How long do you think a man with a happy face would have lasted in my old business, running a boxing gym?

Everybody called Stillman a grouch, a crab, a cranky guy who never smiled. Well that's what scared off the chiselers, moochers and deadbeats. A good-natured guy would have been played for the biggest sucker in the world."[12]

Stillman's gym appeared in two Hollywood movies: *Somebody Up There Likes Me* (1956), which depicted the life story of former middle-weight champion Rocky Graziano, and *The Naked City* (1948), a film shot entirely on the streets of New York. In the Graziano biography, character actor Matt Crowley portrayed Lou Stillman and did a good job capturing the acerbic gym owner's gruff exterior.

The Stillman's Experience

It's estimated that some 30,000 fighters and near fighters passed through Stillman's grimy but hallowed environs, including yours truly. In the fall of 1959 my father took this 14-year-old boxing fan to Stillman's Gym for lessons in the manly art of self-defense. Lou Stillman was no longer there, having retired a few months earlier after selling the building to a real estate syndicate. The gym remained open for two more years under the management of Irving Cohen, a prominent boxing manager.

I didn't know quite what to expect as I entered into a dimly lit hallway that led to a wide and steep wooden staircase. Twenty-one steps later I entered into a world I had never seen before and could not have imagined. I was as excited as a kid going to the circus for the first time.

Arriving on the second floor (the first floor of the gym), I went through a short corridor, past a man standing by a turnstile who collected the admission fee. My attention was immediately drawn to the two full-sized elevated boxing rings. Both added a dramatic touch to the main room. In front of the rings were several rows of wooden folding chairs that by the look of them could have been the same ones that were there when the gym first opened. The walls were in need of a fresh coat of paint, and the large windows on either side of the two rings appeared not to have been cleaned in years. But all that seemed just right. This was no sterile, chrome-and-mirrored fitness salon with a slew of fancy and expensive exercise apparatus. This was a boxing gym with character and history.

Walking into Stillman's was like entering a time warp. I felt like I had suddenly found myself in an old black-and-white movie. All of my senses were engaged in taking it all in. First there was the aroma of the place—a combination of liniment, stale cigar smoke, leather, and sweat. The place was alive with constant movement and motion. I didn't know where to look because wherever I looked there was something to watch: people walking around, fighters sparring in the two rings, others hitting the speed bags or jumping rope, doing calisthenics, or going up and down the metal staircase that led to the second level where the punching bags were located.

A cacophony of sounds echoed throughout the gym: the rhythmic *rat-a-tat-tat* of the speed bags; jump ropes slapping against the hardwood floor; the thump of leather-covered fists hitting the heavy bags, and, if hit hard enough, the jangling sound of the chains that bolted them to the ceiling; fighters snorting and grunting as they shadowboxed and threw punches at imaginary opponents; trainers giving advice and instruction; someone yelling out the name of a trainer or manager who was wanted on the phone. There was a distinct rhythm to it all. It was a symphony of movement and sound that is unique to a boxing gym. And then . . . just as swiftly as it began . . . the tumult would suddenly halt as the automatic bell rang, signaling the end of yet another three-minute round and the start of the one-minute rest period. Sixty seconds later the bell would ring to start another round and it would begin all over again.

If boxing had a voice, it would be the sound of Stillman's on a busy afternoon.

You could spend hours at Stillman's just looking at the interesting faces of some of the characters who always showed up. I had never seen so many dented noses in one place. Half the guys standing around, whether fighters, trainers, or managers, had mugs that could have filled the cast of a *Guys and Dolls* production. To quote Norma Desmond in the classic movie *Sunset Boulevard*: "They had faces then." (For whatever reasons, I have yet to see the same interesting faces in any of today's boxing gyms.)

Stillman's was a decidedly male enclave; I would rarely see women in the gym. But I do remember seeing a woman artist sketching a boxer working out on the heavy bag. I was told it was not uncommon for artists and photographers (male and female) to visit the gym looking for interesting subjects.

Fighters were not the only people worthy of attention and respect at Stillman's. Some of the gym's trainer-teachers were celebrities in their own right. By the late 1950s many of the original retinue that were there when the gym first opened had already retired or passed on, but there were still a few left from the old days whom I was privileged to meet. These "professors of pugilism" taught the art of boxing. As Ray Arcel, the great trainer who was present at the founding of the gym (at the time of my arrival he was on hiatus from boxing), put it: "Stillman's Gymnasium was a school; it was not a gym. You went there, you learned—you learned your lessons."[13]

Fortunately, Charley Goldman, the derby-wearing gnome-like master trainer, was still there, imparting his wisdom to a new generation of boxers. Goldman, himself a veteran of some 400 fights, was renowned for sculpting Rocky Marciano into an undefeated heavyweight champion. And little Whitey Bimstein, another famous trainer, was a constant presence in the gym, as were Freddie Brown, Chickie Ferrera, Jimmy August, Johnny Sullo, and Freddie Fierro.

On my first day in the gym I was introduced to "Hurricane" Jackson, once a top contender who fought Floyd Patterson for the heavyweight championship, and now a washed-up journeyman fighter attempting a comeback. No matter, he still rated a private dressing room.

On another memorable occasion I met Kid Norfolk, one of the greatest African American fighters to never win a title. Kid Norfolk (real name William Ward) had well over 100 fights and was a top-ranked light heavyweight contender in the 1910s and 1920s. During his Hall of Fame career he took on all comers, including several legendary wars with the great Harry Greb. Kid Norfolk (at the time in his mid-60s) was an impressive presence. He wore a long black overcoat and had on dark glasses. Standing ramrod straight, the former ring great projected an air of dignity and pride. He also appeared to be made out of steel. I had just started taking boxing lessons at Stillman's and my trainer, a strict old-school type named Willie Grunes, encouraged me to ask Kid Norfolk any question about boxing.

I tried to think of an intelligent question, and all I could come up with was "What is the most important thing in boxing?" Kid Norfolk put his left foot forward and raised his fists to affect the boxer's traditional "on guard" stance. Then, in sonorous deep tones, came the words: "Balance, son . . . balance!" It was an unforgettable moment.

Once Ingemar Johansson, the heavyweight champion of the world, made a surprise visit. Every spectator in the gym went upstairs to watch the very popular and charismatic Swede hit the heavy bag, shadowbox, and do calisthenics. I couldn't believe my luck. I was only a few feet from the heavyweight champion of the world!

I regularly worked out alongside other well-known boxers whom I often saw on the weekly nationally televised fights: Dick Tiger, Gaspar Ortega, Emile Griffith, Jorge Fernandez, Joey Archer, Rory Calhoun, Alex Miteff, Ike Chestnut, and others. Is there any other professional sport where a fan can get so close to its stars? This was the magic and allure of Stillman's, and I thank my lucky stars I was able to experience it.

End of an Era

By the time I got to Stillman's, boxing had already begun its long, gradual decline, a decline that was exacerbated by a combination of internal corruption, misuse of television, societal and demographic changes, the growing popularity of other sports, and the public's changing tastes. During the golden age the gym's monthly membership had risen to nearly 400 boxers. When it finally closed on December 31, 1961, only about 75 fighters were utilizing its facilities.

Six months later the structure that housed Stillman's and two adjoining buildings was demolished to make way for a nondescript 19-story apartment building. About ten years later I decided to walk into the building. In the lobby I struck up a conversation with a tenant and asked if she had ever heard of Stillman's Gym. Not surprisingly, the answer was no. I was then told she couldn't wait to move out as the building had become infested with prostitutes and pimps. I found that somewhat ironic. I wondered, was it karma? Far too many pro boxers wind up physically damaged, exploited, and broke. Of course professional fighters are not prostitutes. They are proud, hardworking, and disciplined athletes who are courageously trying to make something of their lives in the toughest of all sports. However, when it comes to the lowlife mobsters, crooked managers, and promoters who have controlled and exploited so many boxers without any concern for their health or well-being, then comparison to their like-minded pimp brethren is entirely valid.

In the late 1970s, New York City gave up its position as the epicenter of the sport to the gambling hot spots of Las Vegas and Atlantic City. By that time only Madison Square Garden was presenting regularly scheduled biweekly boxing shows in its smaller 4,500-seat venue located adjacent to the main arena. A generation earlier, at least a dozen small arenas (or "fight clubs" as they are known in the boxing vernacular) had operated on a weekly basis within a ten-mile radius of Times Square. Now there are none.

The glory days of New York boxing are long gone, as are the many monuments to that singular era that were so much a part of the city's culture: St. Nicholas Arena, the old Madison Square Garden on 50th Street, Dempsey's restaurant, Ridgewood Grove, Broadway Arena, Queensboro Arena, the Bronx Coliseum, Coney Island Velodrome, Eastern Parkway Arena, even the old baseball stadiums that during the summer months were the site of dozens of championship boxing matches.

If ever a building deserved to be preserved as a national historic site, that building was Stillman's Gym. Sadly, there isn't even a plaque to commemorate the site of one of New York City's most historic landmarks.

The last vestige of the golden age was Sunnyside Gardens in Long Island City. The old fight club met the wrecking ball in 1977. At least someone had the good sense to put a plaque in front of the hamburger joint that now occupies the space.

Except for the occasional pay-per-view megafight, boxing today is a fringe sport, and vastly inferior as an art form when comparing the skill level of the current champions to the best boxers of decades past. That's aside from the absurdity of having so many multiple world champions in each weight class. Over the past 35 years, the greed and arrogance of boxing's quasi-official "sanctioning organizations," in cahoots with rapacious promoters, have all but destroyed whatever credibility the sport once possessed. When I first walked into Stillman's Gym in 1959 there were ten world champions and ten weight classes. Now there are over 100 "champions" inhabiting 17 weight classes.

Once upon a time everyone, even housewives and schoolchildren, knew the name of the heavyweight champion of the world. That title was the most important in all of sports. Can anyone today name the current heavyweight champion of the world? Does anyone care? I rest my case.

Even without places like Stillman's, or the hundreds of other extinct gyms and arenas that once dotted the American boxing landscape during boxing's golden age, the sport's ability to produce outstanding fighters did not suddenly come to an end. The decline of boxing's infrastructure and importance that began in the post–World War II period was more like a spinning top that slowly winds down. There were some great fighters in the 1960s, less so in the '70s and '80s, and perhaps one or two in the 1990s. I can't name one truly great fighter today.

Within the past 20 years, boxing has deteriorated to the point where I and most of my contemporaries (in addition to many younger fans) have lost almost all interest in what has become, for all intents and purposes, a brutal burlesque of a sport. It is very difficult to support or help a sport that refuses to help itself.

From top to bottom, inside and outside of the ring, from the fighters to the fans, to the commentators, trainers, referees, managers, and commissioners, the level of ignorance is pervasive. If 95 percent of today's trainers showed up at Stillman's, they would be laughed out of the gym or assigned as bucket carriers since that low-level job would result in them doing the least damage.

Am I being too harsh? I think not. My observations are based on my particular frame of reference and perspective. To me, the glory and romance of boxing resides in its past history and I'm content to leave it at that.

I am now more aware of boxing's flaws and dangers than ever before. I realize that professional boxing has never been, and will never be, completely free of the exploitation, greed, and brutality that has marked its existence since time immemorial. It's the nature of the beast. But, in its defense, there once was a brief moment in time when the good in boxing actually outweighed the bad; when great fighters possessing extraordinary skills and seasoning fought other great fighters; when managers and trainers understood their business; when every sports fan could name the heavyweight champion of the world; when *The Ring* magazine was still the "Bible of Boxing"; when baby boomer sons (and even some daughters) bonded with their dads over the televised Friday Night Fight ritual. It was the time of Dempsey, Louis, Marciano, and Robinson . . . and Satchmo, Goodman, Miller, and Elvis.

It was the time of Stillman's Gym.

2

THE NIGHT THE REFEREE HIT BACK

(June 11, 2014)

The date is January 27, 1970. Sammy Luftspring, a 54-year-old one-eyed former welterweight contender, is assigned to referee a ten-round main bout in the ballroom of Toronto's Royal York Hotel between Canada's Clyde Gray and a Panamanian fighter named Humberto Trottman. During the course of the fight Trottman has become angered at what he thinks is Luftspring's biased officiating. Seconds before the start of the sixth round, without warning, Trottman throws a sucker punch right hook to Luftspring's jaw!

In his very readable and informative 1975 autobiography *Call Me Sammy*, Luftspring describes what happened next:

> What was going on in my head was that I was in a boxing ring with a boxer who had just thrown one punch and probably intended to give me a sample of a few more. How I had ever managed, purely by instinct, to dodge his right I will never know. But I had no intention of letting it go unreturned. His next was a left lead, which I slipped, and punched him one on the heart. And the next thing I knew, I had popped him three or four more times without getting touched again myself.
>
> For those few split seconds, thirty years had magically vanished and I was a boxer again, doing my thing. Then a swarm of people—George Chuvalo, and several other heavyweights among them—came swarming over the ropes and the impromptu match was over.[1]

Fifty-four-year-old referee and former welterweight contender Sammy Luftspring takes a right to the chin from boxer Humberto Trottman, January 27, 1970. *Author's collection*

Fans agreed that the old welterweight contender had scored another (albeit unofficial) victory. Sammy also kept his record intact of never having been floored in over 140 amateur and professional bouts.

Trottman was of course immediately disqualified and issued a lifetime suspension. On only two other occasions had a boxer ever turned on a referee, both times in Europe. But only one referee has ever hit back. The incident was reported in newspapers throughout Canada and the U.S. Sammy hadn't seen that type of attention and publicity in years. But there was far more to his story than an impromptu match with an unhinged Panamanian boxer.

Sammy Luftspring began his boxing career in 1932 at a Toronto Jewish community center. Over the next four years he established himself as one of the best amateur boxers in Canada, compiling an outstanding 100–5 won-lost record that included Golden Gloves titles from bantamweight to welterweight. He was Canada's best hope for a gold medal at the upcoming Olympics in Berlin, Germany. But Luftspring and his buddy Norman "Baby" Yack, another outstanding Canadian Jewish boxer, decided to boycott the Nazi Olympics to protest Germany's treatment of its Jewish population.

After their decision was made public, both Luftspring and Yack were invited to participate in an alternate Olympic Games planned for Barcelona, Spain. They were on their way to Barcelona, waiting for a boat to

Luftspring retaliates with a right of his own. Trottman is disqualified.
Author's collection

take them from the southern coast of France to Spain, when the event was abruptly canceled due to the outbreak of the Spanish Civil War. Luftspring returned to Canada and turned pro.

From 1936 to 1938 Sammy won 23 of 27 bouts, including victories over Baby Salvy Saban, Billy Townsend, and a 13th-round KO of Frankie Genovese for the Canadian welterweight title. In January 1939 he moved his base of operations to New York City where Al Weill became his manager and Whitey Bimstein his trainer.

The young fighter was in good hands. Weill was a brilliant and influential manager, and Bimstein had already trained scores of top pros and several champions. Over the next year Sammy won eight of ten fights. Victories over Phil Furr, Johnny McHale, and Andre Jessurun earned him a rating among the top five welterweights in the world. His only losses were by decision to middleweights Steve Mamakos and Vic Dellicurti.

By 1940 Sammy was on a fast track to a title bout with the great Henry Armstrong when disaster struck. In a tune-up bout against Steve Belloise, in front of 12,000 fans crammed into the Bronx Coliseum, he was unintentionally thumbed in the left eye.

Despite fighting half blind for the next seven rounds against the murderous punching Belloise, Luftspring pressed the action and appeared to have won the eight-round decision. But two of the three judges voted for Belloise.

The loss was a serious setback for Luftspring, but worse news was in store for the 24-year-old fighter. He had suffered a detached retina and within weeks lost total vision in his left eye. The injury was permanent. Sammy's career as a professional fighter was suddenly over. His final stats: 31–8 (13 KOs).

The young fighter was devastated. His dream of winning the welterweight championship of the world was gone forever. Now unemployed, and recently married, he had to find a new career that could support his family. After a few false starts, including stints as a cabdriver and liquor salesman, he eventually found his niche as a partner in a successful Toronto supper club. With Luftspring acting as its congenial host (he often took the microphone to croon sentimental ballads), the Mercury Club quickly became a Toronto landmark and a popular destination for locals, tourists, and visiting celebrities. The club operated successfully for 21 years.

While running the club, Sammy remained involved with the boxing world as a referee. He officiated in hundreds of amateur and professional bouts, including the heavyweight title bout between Ernie Terrell and George Chuvalo in 1965.

Luftspring remained a very popular figure in his native Toronto for most of his life. In 1985 he was inducted into the Canadian Boxing Hall of Fame. He passed away in 2000 at the age of 84.

3

ALI VS. SHAVERS: THE MORNING AFTER

(September 30, 1977)

On September 29, 1977, 35-year-old Muhammad Ali stepped into the Madison Square Garden ring to defend his heavyweight championship against hard-punching Earnie Shavers. This was his tenth defense of the title he regained from the seemingly invincible George Foreman in 1974. Since then Ali had fought nine more times, including his exhausting "Thrilla in Manila" victory over nemesis Joe Frazier on October 1, 1975.[1] What more was there left to accomplish? Yet despite his diminishing athletic skills, the most celebrated athlete on earth refused to leave the stage. Ali won the 15-round decision but in the process had been hammered again and again by Shavers's wrecking-ball punches aimed at his head. In a newspaper column appearing the day after the fight, I pleaded with Ali to either retire or take a long rest from boxing. He did neither. Ali would have four more fights before finally retiring a month shy of his 40th birthday. But the damage had already been done and the early stages of CTE (chronic traumatic encephalopathy) were already apparent.

The morning after a particularly tough fight is always the most painful in a boxer's life.

During and immediately after the fight—as pained as he is—his mind is distracted by the cheering mob and the consolation of well-wishers and friends in the dressing room. As bad as it is then, it is always tougher the morning after—when the pain sets in. Then there are no distractions, only the fighter and his brutalized body to keep him company. Skin, muscles, organs, bones, even fingernails and hair seem to have been

Earnie Shavers catches 35-year-old Muhammad Ali with yet another right-hand bomb, September 29, 1977. *Associated Press/Marty Lederhandler*

punished. The simple act of tying one's shoelaces becomes a monumental and arduous task.

This is what Muhammad Ali feels after his latest title defense against Earnie Shavers.

How many more times can Ali allow himself to be put through this torture? More to the point, how long will Ali's body allow him to continue this self-abuse?

Not Built for Punishment

To look at Ali's body it becomes obvious that his was not built for punishment—yet he takes it. When other, seemingly sturdier men would falter and go down—he takes it, subjecting his body to an awesome battering. Ali's strength to withstand this type of battering comes not from his fattening, formerly sleek athlete's body.

Inside that body, once built for dancing and effortless grace, beats the heart of a champion. No, not just your ordinary run-of-the-mill champion, but a champion chosen for immortality.

Ali's pride and vanity is too great to let him suffer the indignity of quitting and going down for the count. This same pride and vanity, this overconfidence, almost proved his downfall Thursday night. Ali says he is getting old, that he no longer can dance anymore. He does not seem to realize that the one sure way to compensate for his slowing up is to work his aging body into good shape.

After all, Ali, Martha Graham is still going strong well into her 80s. Rudolph Nureyev is no kid either. They don't dance like they used to, but would they ever consider exhibiting their skill in front of millions—fat and out of shape?

Ali, you are an artist, so at least make an attempt to remain one. Please don't make excuses like you can't dance anymore. We know that. But we don't expect a charade either.

How do you expect to do any kind of dancing or punching, or much of anything, when you train for a championship bout as if it is a four-round prelim? I take that back. All the four-round prelim boxers I know train much harder than you do.

Granted it is harder to train as you get older, and a pas de deux is not to be compared to a solid left hook to the jaw, but you make 35 sound like 75. Face it, you hate the agonizing hours of drudgery, the endless miles of roadwork, etc. Boxing is not your whole life anymore.

Tell Me, Ali

I don't blame you—you have been at it for over 20 years. But tell me, Ali, feeling as you do now, would you trade the pain you feel today in exchange for those 50 extra miles of roadwork you should have done, the 45 more rounds of real sparring you should have undertaken? Would you exchange that annoyance for the maddening pain you feel today? I'll bet yesterday morning you felt more like 175.

We all know you're not nearly the fighter you once were, but whatever you have left—it should have been enough to beat Earnie Shavers. You made Shavers look much better than he is and much better than he deserved to look.

You didn't really misread Earnie as a fighter. His weaknesses were all there—a slow-moving, unimaginative boxer. However, there is one thing that Earnie does very well, as you painfully found out Thursday night, he hits hard . . . very hard.

You are a boxer, Ali, and you know the answer to that: you don't let the strong guy hit you. Only one thing, you've got to be able to be in shape to time the punches coming at you correctly. I'd say that last night you were only about 75 percent of what you could be at 35. What you could have been would have been enough to take care of Earnie Shavers fairly easily.

Instead, you opted for the easy way out and paid the price. Earnie was not just catching you with rights; he was catching you with oh-so-slow rights. Those extra six pounds you were carrying really cost you.

You should have studied the films of Shavers's first fight with Henry Clark—the one that went ten rounds. Shavers did not collapse from exhaustion at the end of this fight. Why? Clark can't punch so Shavers did not have to worry about being hurt. And Clark put no pressure on Shavers. He didn't make him work. Earnie was the aggressor when he wanted to be, and could rest as he pleased. In other words, he was allowed to control the pace of the fight.

So Long, Earnie

Ali, Ali, you did the same thing! Shavers has a stamina problem (the lack of it resulted in several losses to much lesser fighters than you) and what little confidence he has leaves him when he gets hit hard or he starts to suck air. You would not have stopped Shavers with one punch, but by being more active and forcing him to move he would not have been able to rest and control the pace of the fight. Making the man exert himself was the key.

Only you were unprepared to do it. The last 30 seconds of the 15th round proved what you could do with a tired Earnie Shavers. Had you gotten him that tired around the tenth round, it would have been "So long, Earnie."

Face it, Ali, it was not just your age that caused you to look so bad against a hard-punching mediocrity like Shavers, it was you. You were in lousy shape.

I have no doubt that the last thing you want now is to step into a ring for a serious fight. You need a long rest from fighting—anybody. It could be six months, possibly a year. Let the others fight it out, and then—if you feel up to it—maybe consider taking one more crack at it.

But this time be in shape, or else forget the whole thing. Spare us, and more importantly, spare yourself the agony.

4

NO HEART-SHAPED BOXES ON THIS VALENTINE'S DAY

(February 14, 2003)

"I fought Sugar Ray Robinson so many times, it's a wonder I don't have diabetes."

—Jake LaMotta

The first televised championship fight of 1951 featured the incomparable Sugar Ray Robinson vs. the indefatigable "Bronx Bull" Jake LaMotta. Robinson had ruled the welterweight division for the past five years. Now he was attempting to add the middleweight championship to his spectacular resume. He faced a formidable roadblock. Two legendary superstars of the golden age of televised boxing were about to clash for the sixth and final time.

When the elegant welterweight champion of the world Sugar Ray Robinson slid gracefully through the ropes of the Chicago Stadium ring on February 14, 1951, St. Valentine's night 50 years ago, he was generally acknowledged to be the greatest fighter, pound for pound, of the modern era. Since turning pro ten years earlier he had lost only once in 123 professional fights, winning 79 by knockout. It is an incredible record that, it is safe to say, will never be equaled. The Neanderthal-like individual in the opposite corner was the one person responsible for that lone blot on his otherwise perfect record—the "Bronx Bull," Jake LaMotta, reigning middleweight champion of the world.

Sugar Ray was not about to send him a heart-shaped box of chocolates.

The rough-hewn Jake had his own perfect record to protect. In 95 pro fights he had never been knocked off his feet. It was a proud boast made even more impressive by the fact that this iron man had met the hardest punchers in both the middleweight and light heavyweight divisions.

This was the sixth and final chapter of a bitter rivalry that had begun almost eight years earlier. Their first encounter took place in Madison Square Garden on October 2, 1942. Even then Robinson was considered a boxing phenomenon. He could box, punch, dance, take a punch, and fight inside or at long range. He also possessed a breathtaking repertoire of combination punches that were thrown with extraordinary speed and power. Within a year of turning pro he was ranked the number one welterweight contender. By the end of his second year, having won 35 straight fights (27 by KO), he was running out of competition. Since the welterweight title was frozen for the duration of World War II (the current champ was in the navy), he decided to take on middleweights even though he would be giving away close to 20 pounds to some opponents.

Around this same time a Bronx-born human tank named Jacob LaMotta was on the rise wreaking havoc in the middleweight division. Turning pro five months after Sugar Ray, the appropriately nicknamed Bronx Bull had won 26 of 31 fights, including one draw. LaMotta was a big middleweight whose frame could easily support 160 to 170 pounds. Jake was a special fighter, but how special really wouldn't become apparent until his second fight with Robinson.

Their first fight was somewhat anticlimactic. The usually aggressive LaMotta did not follow his game plan. He was overly cautious and tentative, respectful as he was of Robinson's awesome reputation. Although he lost the ten-round decision, the fact that he managed to win three rounds and was still standing at the end bolstered his confidence.

LaMotta's trainer, Mike Capriano, the man who had fashioned and refined Jake's unique bend-and-weave style of fighting, decided his fighter needed some fine-tuning before accepting a rematch with Robinson. Over the next four months Jake fought five contenders, including the highly touted Jackie Wilson, who had won 50 of 52 fights. Jake beat them all.

The rematch with Robinson was fought in Detroit's Olympia Stadium on February 5, 1943. Robinson weighed 144 to Jake's 160 pounds. Despite the obvious weight advantage, the odds makers made LaMotta a

9-to-2 underdog, which at least was better than the 10-to-1 odds of the first fight.

Jake's strategy was the same for every fight with Robinson: LaMotta, 5'8" tall to Robinson's 5'11", was to constantly attack out of a low crouch, forcing Robinson backward so he could not get set to unleash his deadly combinations. LaMotta, who had surprising speed, had to move quickly. As Robinson started his jab LaMotta would step in and weave under and inside. Once inside the jab, LaMotta, bending low, would drop a right hand to Robinson's side and bring up a quick left hook to the head. He would then attempt to stay inside, burying his head in Robinson's chest, and whale away with body punches and combinations in an attempt to slow him down. LaMotta knew how to utilize his great strength to full advantage. In his low crouch, bobbing and weaving, he presented a difficult target. He never stood straight up and always kept his chin tucked in behind his left shoulder.

Jake fought brilliantly. He pressured Robinson throughout the fight. Ray's strategy was to try and outbox LaMotta by keeping the action at long range, spearing him with left jabs while trying to set him up for the right cross, uppercut, left hook, or combinations. But many of Robinson's best shots missed their mark as Jake rolled with the punches, taking the sting out of them. In the eighth round, Jake sent Robinson through the ropes for a nine count. It was the first time Robinson had ever been knocked down. At the end of ten exciting rounds, Jake was awarded a close but unanimous ten-round decision.

Exactly three weeks later they fought again. Same arena, same fight. Jake even managed to floor Robinson again. But this time the unanimous decision went to the Sugar Man. At least that is what the record book says. The consensus among fans and reporters was that LaMotta deserved the win. They had two more fights in 1945, both hotly contested, but with Robinson having the edge both times.

It would be almost six years before these two magnificent gladiators would square off against each other one more time.

Over the next five years both men went their separate ways, fistically speaking. Robinson won the welterweight title in 1946, defended it until he ran out of challengers, and by 1949 was campaigning for a shot at the middleweight crown

LaMotta, meanwhile, was fighting virtually any middleweight, or light heavy willing to step into the same ring with him. By 1946, he was rated the number one middleweight in the world. Yet he could not secure a title shot. The problem was that Jake had wanted to remain a free agent in a business controlled by mobsters. It was an impossible situation. Finally, after agreeing to throw a fight against Billy Fox in 1947, LaMotta was given the green light to arrange a title match. This unfortunate chapter in LaMotta's career is accurately portrayed in the film *Raging Bull.*

Winning the middleweight championship of the world from Marcel Cerdan in 1949 was certainly the highlight of Jake's colorful career. By the time he won the crown, though, the wear and tear of numerous ring wars, his constant battle to control his weight, along with marital and managerial problems, had begun to take their toll. At 29 years of age, the Bronx Bull, while still a nightmare for any middleweight alive, had seen his best days. Yet, when the chips were down, LaMotta could still call upon his amazing resilience and determination to snatch victory from the jaws of defeat, as was demonstrated in his dramatic 15th-round KO of leading contender Laurent Dauthuille on September 13, 1950. With 30 seconds left to go in the fight, and hopelessly behind on points, Jake suddenly exploded and flattened Dauthuille. Five months later LaMotta put his title on the line against Sugar Ray Robinson who, aside from holding the welterweight title, had earned a number one ranking in the middleweight division.

Fifteen thousand fans filled the Chicago Stadium, and millions more watched the fight on network television—for free. There was also an international radio hookup for Europe and South America.

Robinson, now 30 years old, was still a magician with his fists despite having passed his peak within the previous year. He was bigger now, at 155 pounds, and, although he may have slowed down a bit, he could still dazzle fans and opponents alike with his spectacular six- to ten-punch combinations.

Robinson's strategy was based on LaMotta's struggle to make the 160-pound weight limit. (Indeed, the night before the fight Jake was sitting in a steam room sweating off four and a half extra pounds.) As LaMotta chased him around the ring, Ray, playing matador to the Bull, would punish him with sharp jabs and damaging counterpunches. The Harlem Dandy's footwork would be put to the test. And if he was gored, which was sure to happen, Robinson was not overly concerned as he had, along with his other attributes, one of the best chins in the business. When the time was right, and a tired LaMotta was ready to be taken, Robinson would open up with everything he had. The odds favored Robinson 3½-to-1.

Although the fight followed the same basic pattern of their previous encounters, there were significant differences. Both men had aged and slowed up a bit, but whatever athleticism they had lost was more than made up for with experience and craft. But it was LaMotta who was the more shopworn of the two. The Bull was still a formidable foe, strong and determined, yet . . . something was missing. He was able to nail Robinson with his left hooks and jabs but was not getting under and inside in the way that he had in the past. He was a step slower and his punches did not fly as fast or as frequently as they once had. Unlike their previous fights, he seemed to be targeting Robinson's head more than his body, a change in strategy that could cost LaMotta if he failed to score a knockout and the bout entered the late rounds. Worse, LaMotta's fabled durability seemed lacking. By the sixth round he appeared to be growing tired.

Robinson sensed LaMotta's weakening condition. Like a matador preparing a bull for the final thrust, he landed brutal shots to the body while waiting for the right moment when it would be safe to attempt the impossible and knock out Jake LaMotta. But he had to be careful. Robinson knew Jake only too well not to be. He was reminded of this in the sixth round when LaMotta shook him up with a solid left hook to the jaw and bloodied his nose and mouth.

At the end of the tenth round, the fight was dead even. But LaMotta was near exhaustion. The effort to make the weight coupled with the grueling pace of the fight had taken too much out of him. With what little reserve he had left, he went for broke in the 11th round. For 30 seconds, he looked like the LaMotta of old as he rushed Robinson and pinned him against the ropes, throwing punches from all angles in one last desperate attempt to end the fight. Robinson survived and by the end of the round had LaMotta in serious trouble as he raked him with combinations to both head and body.

The 12th round was hard to watch. It wasn't a competitive fight anymore. It was slaughter. LaMotta had absolutely nothing left except his fighting heart, grit, and the determination not to go down. He could barely keep his hands up, much less throw a punch. Robinson was tee-

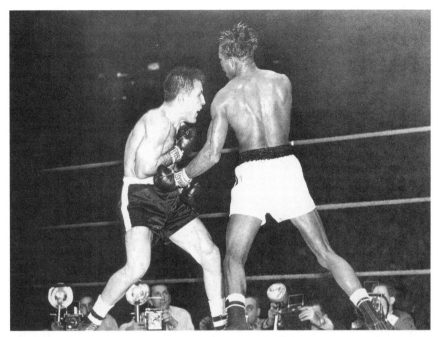

Sugar Ray Robinson digs a left into the Bronx Bull's midsection during their memorable St. Valentine's Day brawl, February 14, 1951. *Steve Lott/Boxing Hall of Fame Las Vegas*

ing off on his head, doing everything within his power to bring LaMotta down. Uppercuts, right crosses, left hooks . . . double and triple left hooks! It was amazing, cruel, disgusting, yet awe inspiring all at the same time. What the hell was keeping LaMotta up? He could have easily taken a nine count, at least to interrupt the savagery, but no, he would not give Ray the satisfaction. The doctor visited Jake's corner before the start of the 13th round and allowed the fight to continue.

Jake was a human punching bag. For two minutes straight he was subjected to a horrific beating yet he still refused to go down! Two things were about to happen: either Jake would finally drop, or Robinson, who was becoming exhausted from hitting him, would collapse. Thankfully, mercifully, the referee stepped in between them as LaMotta lay helpless against the ropes, and finally stopped the thing at 2:04 of the 13th round.

So ended a fight that in lore and legend came to be known as boxing's "St. Valentine's Day Massacre."

5

WHERE WERE YOU ON MARCH 8, 1971?

(March 8, 2003)

I know where I was that night of nights—I was among the 20,455 spectators in a sold-out Madison Square Garden who were about to witness an electrifying contest of will and skill between two undefeated heavyweight champions.

It was advertised simply as "THE FIGHT." No other words were necessary. The stupendous Muhammad Ali vs. Joe Frazier showdown of March 8, 1971, was perhaps the most anticipated event in all of sports history.

It was a match between two great undefeated heavyweight champions that by itself would have been enough to capture the attention of millions of fans. But it was the added dimensions of politics, religion, race, and ego whipped to a frenzy by the most charismatic and controversial athlete of the 20th century that would capture the attention of hundreds of millions of people throughout the world, most of whom had never even seen a professional boxing match.

It was an event that transcended sport.

Boxing, in its naked violently simplistic mano a mano way, was the perfect metaphor. To the masses, Frazier and Ali had come to represent more than themselves.

It all began innocently enough. Ali, fighting under his given name of Cassius Clay, had won the Olympic light heavyweight title in 1960 and the heavyweight championship of the world at the age of 22 by defeating the seemingly invincible brute Sonny Liston in 1964. Spouting poetry and predicting the round in which his opponents would fall, the brash youngster was colorful, engaging, quick witted, and a master showman.

The self-proclaimed "Greatest" was a boxing phenomenon. He had incredibly fast hands and catlike reflexes. His handsome face was rarely hit. Clay personified his motto to "float like a butterfly and sting like a bee." The boxing world, indeed the sports world, had never seen anything like him.

But everything changed the day after he won the title. He announced to the world he was a member of the Black Muslims, a hitherto little known black separatist movement that practiced the religion of Islam, espoused self-help for the Negro race, and preached that the white man was the devil.

The new champion said that he would no longer be known by his slave name Cassius Clay. He would now be known as Cassius X. He spoke to the assembled reporters, but his words were aimed at the white establishment when he stated that "I don't have to be what you want me to be. I am free to be who I want."

Three weeks later the leader of the sect, Elijah Muhammad, conferred upon Cassius X his new Muslim name—Muhammad Ali.

Ali, backed by the Black Muslims, was announcing to the world that he was breaking free of the role that had traditionally been assigned to black heavyweight champions.

Yet, in many ways, Ali never really stopped being Cassius Clay. He could still be funny and creative when promoting his fights just as he was before he won the title. Then again, when preaching Black Muslim dogma, he could be humorless and petulant even to the point of taunting and cruelly punishing black opponents (Floyd Patterson and Ernie Terrell) who refused to call him by his Muslim name. Boxing's established old guard felt betrayed and angry and hoped that he would soon be dethroned. No such luck. Ali was just too good a fighter.

From 1965 to 1967 he defended his title nine times. No challenger ever came close to defeating him. He was proud of his defensive skill, often boasting that no one would ever know if he could take a punch because he did not intend to ever have to prove that he could.

Muhammad Ali, boxer and public figure, had his detractors and his supporters, but whatever criticism and controversy he had encountered in the past was nothing compared to what was to come. He was about to be thrust onto a stage much larger than a boxing ring. The turbulent, crazy decade of the 1960s was about to shift into high gear.

In 1967, with the United States fighting a war in Vietnam, Muhammad Ali, the heavyweight champion of the world, refused to step forward and accept induction into the army. Ali, stating that he was a Muslim minister, claimed conscientious objector status on the grounds that his religion forbade him to participate in a war. It should be understood that there were already hundreds of thousands of Americans doing service in the jungles and rice paddies of Vietnam. Almost 30,000 had already been killed. Ali was denounced as a draft dodger. Several congressmen took the opportunity to vilify him and questioned his patriotism and motives. Boxing commissions throughout the country were quick to strip him of his title and suspend his license to box.

Two months later, on June 20, 1967, Ali was convicted of draft evasion and sentenced to five years in prison. While Ali was free on bail, pending the appeals process, his lawyers tried to restore his boxing license. It was to no avail; Ali was a pariah.

But not to everyone.

The controversial war in Vietnam had created an active antiwar movement composed mostly of college students. Ali, running low on funds, accepted invitations to speak on college campuses. The defrocked champion may have been barely literate, but he certainly was not verbally challenged. His lively lectures were well received. He spoke about his views on race, religious philosophy, and the war. Since the boxing establishment had already started the process of crowning a new heavyweight champion, Ali always ended his speeches by asking the audience to tell him who the real heavyweight champion was. He was obviously pleased to hear the familiar chant of "Ali, Ali." The counterculture had a new hero.

The country was split between those supporting our efforts in Vietnam and those opposed to the war. Hawks, doves, hard hats, flower children, black power, Woodstock, Kent State, and the silent majority were bywords for the most divisive American decade since the American Civil War some 100 years earlier.

This was also a time of activism and militancy for many black Americans involved in the civil rights movement, especially after the assassinations of Martin Luther King Jr. and Bobby Kennedy in 1968.

While all this was going on, the boxing promoters were conducting a series of tournaments to find a successor to Muhammad Ali.

Rising to the top of the heavyweight heap like some unstoppable force of nature was a human wrecking ball named Joe Frazier. He was one of 13 children born dirt poor on a farm in rural South Carolina. He had come to Philadelphia as a married 16-year-old and was working in a kosher slaughterhouse when he first took up boxing. As an amateur Joe won three Golden Gloves titles and, in 1964, the Olympic heavyweight championship. Over the next five years, using his feared left hook like a meat cleaver, he knocked out 23 of 26 opponents.

In many ways he was the exact opposite of Ali both in style and personality. Frazier was a pure puncher. He constantly pressured opponents, hands always in motion, head down, moving ever forward out of a low crouch and throwing his destructive left hook out of a bob and weave. He never stopped throwing punches until his opponent dropped. It was a style that was meant to vex a stand-up boxer like Ali.

Frazier was a decent, hardworking, law abiding, churchgoing family man, who was too busy trying to support his growing family to get involved in any causes.

The anti-Ali crowd had found their man, although Joe did not care to be looked upon as a symbol of anything other than who he was.

So impressive was Frazier in victory that many fans thought he had a good chance to defeat Ali on the best day the ex-champion ever saw. Ali instinctively sensed that this was the perfect opponent for him physically and psychologically. And even though he now had been out of the ring over three years, he was as confident of victory as was Frazier.

Ali never lost an opportunity to demean and belittle Frazier's ability and insist that he and not some pretender was the real heavyweight champion. Of course, it was meant to hype the gate for a possible fight. But try as he might, Ali was never able to ruffle Joe's feathers. Smokin' Joe was a cool customer who was happiest and most comfortable beating up opponents. He would silence this braggart in the ring. The stage was being set for an epic confrontation.

It was now the summer of 1970. Ali had not fought in almost three and a half years. Even if he was allowed to come back, how much had the layoff affected his magnificent skills?

The world was about to find out.

Through a quirky set of circumstances, helped by a changing political climate and a friendly black state senator, Ali was granted a boxing license in Atlanta, Georgia, of all places. Not wanting to go in against Frazier without some tune-up fights, Ali chose to meet the number one contender, Jerry Quarry, on October 26, 1970, in the 6,000-seat Municipal Auditorium.

What irony! A controversial black activist and war resister meeting a white opponent in Atlanta, Georgia. It was the biggest night Atlanta had seen since the opening of *Gone with the Wind* some 30 years earlier.

The 28-year-old Ali dominated Quarry for the three rounds the fight lasted until a bad cut over Quarry's left eye forced a stoppage. Although an impressive victory, it was too short a fight to evaluate Ali's true condition.

Ali's situation was steadily improving. A New York State judge ruled that his boxing license had been revoked unfairly and ordered it reinstated. This opened the way for another tune-up fight in New York against top-rated contender Oscar Bonavena.

On December 7, 1970, in New York's Madison Square Garden, Muhammad Ali knocked out the awkward and very strong Argentinean in the 15th and final round for his 30th straight victory. Up until the spectacular knockout it had been a tough and grueling fight. Boxing people saw that Ali's legs had slowed down and he did not move with the same fluid speed and accuracy that he had before his long layoff. But he did win, was still undefeated, and had three months to prepare for his showdown with Joe Frazier.

The countdown had begun.

The Fight

The match was set for March 8, 1971, at Madison Square Garden. Each man was guaranteed $2.5 million, the largest single payday for any entertainer or athlete at the time. Tickets to the Garden would be made available to the general public by mail on a first-come-first-served basis. Prices in the arena ranged from $20 for a balcony seat to $150 for ringside. Hundreds of other locations throughout the U.S. and Canada would screen the fight via closed-circuit television to fans paying $5 to $15.

Interest in the event was incredible. Radio, television, and the print media were filled with stories discussing the upcoming fight. Tension and anticipation were building by the hour. Few athletic events, be it World Series, Super Bowl, or World Cup, had come even close to generating the type of excitement and attention that this prizefight was getting.

Fifty countries had purchased rights to the telecast.

The fight was broadcast from ringside in 12 different languages. When the final tallies were added up, it was estimated that 300 million people around the globe had watched the fight. It was the largest audience ever for a television broadcast up to that time. In the end, the fight grossed between $18 and $20 million worldwide, of which less than $1.5 million came from television money outside the United States and Canada. But the United States and Canada provided only 1.5 million viewers.

Although oddsmakers made Frazier a slight 6-to-5 favorite, Ali's supporters were not perturbed. Their belief in him was total. It went beyond his skill as a boxer. To them he was more than just a boxer—he was a symbol. He could not lose. Ali agreed and predicted that Frazier "will fall in six."

Ali had an 8½-inch advantage in reach, four inches in height (6'3" to 5'11"), and weighed 215 pounds to Joe's 205½.

The night of the fight was electric. As the fighters made their way toward the ring, hearts pounded and pulses raced. Everyone was on their feet. The Garden, filled to capacity with 20,455 spectators, was brimming with celebrities. But not everyone of note was able to get choice seating. Hubert Humphrey, the ex–vice president of the United States, was sitting in the mezzanine! Frank Sinatra had one of the best seats in the house. He was hired by *Life* magazine (although he would gladly have paid them for the privilege) to photograph the fight from the ring apron. The overflow of stars who couldn't get into the Garden, like Bing Crosby, were to be found at Radio City Music Hall, whose 6,500 seats had sold out three weeks earlier. Virtually every other closed-circuit television location was also filled to capacity.

While both fighters waited for the introductions, Ali, gliding around the ring, twice brushed Frazier's shoulder as he moved past him. The crowd reacted with a roar. Frazier glared at Ali contemptuously.

Then the house lights dimmed. The tension was almost unbearable. The fans were still on their feet when the bell rang. The fight was on!

Joe came out bobbing and weaving, edging in toward Ali, trying to get under his jab and land the hook to his body or head. Ali was using his footwork to keep Joe at a distance. But most of his jabs were missing the target as Frazier's head moved quickly to avoid them. Ali seemed surprised by Frazier's speed.

By the third round Ali had come off his toes and was fighting uncharacteristically flat-footed, perhaps to save energy. Frazier was setting an incredible pace. He seemed almost maniacal, throwing more punches in one round than most heavyweights throw in an entire fight. But Ali was picking his spots and landing hard counterpunches and powerful jabs.

The sixth round came and went and with it Ali's predicted knockout. Frazier laughed derisively at him at the end of the round.

The fight was being fought with a brutal intensity rarely seen in any prizefight. Each man was fighting as if he had a point to prove. This was a genuine grudge match and it was being fought like one.

Ali could not keep up the torrid pace. He was allowing Frazier to pin him against the ropes, something he would never have done in previous fights. It appeared that Ali could no longer move with the old speed and lightness of foot. Even so, as the bell rang for the start of the 11th round, it was still anybody's fight.

Suddenly, with a minute to go in the round, Frazier caught Ali with a tremendous left hook to the jaw that caused his knees to sag. He tried to fool Frazier into thinking he was just playing possum, but he was genuinely hurt. He barely made it to the end of the round. The pace slowed a bit in the next two rounds as both men seemed to be conserving what energy they had left for the homestretch. In the 14th round Ali, drawing on some mysterious inner resource, staged a miraculous comeback and pounded Frazier with some of his best punches of the fight.

Now entering the final round, both men were exhausted but still punching.

And then it happened.

Frazier lashed out with another of his countless left hooks, only this one landed flush on Ali's exposed jaw. He went down hard, flat on his back, legs in the air. Incredibly, Ali bounced up at the count of three and made it to the final bell.

If anyone still had any doubts as to who deserved to win the fight, it was settled with that one left hook that dropped Ali for only the third time in his career.

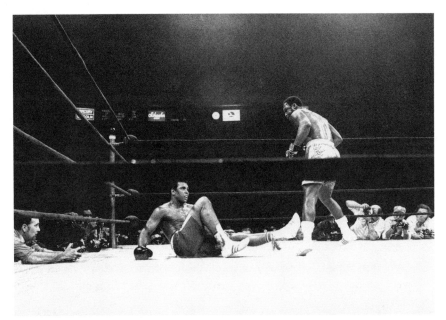

Joe Frazier's knockdown of Muhammad Ali in the 15th round was the climactic moment in an epic fight. Frazier won a unanimous decision, March 8, 1971. *Associated Press*

The unanimous decision went to Frazier. He deserved it. But Ali, too, deserved the accolades due him for a tremendous effort. No one would ever again question his ability to take a punch.

The fight ranks as one of boxing's all-time classics.

Epilogue

On June 27, 1971, by a vote of 8–0 (Justice Thurgood Marshall abstaining), the United States Supreme Court overturned Ali's conviction for refusing induction into the United States Armed Forces.

6

BENNY VALGAR:
FORGOTTEN BOXING MASTER

(September 2008)

"When it came to all around ring generalship, Benny Valgar was on a par with Benny Leonard, though Leonard packed the better punch."

—Ray Arcel

There are times when an individual's greatness is underappreciated or forgotten with the passage of years. Achievements that deserve to be recalled and celebrated are allowed to fade into obscurity. So in the spirit of "attention must be paid," here is one of those stories.

The above quote by legendary trainer Ray Arcel appeared in the January 13, 1935, issue of the *New York Enquirer*. It is quite an accolade when one considers that Benny Leonard (lightweight champion 1917–1925) is universally regarded as one of the greatest boxers of all time.

Ray Arcel spoke from a unique vantage point. He trained Valgar (sometimes spelled "Valger") throughout the 1920s. Ray also saw Leonard in action many times and had trained the former lightweight champion for his comeback in the early 1930s.

In 1978 this writer interviewed Ray Arcel. He still reserved the highest praise for both fighters. "I've seen every great fighter from 1915 to the present and to me {Benny} Leonard was the best," said Arcel. "He was without question, the fastest thinking fighter I ever saw. I class one other fighter with him as far as cleverness and that was Benny Valgar, a lightweight contemporary of Leonard's."[1]

I first became aware of the French-born Benny Valgar (nicknamed "the French Flash") in the early 1960s. I was a wet-behind-the-ears amateur when I overheard my old-school trainer, Willie Grunes, say that in his opinion Valgar had a better left jab than Leonard. Willie did not hand out compliments easily, so his comment made a strong impression on this boxing neophyte.

My friend and fellow historian Tony Arnold recalls meeting an old armory fighter in Stillman's Gym who insisted the French Flash was the greatest boxer he'd ever seen. This fighter had often appeared on the same cards with Valgar. He related the following story to Tony: A participant in the evening's main bout failed to show, and the desperate promoter, spotting Benny Valgar in the audience, asked him to substitute. He was provided with trunks and gloves, but they couldn't find a pair of boxing shoes that fit, so he fought in his wing tips and garters. Although the street shoes limited his footwork a bit, he still managed to win an easy decision.

The Facts

Benny Leonard and Benny Valgar were both managed by Billy Gibson, an astute handler of fighters who also managed the career of future heavyweight champion Gene Tunney. The two Bennys often sparred with each other in the gym (what a fan treat that must have been!) but never met in an official fight.

Valgar turned pro in 1916, following a successful amateur career that saw him win the national AAU (Amateur Athletic Union) bantamweight title. His rise in the professional ranks was swift. By 1920 he was considered good enough to challenge the great featherweight champion Johnny Kilbane.

The title bout was a "no decision" affair limited to eight rounds. At the time New Jersey law did not permit decisions or bouts scheduled beyond eight rounds. (The limit was raised to 12 rounds later that year.) It was understood that Valgar would have to knock out Kilbane in order to claim the title. It was a tall order for the light-hitting challenger. In 132 previous fights, only Benny Leonard had been able to knock out Kilbane.

As was the custom, the unofficial winner of a "no decision" bout that did not end in a knockout was determined by a consensus of newspaper reports. The next day, five of six New York dailies (and three of four

Virtually untouchable in 234 professional fights, Benny Valgar was never knocked out or stopped. In the 1920s and early '30s his ring artistry dazzled fans on two continents. *Author's collection*

out-of-town papers) reported that Valgar had won a close decision. The headline "Johnny Kilbane Outpointed by Benny Valger in Their Eight-Round Bout at Newark" took up all eight columns of the *New York Times*' sports page, reflecting both the importance of the bout and its outcome.

The article stated that both contestants exhibited "brilliant footwork" and "showed knowledge of the scientific side of boxing and feinted and parried with the skill and effectiveness of veteran fencers."

In the final two rounds Valgar became very aggressive in a desperate but vain attempt to end the bout and win the title. The challenger "pounded Kilbane hard about the stomach, and frequently reached the champion with stinging rights and lefts which went through Kilbane's guard as blows have seldom done before." The *New York Times* awarded four rounds to Valgar, three to Kilbane, and called one round even.[2]

There would be no return match. The French Flash soon outgrew the featherweights and spent the remainder of his 16-year pro career fighting in the lightweight division.

The 1920s was a golden era for lightweights. The 135-pound division was dense with talent and the competition at the top brutal. This was the era of Sid Terris, Sammy Mandell, Johnny Dundee, Charley White, Ace Hudkins, Solly Seeman, Lew Tendler, Billy Petrolle, and dozens upon dozens of other formidable contenders and battle-tested veterans.

In his prime, Valgar rarely lost. He won newspaper decisions over future champions Rocky Kansas, Jimmy Goodrich, and Jack Bernstein and contenders Charley White, Leo Johnson, King Tut, and Joe Tiplitz. He officially defeated Frankie Britt, Solly Seeman, Basil Galiano, Alex Hart, Hilario Martinez, Jimmy Fruzetti, and Billy DeFoe. Valgar also lost 12-round decisions to Goodrich, Johnny Dundee, Joe Benjamin, and Billy Wallace.

Like most fighters of his era, Valgar kept to a very busy schedule. Bouts were sometimes spaced just days apart. In 1919, a typical year, he engaged in 16 fights, including six 12-round bouts. Three of the 12-rounders were fought in 22 days.

An Extraordinary Achievement

BoxRec.com credits Benny Valgar with 137 wins (18 by KO), 36 losses, seven draws, and four no contests. Boxing historian Herb Goldman has since found an additional 54 fights, for a total of 234. That number places him among an elite group of fighters who've fought more than 200 times. But more importantly, it makes Valgar one of only two fighters with more than 200 bouts to have never been knocked out or stopped (the other is Harry Stone). It is an extraordinary achievement that, in all likelihood, will never be equaled. For that reason alone Benny Valgar deserves the recognition that has eluded him all these years.

Statistics aside, Valgar's superlative boxing skill was a matter of record. Newspaper accounts of his fights are peppered with words such as "clever," "scientific," "brilliant," "amazing speed," "master boxer," "elusive," "dazzling," "ring wise," "crafty," and giving opponents a "boxing lesson." My guess is a close approximation of his style would be that of the great 1940s-era featherweight champ Willie Pep.

The Ghetto Ghost vs. the French Flash

There were only a few times in his long career when Valgar was stymied by an opponent. One of those opponents was the brilliant "Ghetto Ghost" Sid Terris.

On August 19, 1924, over 14,000 excited fans jammed into Brooklyn's Henderson Bowl to see their highly anticipated bout. Both boxers were experienced and consummate ring technicians, but it was Terris's edge in speed that carried him to victory. In a fight that brought together the world's fastest lightweights, Terris outpointed his East Side rival and won a unanimous ten-round decision.

The *New York Times* praised Terris's "remarkable speed and cleverness" and cited his performance as "one of the most skillful exhibitions of boxing seen here in recent years."[3]

Terris was doing the "Ali Shuffle" at least 40 years before Ali made the move famous and gave it a name. Like a pugilistic Michael Jordan, the 5'10" 130-pounder seemed to defy the physical boundaries of gravity. Old-timers were in awe of his phenomenal speed and agility, including legendary trainer Cus D'Amato, who saw Terris perform in his prime. Cus's protégé, Teddy Atlas, recalls his mentor telling him that he once saw Terris distract an opponent by jumping off the canvas and in the fraction of a second that both feet were in midair land three left jabs!

The Great Lightweight Title Tournament of 1925

The Terris defeat was a temporary setback for Valgar. Fate was about to present him with one last opportunity for championship glory. In January 1925, only a few days after Benny Leonard retired as undefeated lightweight champion, the powerful New York State Athletic Commission announced that it would sponsor an open tournament to determine his successor.

The commission sent invitations to 18 top lightweight contenders requesting their participation. Many other established boxers, including foreign champions, were also invited. Sid Terris and Johnny Dundee, the two top-rated lightweights, declined the offer (much to the relief of every other entrant). They thought it made more economic sense to challenge the eventual winner. In all, over 50 of the world's finest lightweight boxers took part in the tournament. From February to July, promoters were kept busy staging a series of round-robin elimination bouts.

In his first bout, Valgar scored an easy win over Alex Hart in ten rounds. Ten days later he dominated Basil Galiano in a 12-round bout at Madison Square Garden. Two months later, in the quarter final match, Valgar proved too ringwise for young Solly Seeman, winning a unanimous ten-round decision. Seeman was a former national amateur champion and a superb boxer in his own right.

According to the *New York Times*, Valgar gave his less experienced opponent "a boxing lesson." Seeman's efforts were "overshadowed by the steady consistent boxing of Valger," who won six of the ten rounds "by blocking Seeman's blows or parrying them and blinding the Harlemite with a dazzling attack characteristic of the master boxer that is Valger."[4]

After these impressive victories, oddsmakers established Valgar as the favorite to win the vacant title. But it all came to naught in his 12-round semifinal match against the tough and experienced veteran Jimmy Goodrich.

Two years earlier he had won a 12-round decision over Goodrich in Goodrich's own hometown of Buffalo, New York. This time it was different. Perhaps it was just an off night, but for whatever reason the French Flash could not get his act together against Goodrich. He lost the 12-round decision. James P. Dawson, covering the fight for the *New York Times*, wrote that Valgar's showing was "far below the form expected of him."[5]

Goodrich advanced to the finals at Madison Square Garden where, on July 13, 1925, he won the title with a victory over Stanislaus Loayza of Chile. Goodrich and Loayza had fought a total of 11 tournament bouts in five months.

Boxing had a new lightweight champion—not two, or three, or four—just one. The idea seems almost quaint today.

The late 1920s saw Valgar's career wind down. He won more than he lost, but he was not the whippet of old. Fortunately, his superb defensive skills kept him from taking a beating. Other than a slightly flattened nose, his face bore none of the facial scar tissue so prevalent among his contemporaries. Valgar's nickname "the French Flash" paid homage to both his birthplace and his speed. His parents fled the anti-Semitic pogroms of Russia and immigrated to Paris around 1894. Benjamin (Benny), one of five children of Etta and Menachem Valger, was born in Paris in 1898. In 1913 his widowed mother moved to New York City. The following year Benny and his younger sister arrived.

Benny spoke fluent French, but if you listened closely you could detect a slight Yiddish lilt to his accent. From 1929 to 1931 he made several trips back to Europe where he took on the local stars. He fought in London, Liverpool, Manchester, Prague, Bologna, Milan, and Liege (Belgium). He also won five of seven bouts in Paris—all 12-rounders. Wherever he fought he impressed the foreign fans with a brand of scientific boxing rarely seen.

Valgar's reputation preceded him. Before his first fight in Paris, the French sports newspaper *L'Auto* devoted several columns to the American "pugiliste." Proudly the newspaper declared, "He is of ours. . . . Benny Valger has had a very brilliant career in the U.S.A. where he began boxing in the ring in 1916 . . . he is considered as one of the most scientific lightweights of the U.S.A."[6]

In a recently published biography of Ray Arcel titled *Champ in the Corner: The Ray Arcel Story*, author John Jarrett relates an amusing story that took place in the waning days of Benny Valgar's career. It captures the essence of his boxing persona:

> One night Benny looked around the arena and saw only a handful of customers, recalled Arcel. Benny looked at me and said, "Ray, what's the matter? Why ain't we drawing?"

I said, "Benny, the fans want action. They don't want to see any of that fancy jab and run stuff. Get out there and slug."

Benny went out with a rush but did nothing but box. When the round was over, I said to Benny, "Why didn't you go out there and slug?"

Benny looked at me and said, "I tried, Ray, honestly I did. My arms were willing, but my brain wouldn't let me do anything wrong!"

That was my Benny.[7]

Valgar finally retired in 1932, at the age of 34, with his intellect intact. He led a quiet life after retirement, although he remained active in veteran boxers' organizations. With his wife, Rose, whom he married in 1919, he settled in Brighton Beach, Brooklyn, and opened a dress shop in the Brownsville section of that borough. He passed away in 1972.

7

BOXERS 2, STRONGMEN 0

(April 18, 2013)

Acquiring proficiency in any demanding profession is no easy task. Developing highly refined skills takes years to master. For a boxer, the journey from the amateur ranks to professional status involves a grueling and brutal apprenticeship. Being the strongest and toughest athlete in another sport in no way guarantees success as a professional boxer. A painful lesson awaits those who think they can compete without the necessary preparation.

It is not surprising that champion athletes in strength sports like weight lifting or the shot put might get it into their heads that they could use their incredible strength to achieve success in the prize ring. Such was the case with Olympic gold medal winners Paul Anderson and Bill Nieder.

Paul Anderson is a legend in the sport of weight lifting. In 1955 the 5'9", 320-pound strongman won the world weight lifting title with a clean and press of 408.5 pounds. No human being had ever done that before. One year later he won a gold medal in the super heavyweight class at the Melbourne Olympic Games. His Olympic triumph combined with an astounding back lift of 6,270 pounds earned him the title of "World's Strongest Man." He is still considered the greatest power lifter of all time.

Anderson lost his amateur status because he had accepted money for some of his strength exhibitions, thereby barring him from competing in the 1960 Olympic Games. A Russian weight lifter broke Anderson's 1956 record and took home the gold medal. Anderson, in a demonstration to prove he still owned the title as World's Strongest Man, gathered witnesses to watch as he lifted the same weight as the Russian three times in quick succession!

Three years after winning Olympic gold, Anderson, the World's Strongest Man, decided to add the heavyweight championship of the world to his already superlative list of athletic credentials.

On April 25, 1960, Anderson, trimmed down to a svelte 290 pounds (he went as high as 370 while competing as a weight lifter), took the first step on his road to a world boxing title. He made his professional boxing debut in Charlotte, North Carolina, against a preliminary boxer named Attilio Tondo (3–7). The bout was scheduled for six rounds.

Anderson was an awesome sight to behold. He looked like a human tank as he entered the ring with his 58-inch chest, 22½-inch biceps, and 36-inch thighs. The Georgia strongman outweighed his opponent by 94 pounds and probably could have benched-pressed him with one hand and then heaved him into the seventh row. But this was a different ball game, so Paul had to play by the rules.

The great weight lifter came out punching and managed to floor his much lighter opponent three times. But every time Attilio was knocked down he got up. By the third round Paul was gasping for air and wheezing like a wounded rhinoceros.

Two-hundred-ninety-pound former Olympic weight lifting champion Paul Anderson made his professional boxing debut against 194-pound Attilio Tondo on April 25, 1960. Paul ran out of gas in the third round. *Author's collection*

Not content to end his brief boxing career with a loss, Anderson went to the post three more times. He knocked out two obscure opponents and then lost to one Billy Walters (6–5–1). In the fourth round, Anderson confused Walters with a dumbbell, picked him up, and threw him to the mat. He was immediately disqualified.

In 1961 Paul and his wife, Glenda, founded the Paul Anderson Youth Home, a residential home for troubled youth, in Vidalia, Georgia. It was supported by his speaking engagements and strength exhibitions. Paul passed away in 1994 at the age of 61 from kidney failure. Through private and public donations the home continues its mission.

One year after Anderson's disastrous professional boxing debut, another Olympic gold medalist and legendary strongman was about to enter the professional prize ring for the first time. Bill Nieder was the 1960 Olympic shot put champion. He won the gold medal by hurling a 16-pound iron ball nearly 65 feet, setting a new world record.

To say that Nieder was uncommonly strong is an understatement. His prodigious feats of strength included holding, at arm's length in front of his chest, a barbell weighing 300 pounds! He was also reputed to have killed a cow with a single blow. When asked about this by a *Sports Illustrated* reporter, Nieder responded with, "I'd rather not talk about that."[1]

As it turned out, Nieder might have been better off fighting the cow.

The 26-year-old Olympic champion stood 6'3" tall and weighed 242 pounds when he won the gold medal. Three months of training for his boxing debut brought Nieder's fighting weight down to 216 pounds. His opponent was a six-foot, 198-pound preliminary boxer named Jim Wiley who sported a 6–15–3 (1 KO) record.

Wiley had been KO'd nine times, but most of his opponents were legitimate professionals including several recognizable names. Despite his dismal record, Wiley was far more experienced than Nieder, whose press release claimed he had knocked out six amateur opponents.

The Fight

The bout took place in Philadelphia's Alhambra Arena, an old theater that had been converted into a boxing venue. As reported in the May 29, 1961, issue of *Sports Illustrated*, Nieder was severely overmatched: "At no time in the two minutes the fight lasted did Nieder throw a worthwhile punch, but worst still, and sadly, he had not the faintest notion how to defend himself. . . . In the ensuing melee Wiley hit the incredibly hapless Nieder at will, or would have but for the collisions and entangling misalliances."

Nieder was knocked down but bounced up at the count of one. Wiley then landed a right that sent his startled opponent through the ropes and out of the ring. For a few moments Bill was out of sight, disappearing below the first row of spectators. Finally, aided by a few ringside fans, he made it back in but stumbled over the middle strand "and went flying into the ring much as he had gone out, as though a film of the fight had been reversed."[2] By the time he clambered to his feet, the count had been completed.

Jersey Joe Walcott, the old champ who'd been involved in preparing Nieder, put in a few positive words. "The kid got fighting heart," he said. "But he shouldn't have been fighting for another three or four months." Nieder was embarrassed but philosophical about his only experience as a pro boxer: "I have no one to blame but Ole Bill Nieder. . . . I want one more fight to prove to myself this isn't a fluke. Patience and relaxation is the key. It's a matter of conquering the mind. You know, when you throw an iron ball it doesn't come back at you."[3]

As for Jim Wiley, some fool got the notion that he was now ready for some serious competition. In his very next fight he was matched against the murderous-hitting heavyweight contender Cleveland Williams. The fight lasted all of 44 seconds.

Bill Nieder did far better outside of the ring. He was employed by the 3M Corporation for many years and was instrumental in developing artificial athletic turf, which is now standard at all major track meets.

On May 8, 2011, Bill Nieder's name appeared in newspapers across the country. At the age of 77 he helped subdue a passenger attempting to enter the cockpit of an American Airlines flight headed to San Francisco.[4]

8

THE PRESIDENT BOXER

(November 17, 2015)

No U.S. president, past or present, was more associated with the "sweet science" than Theodore Roosevelt. It was not by accident that TR developed his interest in boxing. In Roosevelt's formative years, young men from the best families practiced the manly art. In the late 1800s amateur boxing "in gentlemanly fashion" (fought with gloves under Queensberry rules) was included in the athletic programs of Harvard and Yale. (Both institutions were among a handful of colleges that offered boxing instruction to their students.)

The future president boxed as a 135-pound lightweight while attending Harvard. He entered several tournaments, and though he was only moderately successful, his courage and tenacity were admired by his classmates.

During one tournament match he was hit hard by his opponent just after the referee yelled, "Time." The crowd hissed and shouted, "Foul, foul!" Roosevelt is supposed to have cried out, "Hush! He didn't hear." Years later, during his campaign for the presidency, his supporters would frequently reference the incident as an example of his extraordinary character.

In his junior year at Harvard (1879), TR fought for the university cup against a senior and was "severely punished" according to the *New York Times*.[1] The *Times* often reported on the athletic exploits of Ivy League athletes as these schools were considered incubators for the future economic, social, and political leaders of America. His opponent was two or three inches taller and had a much longer reach. "When time was called after the last round," one spectator recalled, "his face was dashed with blood and he was much winded; but his spirit did not flag, and if there had been another round, he would have gone into it with undiminished determination."[2]

The future president at Harvard, 1879. *Theodore Roosevelt Collection (520.12-002), Houghton Library, Harvard University*

TR was at best a fair boxer and athlete, but he loved boxing and was a steadfast supporter of the sport as long as it remained free of gambling and corruption. In 1896, while serving as police commissioner of New York City, Roosevelt endorsed a bill that legalized boxing in the state. He believed that under the right circumstances boxing had value as a "vigorous healthful sport that develops courage, keenness of mind, quickness of eye, and a spirit of combativeness that fits every boy who engages in it for the daily tasks that confront him."[3] But the professional side of the sport remained a problem for him.

In 1899, during his term as New York's governor, boxing was rocked by a number of major betting scandals and fixed fights. The following year, he reluctantly signed a bill outlawing professional prizefighting in New York State. (The ban lasted four years.)

Roosevelt's interest in athletics, and specifically boxing, was the result of a lifelong pursuit of what he called "the strenuous life." TR exercised daily and was constantly challenging himself to do better. His favorite sports were boxing, tennis, hiking, rowing, polo, and horseback riding. He greatly admired boxers and formed friendships with John L. Sullivan, Bob Fitzsimmons, Battling Nelson, and Mike Donovan.

Even while occupying the White House (1901–1909), Roosevelt enjoyed boxing with an array of sparring partners, including former professionals, several times each week. By then the president was a full-fledged heavyweight, weighing around 190 pounds.

During a sparring session with a military aide, Roosevelt took a hard punch to his left eye. He gradually lost sight in the damaged orb, but that information was not made public until many years later. Although the injury failed to dampen his enthusiasm for boxing, he thereafter confined his physical jousts to practicing judo, attaining a third-degree brown belt.

Of all the fighters Roosevelt knew, he was closest to Sullivan, who reigned as heavyweight champion from 1882 to 1892. They first met in the mid-1890s when TR was a crusading police commissioner in New York City. Sullivan had retired in 1892 after losing the title to James J. Corbett, but the public's adulation for "the Great John L." endured well after his last bout. During that time he earned his living as a professional entertainer and temperance lecturer.

The patrician Roosevelt and the rough-hewn Sullivan, an Irish American from an urban, working-class background, formed a sort of mutual admiration society based on their common interests. They were the same age, and as noted by Sullivan biographer Michael T. Isenberg, "Each worshipped the shrine of masculinity and had, in his different way, been a missionary of the strenuous life; each was his own brass band."[4]

Roosevelt's friendship with Sullivan remained strong during and after his presidency. In later years Sullivan was a frequent guest at Roosevelt's Sagamore Hill estate. Both of these fascinating and charismatic individuals were perfect symbols of their era. They were energetic, confident, assertive, and occasionally reckless, and their colorful personalities embodied the qualities of a country ascending to greatness at the turn of the last century.

The 26th president of the United States would have made a wonderful boxing commissioner, but after his "Rough Rider" campaign in Cuba during the Spanish-American War of 1898, bigger and more important responsibilities awaited him. But if there ever was an individual with the wherewithal, honesty, and courage to clean up professional boxing, that man would have been Theodore Roosevelt.

THE OTHER BILLY GRAHAM

(March 2, 2016)

*Boxing has always lacked the type of effective regulation common to other pro-
fessional sports. In the 1950s, many contenders and champions were pawns of
a hoodlum element that had infested the sport. By the end of the decade, Senate
investigations and federal prosecution finally ended the mob's stranglehold on
the sport, but too late to rectify the injustice done to the subject of this story.*

Billy Graham, the world-famous evangelist, has preached to more
people than anyone in the history of Christianity. Graham has been
a national figure since first coming to the public's attention in 1949,
and his estimated lifetime audiences (including his worldwide crusades
and countless radio and television broadcasts) have topped 2.2 billion. The
97-year-old retired preacher has been the spiritual adviser and confidant
to former presidents Dwight Eisenhower, Lyndon Johnson, and Richard
Nixon. He has repeatedly been on Gallup's list of most admired men and
women. By the mid-1970s, many deemed him "America's pastor." But this
is not a story about the Reverend Billy Graham; it is a story about his name-
sake, a professional prizefighter also named Billy Graham, whose fame and
popularity predated the popular preacher's celebrity by several years.

The boxer Billy Graham was born in 1922, in the Murray Hill section
of Manhattan. Billy first laced on the gloves as an 11-year-old member
of his local Police Athletic League's boxing team. His amateur career included a win over a very young Sugar Ray Robinson. When he attempted
to enter the New York Golden Gloves tournament, the examining physi-

cian discovered a heart murmur and disqualified him. The following year Billy applied for a professional boxing license and passed the physical without incident.

Shortly before his 19th birthday a neighborhood acquaintance, Jack Reilly, introduced Billy to boxing manager Irving Cohen. It was a fortuitous meeting. Irving Cohen was the antithesis of the cigar-chomping, in-your-face boxing manager. Before he began his career as a boxing manager, Irving had spent several years in New York's garment industry, selling women's lingerie—not exactly the ideal preparation for a boxing manager. But Irving was a former amateur boxer with a love for the sport and a discerning eye for ring talent. He was a soft-spoken gentleman who rarely raised his voice, yet he possessed the most important attribute of a competent fight manager: compassion combined with the knowledge of how to develop a young fighter without getting him ruined by careless matchmaking.

Taking the young fighter under his wing, Cohen hired the capable Whitey Bimstein to train him. Billy was brought along slowly. There would be plenty of opportunities to gain professional experience while learning his trade in the myriad of boxing clubs that dotted the New York City landscape.

Irving Cohen did not believe in rushing his fighters. Billy's first 16 bouts were all four-rounders, followed by 17 bouts limited to six rounds before Cohen put him into an eight-round semifinal. Graham went to the post 42 times before engaging in his first ten-round bout—almost four years after turning pro. This was the pattern for every fighter Cohen managed, including future middleweight champion Rocky Graziano, who had close to 40 bouts before his first ten-rounder.[1]

By then Billy had grown into a solid 145-pound welterweight with a superb jab, good infighting skills, excellent footwork, and the ability to adapt to a variety of different styles. His clever boxing technique more than compensated for his lack of a big punch. On those rare occasions when he was tagged with a haymaker, Billy's rock-solid jaw stood the test. Clean cut and handsome, the young fighter had become a hot attraction in the local fight clubs. He continued to improve with every contest, remaining undefeated through 58 bouts (52–0–6 with 19 KOs).

Graham's 59th bout resulted in his first loss—a split ten-round decision to tough Tony Pellone at the Queensboro Arena on September

11, 1945. Over the next four years he won 31 of 35, including wins over Aldo Minelli, Terry Young, and Fritzie Pruden. Those victories earned him a rating among the top ten welterweight contenders. His four losses were to Pellone, Tippy Larkin, Paddy DeMarco, and England's Eddie Thomas, all of whom were top fighters. He considered those losses learning experiences, especially his bout with Larkin, one of the finest boxers of his generation.

Graham opened his 1950 campaign with a win over previous conqueror Tony Pellone and followed 23 days later with a split ten-round decision over the great Cuban boxer Kid Gavilan. He was now the top-rated welterweight contender in the world. After winning his next five bouts, Graham lost his rematch with Gavilan via another split decision.

Eight months later Kid Gavilan won the world welterweight championship with a 15-round decision over Chicago's Johnny Bratton. Having split two close decisions with the Cuban Hawk, Billy should have had the title shot and not Bratton. But there was a fly in the ointment. Gavilan and Bratton were IBC fighters. Graham was not. The International Boxing Club (IBC) monopolized the promotion of big-time boxing in the United States during the 1950s. Although the IBC's titular head was James D. Norris, a wealthy sportsman who owned several major arenas and stadiums, the real power behind the IBC throne was the notorious mafia hoodlum and racketeer Frankie Carbo. In silent partnership with Norris, Carbo and his cohorts used front managers to control the destinies of many top contenders and world champions. Carbo was the sport's unofficial dictator, czar, and commissioner all rolled into one. Under Carbo the IBC oozed corruption. Fighters controlled by the IBC were sometimes ordered to throw a fight in order to facilitate a betting coup for the mob. The organization had a stranglehold on the sport. Managers and boxers who preferred to remain independent and refused to follow the edicts of the all-powerful IBC were denied lucrative television dates and the opportunity to advance their careers.

Shortly after Graham's second bout with Gavilan, Norris had met with Irving Cohen at New York's Forrest Hotel to discuss a title bout between Gavilan and Graham to determine a new welterweight champion. (The former champion, Sugar Ray Robinson, had abandoned the title after defeating Jake LaMotta for the middleweight crown.) Present at the meeting was the ubiquitous Carbo. They told Cohen he could have the title match on the condition that Carbo would take over the management of Graham. Cohen was no neophyte; he understood that not giving up control of his fighter would jeopardize the chances of Graham ever getting a title shot. He decided to let his fighter decide. If Billy wanted the fight under those conditions, Cohen was willing to step aside. Billy's loyalty to the man who had steered his career from the very beginning was unwavering: "Irving, I started with you and I will finish with you. I will not take the fight under those conditions." As Cohen expected, Billy was left out in the cold and Bratton was given the title shot.[2]

Over the next six months, Graham maintained his number one contender status. Whenever he fought, ring announcers would introduce him as the "uncrowned welterweight champion." The fans and sportswriters wanted to see him challenge Gavilan for the title. Public pressure finally forced Norris's hand, and he agreed to stage the bout on August 29, 1951, at Madison Square Garden. The fight would be televised nationally (CBS network) on the Pabst Blue Ribbon–sponsored fight of the week program. This was a time when televised main events were shown every night except Sundays. Billy had already appeared in almost two dozen televised matches. He was a familiar name to the millions of armchair fans who tuned in each week.

Cohen knew the deck would be stacked against him and that Carbo would probably coerce the judges and referee to vote against Graham if the bout went to a decision. In 1995 I interviewed Herb Cohen, Irving's son, for *The Ring* magazine. He said that an anonymous caller phoned his father the day before the fight and told him who would be judging and refereeing the fight. The New York State Athletic Commission's policy was to assign the referee and judges on the same night the fight took place so as to discourage bribes. Irving Cohen went directly to the commission office to express his concern and go on record that an anonymous caller had already named the officials for the fight. He asked, as a precaution, that the judges and referee named by the caller not officiate the following evening. Commission officials assured him this would be done. He was told not to worry and that all precautions would be taken to protect his boxer and the integrity of the sport.

To Cohen's dismay, on the night of the fight, the commission did not switch the two judges and referee. The same people named by the anonymous caller were assigned to the fight. Adding to his alarm was a late shift in the odds that made Gavilan a 14-to-5 favorite to retain his crown. Considering that their first two fights could have gone either way, the odds made no sense unless word had gotten out that the fix was in.[3]

It was a tough, competitive fight. At the end of 15 hard-fought rounds, Gavilan retained the title on a split decision by the narrowest of margins. One judge had it for Graham, but he was outvoted by the referee and the other judge. As soon as the decision was announced, the jeers and hoots of thousands of spectators echoed throughout the Garden. Cigar butts, beer containers, programs, and other assorted debris were thrown into the ring by irate fans. A near riot ensued. The referee and judge who voted for Gavilan needed a police escort to get back to the safety of the dressing rooms.

There is no denying that it was a close fight, but most observers thought Graham had done enough to win the decision, including 12 of the 15 reporters at ringside. The real question was, how could a very popular New York boxer lose a close decision for the championship in his

Billy Graham (right) lost a controversial decision to welterweight champ Kid Gavilan on August 29, 1951. Graham's refusal to accept mob management may have cost him the title. *Associated Press*

own hometown? Although a fix was never proven, it certainly would not have been the first time that Carbo and company had prearranged the outcome of a major fight.

There was one more bout with Gavilan. Thirteen months after their controversial title bout, Billy traveled to Havana, Cuba, Gavilan's hometown, where he lost an uncontested 15-round decision.

In Teddy Brenner's book *Only the Ring Was Square* (1981), he talks about the Gavilan-Graham bout. The book is a 163-page gossipy tome that lacks depth. It is based on Brenner's experiences as Madison Square Garden matchmaker in the 1960s and 1970s. In it he states that years after the controversial title bout, the judge who voted for Gavilan summoned Irving Cohen to the hospital where he was in the last stages of a terminal illness. In what amounted to a deathbed confession (according to Brenner), the guilt-ridden boxing judge said: "The boys ordered me to do it."[4] The judge's widow later sued both Brenner and the publisher for defamation, stating her late husband had never confessed to anything and had not been hospitalized but had succumbed at their home to a fatal heart attack.

Deathbed confession or not, there is virtually no doubt that short of scoring an unlikely knockout (in 143 fights Gavilan never came close to being KO'd), Graham had no chance of winning the fight once he decided not to go with Carbo.

In 1957, nearly a decade after the formation of the IBC, the Justice Department ordered its dissolution for operating a monopoly in restraint of trade. Four years later Carbo and his chief lieutenant, Frank "Blinky" Palermo, were convicted of extortion and racketeering and received lengthy prison sentences. Unfortunately, their imprisonment came years too late for Graham and who knows how many other exploited victims of their pernicious greed.

"Billy Graham was really a gentleman, he really was," recalled Herb Cohen in his interview with *The Ring*. "He should have been champion. He earned it. He didn't get it. Yet he never showed any real bitterness. And he never regretted his decision not to leave my father and hook up with Carbo, even though it cost him a world title. I don't know how many fighters would have refused a title fight because their manager was not willing to accept the terms. My father offered his fighters more than just a business relationship. The relationship extended to them as human beings, as sons, as friends. He was devoted to all his fighters. They were like his children."[5]

Such qualities are indeed rare in the business of boxing—as rare as the loyalty shown by Billy Graham in refusing to compromise his principles and integrity.

Echoing Herb Cohen's sentiments is Eddie Foy III, the grandson of the legendary vaudeville performer Eddie Foy. Eddie III (whose father, Eddie Foy Jr., was number six of "The Seven Little Foys") idolized Billy Graham and became his biggest fan. In 1945, when he was just 12 years old, Eddie went up to Stillman's Gym and introduced himself to the welterweight contender. Billy was taken with the young man's sincerity and enthusiasm. They developed a strong bond of friendship that lasted until Graham's death in 1992. "Billy Graham was one of the nicest and most decent men you'd ever want to meet," says Foy. "I was heading in the wrong direction and he straightened me out. He was not only a father figure to me—he was my best friend. Billy wasn't a pug. He was a street-wise, classy man and a truly artistic fighter."[6]

After his final fight with Gavilan, Billy remained active for three more years, fighting the top men in both the welterweight and middleweight divisions. He outpointed Jimmy Herring, Art Aragon, and Paddy Young and fought to a draw with Rocky Castellani. Between 1952 and 1954 he split several wins and losses with future champions Carmen Basilio and Joey Giardello.

Thanks to his superb boxing skills Graham was never seriously hurt or banged up in any of his fights. On April 1, 1955, a slower and older Graham lost a unanimous decision to welterweight contender Chico Vejar. He had been outpointed by Vejar the previous month. The defeat was his fourth straight loss. At age 32 Billy knew he was past his prime as a fighter; it was time to hang up his gloves. He finished his career with a 102–15–9 (27 KOs) record. Seven of his losses were by split decision. In 126 professional fights Billy had never been knocked out or even knocked down.

After he retired from boxing, Billy moved his wife and four children to Long Island where he began a long career as a salesman for National Distillers. Whenever he attended the fights at Madison Square Garden, he was introduced before the main event along with other past and present boxing stars. Johnny Addie, the announcer, always prefaced his name with the words "uncrowned welterweight champion of the world." Billy's name was always greeted with warm applause. It was as if the New York fans still felt bad about the injustice done to this fine fighter and gentleman who was denied the prize he worked so hard to attain because the scum who always seem to rule this rotten sport didn't want it that way.

Once upon a time winning a world boxing championship was a rare and venerated achievement. It really meant something. Today every boxer it seems is wearing some kind of goofy title belt, which of course makes them all worthless. In Billy's day not winning the title was a great disappointment, but it did not define him. Nor did he brood over it for the rest of his life.

It's not an easy task to remain unsullied, uncorrupted, and undamaged in the brutal, unforgiving sport of professional boxing. Billy Graham was one of the few who did. In his excellent biography of former heavyweight champion Gene Tunney, author Jack Cavanaugh recalls a quote made by sportswriter Jim Murray in which he claims that Tunney "was the best advertisement his sport ever had."[7] Billy Graham was cut of the same cloth. No doubt Pastor Billy Graham would agree.

Part II

THE WAY I SEE IT

10

DON'T BLAME RUBY: A BOXING TRAGEDY REVISITED

(July 30, 2012)

"If boxing is a sport it is the most tragic of all sports because more than any other human activity it consumes the very excellence it displays—its drama is this very consumption. To expend oneself in fighting the greatest fight of one's life is to begin by necessity the downward turn that next time may be a plunge, an abrupt fall into the abyss."

—Joyce Carol Oates

From 1945 to 2007 at least 640 professional and amateur boxers have died as a result of punishment received in the ring.[1] Two of those fatalities took place in front of a nationwide television audience, thereby exposing boxing's worst-case scenario to millions of people. In 2011, nearly 50 years after it happened, the story of the first fatality made the news again when the well-known manager of one of the fighters involved died. In recounting the fight, several newspapers and media outlets attributed sole blame to the referee, an accusation that was both unjustified and not based on the facts. My purpose in writing this article was to set the record straight by examining and analyzing the series of events that contributed to the death of a champion.

On March 24, 1962, Benny "Kid" Paret, the welterweight champion of the world, was beaten into a coma in the 12th round by former champion Emile Griffith at New York's Madison Square Garden. Despite emergency brain surgery, Paret never regained consciousness and died ten days later.

Boxers had been killed in the ring before (192 in the previous 16 years), but never in the modern history of the prize ring had a champion died defending his title. And never before had anyone ever been fatally injured in front of a nationwide television audience. (Twenty months later Lee Harvey Oswald, the assassin of President John F. Kennedy, would be the second person killed during a live nationwide broadcast.)

Estimates put the number of people who watched the Paret vs. Griffith fight at 14 million. The tragedy, being so public and involving a world champion, shook the boxing world to its very core. The memory of the fight and its brutal ending—unforgettable to those who witnessed it on television or in person—remains an iconic moment in the history of boxing.

There is an infamous side story to the fight that involves Paret's insulting Griffith at the boxing commission's weigh-in on the morning of the fight. Paret's gay-baiting remark and boorish behavior was meant to unnerve Griffith and it worked. Griffith was furious and had to be restrained from starting the fight then and there. But that ugly incident is not relevant to the purpose of this chapter, which is to set the record straight as to who was really responsible for Paret's death and to determine if it could have been avoided.

Details of the fight resurfaced not too long ago in obituaries of Gil Clancy, the well-known trainer and comanager of Emile Griffith. Most of the articles stated that Paret had died because the referee, Ruby Goldstein, waited too long to stop the fight. This explanation has been repeated so often over the years that most people just accept it at face value. But an examination of the facts leading up to the tragedy reveals a far more complex answer to the question of who bears responsibility for it.

The competence of boxing referees remains an ongoing problem in professional boxing. In no other sport can a wrong decision by an official have fatal consequences for the athlete. It is a very heavy responsibility. There have been a number of previous boxing fatalities that can be directly attributed to a referee acting too late to stop a fight—but this was not one of them.

The Facts

Benny "Kid" Paret won the undisputed welterweight title from Don Jordan in May 1960. His record was a respectable 32–7–3. Paret's ascent to the title was done the old-fashioned way—he earned it. Six months earlier he upset the number one welterweight contender, Charley Scott, in two back-to-back ten-round bouts that were spaced less than six weeks apart. Both bouts were savage affairs with each fighter taking, and dishing out, heavy punishment. At the time Scott was one of the hardest-punching welterweights in the world.

Just two months after his second row with Scott, Paret fought 12 hard rounds with third-ranked Federico Thompson of Argentina. The fight, a title eliminator, ended in a draw.

Federico Thompson is all but forgotten today except by a few boxing purists who remember a very experienced and skilled boxer with knockout power in both fists.

Less than two months after his melee with Thompson, Paret defeated Don Jordan for the title via a 15-round unanimous decision. It was one of the few easy fights of his career.

The new champion would have been justified in taking a rest, but with Madison Square Garden having to fill its summer TV schedule Paret was back in the ring six weeks after winning the championship.

On July 12 he knocked out former contender Sugar Hart in the sixth round of a nontitle fight. The following month he returned to the Garden to face fourth-ranked Denny Moyer in yet another nontitle fight. Paret appeared a bit overweight and fought without his usual fire or conviction and lost the ten-round decision.

Four months later, on December 10, 1960, Paret closed out a very busy year by fighting a return bout with Thompson in defense of his title. The champion absorbed some powerful punches, but youth was on his side and he was able to outhustle the hard-punching Argentinian over 15 rounds and win a unanimous decision.

Barely ten weeks after that tough bout, Paret fought perennial contender Gaspar Ortega in a nontitle ten-rounder. This fight was the first overt clue that Paret's unrelenting schedule and his give-and-take style of fighting was wearing him down. He looked uncharacteristically sluggish and lacked the energy and focus of previous fights. Paret lost a unanimous decision.

To most fans it appeared that Paret was not trying hard enough against Ortega or perhaps he just had an off night. But in truth he was already a shopworn fighter physically and mentally in need of a respite from boxing and training. Yet only five weeks after his bout with Ortega he put his title on the line against top-ranked contender Emile Griffith.

If Paret had been a less durable fighter, his recent poor showings might have been cause for some concern. But throughout his career the tough Cuban expatriate had exhibited a remarkable resiliency and the ability to absorb punches that would have wrecked many other boxers. This was particularly evident in his punishing fights with Scott and Thompson.

It was hard to envision Paret on the canvas. But that is exactly where he landed on April 1, 1961, the day he faced Emile Griffith for the first time. The resiliency that was this iron man's stock in trade suddenly evaporated at one minute and 11 seconds into the 13th round.

Paret will never make an all-time great list, but in his day he was a decent enough fighter and a step above the tough club fighter he was just a few years earlier. His movements were quick and rhythmic. At his best he was a very strong and durable unrelenting pressure fighter who preferred infighting over long-range boxing. If he were active today he could easily steamroll the competition.

Even though he was beginning to show the effects of his punishing ring career, Paret was no pushover and more than a match for Emile. He was the busier puncher and was outscoring Griffith in close-quarter infighting. At the end of 12 rounds Paret had a slight lead on all the scorecards.

What happened next was totally unexpected. In the middle of the 13th round, Griffith suddenly landed a three-punch combination capped off by a solid right cross to the chin. The knockdown took everyone by surprise, including Griffith. Paret stumbled back a few steps after being hit and then sprawled to the floor. He landed on his side with his body propped up by an elbow, in a position similar to that of a reclining beach-goer gazing absentmindedly at the surf.

But Paret's glassy-eyed empty stare indicated a fighter who was completely unaware of his surroundings. Even after being counted out he did not move or attempt to rise. It took several minutes before the woozy fighter was able to leave the ring.

To this observer watching the televised broadcast of the fight, there was something unnatural and disturbing in the way Paret took the count. I have seen countless knockouts since then and have yet to witness anything resembling that knockdown. His body just seemed to suddenly quit on him, as if it had reached the end of its limit and just could not go on anymore.

The Breaking Point

What had happened to the iron man? He'd taken worse punishment from harder punchers in other fights and had not faltered. The answer was that Paret's ability to "take it" had finally been compromised. The Kid had fought too many tough fights in too short a span of time. The iron man had stretched his remarkable physical resources to the breaking point. When those three punches caromed off his head, the champion's neuromuscular physiology went into lockdown. The connection between Paret's consciousness and his indomitable fighting spirit had been temporarily short-circuited.

Beginning of the End

Benny "Kid" Paret was a magnificent physical specimen. Even his sinewy muscles seemed to have muscles. But he did not have the wide lats and oversized pectoral muscles that are useless to a fighter but are common among today's weight lifter/boxers. The Kid never lifted weights. His development was all natural and genetic. As a poor illiterate child and teenager, he'd worked for years cutting sugarcane in Cuba. If he wasn't doing manual labor he was training to be a fighter. His muscular development was perfect for the ring.

But even the best built piece of machinery can only stand so much abuse before breaking down. In the jargon of the fight game, the 24-year-old ex-champ was on his way to becoming a "shot" fighter—meaning that he was punched out, irrevocably past his prime, and vulnerable to further injury.

A Perfect Storm

In a rare break from his hectic schedule, Paret did not fight again for six months. When he did get back into the ring it was for a return match with Griffith in an attempt to regain the title.

The six-month respite had given Benny a chance to recharge his batteries and regain a semblance of his old form. Although a 5-to-1 underdog to Griffith, he still had enough juice left to make it a competitive fight. The one aspect of Paret's fighting persona that had not diminished was his indomitable fighting spirit.

In a hard-fought and exciting battle, the former champion upset the odds and won a 15-round split decision.

The decision did not sit well with the Madison Square Garden audience or the millions of fans watching the fight on television. To most everyone it appeared that Griffith had won the fight. It wasn't a blowout but he definitely deserved the win. The referee saw it that way but was overruled by the two judges who voted for Paret.

Without knowing for sure, I will not impugn the motives of the two judges. But no fewer than 18 of 22 reporters sitting at ringside had scored the fight for Griffith. The controversial win for Paret ensured a third bout between the two adversaries.

A perfect storm of circumstances that would eventually lead to a champion's death in the ring was gaining momentum.

Welterweight or Middleweight?

An often overlooked aspect of Paret's ill-fated career that may have had some bearing on the outcome of his final fight was his difficulty making the welterweight limit of 147 pounds. In the 18 months prior to acquiring the welterweight title he was under 147 pounds only once in 12 fights. Paret's average weight for all of his other bouts hovered around 153 pounds. He'd even gone as high as 157½ pounds for one bout. Eight weeks before his third fight with Griffith, he was still almost ten pounds over the welterweight limit. I'm not saying he was dehydrated for his final fight, just that the extra burden of making weight could have weakened him, especially as the fight entered the later rounds.

The Fullmer Fight

Considering the problems Paret was having making 147 pounds, it seemed logical to move up a division and challenge the middleweight champion Gene Fullmer. Even if Paret lost, he would still retain his welterweight crown. Nevertheless, it was an audacious move.

Gene Fullmer was something else. He was a hard-charging bull of a fighter with an iron chin and an indestructible body. Aside from being extremely strong and durable, his awkward punishing style gave opponents fits. To throw Paret into the ring with him only nine weeks after his grueling 15-round bout with Griffith was really pushing the envelope. A parent can be arrested for child abuse, but there are no laws to stop a boxing manager from abusing his own fighter.

Paret weighed 156¾ pounds for his fight with Fullmer, a good weight for him. Fullmer scaled a quarter pound under 160 for the nationally televised fight. The location was the Las Vegas Convention Center, not far from Fullmer's home base near Salt Lake City, Utah. Everyone expected an exciting fight, but hardly anyone expected Paret to win.

A battle of attrition was the hallmark of almost every one of Fullmer's fights. He seemed to have endless reserves of energy and stamina. Against this type of opponent, Paret's aggressive buzz-saw style and his fondness for infighting would work against him. He would be drawn into a slugging match with one of the strongest and roughest middleweights to ever hold the title. It was a recipe for disaster.

As expected, Paret stood toe to toe with Fullmer for the first four rounds, dishing out as much punishment as he took. It was a tremendous but futile effort. Over the next four rounds the superior strength, punch, and stamina of the middleweight champion wore Paret down. The ninth and tenth rounds were particularly hard to watch as the rampaging middleweight champion connected at will with one brain-rattling punch after another.

In the tenth round the exhausted, bloodied challenger was the recipient of one of the most frightful and sustained beatings this writer has ever witnessed. Seven full-power right-hand punches were landed consecutively to Paret's head before he went down. After getting up from the second knockdown he could barely stand. The referee, Harry Krause, inexcusably allowed the fight to continue for one more knockdown before finally counting him out.

If ever there was a textbook example of incompetent refereeing, this was it. Yet there was hardly any criticism directed toward the referee for his atrocious conduct, mainly because Benny, after being revived, was able to walk out of the ring under his own power.

The fight had also taken its toll on the middleweight champion. Fullmer's face looked like he'd walked into an electric fan. He told reporters he hit Paret harder and more often than any other opponent and could not understand what held him up.

Fullmer did not fight again for ten months. Benny was given no such luxury. He was back in the Madison Square Garden ring three and a half months later for the rubber match with Griffith.

After his punishing bout with Fullmer, the wise decision would have been to either retire Paret or grant him six months to a year off from boxing and sparring. His brain had been traumatized and needed time to heal. But a temporary suspension or neurological testing was not ordered by the New York State Athletic Commission (NYSAC) that licensed Paret, a resident of the Bronx. The commission did not hesitate to approve the bout with Griffith.

Old-school managers shook their heads. They thought it was a reckless move for the Kid's manager, fellow Cuban Manny Alfaro, part owner of a Bronx nightclub, to put his fighter back into the ring with the hard-punching Griffith so soon after such a vicious beating.

Aftermath of the Fullmer Debacle

Boxing history (and medical opinion) has shown that it is the damage sustained in a previous fight that often leads to a fatal outcome in a subsequent fight. A famous case is that of 1930s heavyweight contender Ernie Schaaf, who collapsed in the ring after getting hit with a jab from light-hitting Primo Carnera.

Five months earlier Schaaf had been knocked unconscious by Max Baer, whose murderous right-hand punches had already taken the life of another fighter. It took Schaaf's handlers three minutes to bring the fighter back to consciousness. After the Baer fight Schaaf complained of chronic headaches, yet he continued with a busy fight schedule. At that point Schaaf was an accident waiting to happen. Carnera was just the straw that broke the camel's back, so to speak.

Los Angeles welterweight contender Jimmy Doyle should have retired after being knocked unconscious for several hours by vicious-punching middleweight Artie Levine. (In fact, Doyle was banned from fighting in California after the knockout.) He was never the same after that knockout and was subsequently killed in a 1947 title fight with Sugar Ray Robinson.

Other high-profile ring fatalities happened for the same reason. Check the records of Georgie Flores and Willie Classen and you will find they suffered punishing knockouts only weeks before the fight that ended their lives. All had become accidents waiting to happen. That was Benny "Kid" Paret's situation in early 1962, although no one seemed to notice or care.

Despite the knockout by Fullmer, Benny's reputation as an iron man remained more or less intact. The televised image of a fighter who could "take it" was still fixed in most people's minds. It was obvious he could be stopped, but it took a tremendous effort by a very good fighter to make it happen. The guy was still one tough cookie. Fullmer had to go all out to stop his stubborn opponent in their savagely fought battle.

But warning bells should have sounded. The former iron man had been counted out twice in the previous year, indicating there were definitely cracks in the armor.

In a recently published biography of Emile Griffith, *Nine, Ten, and Out! The Two Worlds of Emile Griffith*, Paret's wife Lucy told author Ron Ross that in the days leading up to the fight her husband complained of headaches and said he did not feel right. She begged him to seek a postponement. But Alfaro told her it was too late to pull out. There was big TV money on the table. So there was no cancellation or postponement.[2]

Split-Second Decisions

Ruby Goldstein, the popular 54-year-old referee chosen by the New York State Athletic Commission to referee the third and final Griffith vs. Paret title fight, was a former outstanding professional boxer. He was also one of the most respected and experienced referees in the world. Over the previous 20 years he'd refereed hundreds of bouts and never experienced a fatality in the ring.

Ironically, Goldstein had been criticized in the past for stopping at least half a dozen major fights too soon. Just five months earlier he stopped a main bout at the Garden when an outgunned fighter was staggered just once.

I do not envy a professional boxing referee's job. Split-second decisions must sometimes be made. The life of the athlete is in his hands. A wrong call during a boxing match can lead to severe injury or worse. Mere seconds could mean the difference between life and death in deciding when is the proper time to stop a fight. If a boxing referee wants to sleep well at night, his mantra should be "Better to stop a fight too soon than too late."

Unfortunately there are referees today who *consistently* make the decision to allow a hurt fighter every opportunity to come back rather than risk criticism for appearing to stop a bout too soon, thereby incurring the wrath of the promoter (who pays his fee) and the fans. These referees are a menace to the health and well-being of fighters and do not belong in the sport. Ruby Goldstein's history showed he did not fit into this category of referee.

Did the Referee Stop the Fight Too Late?

But nobody is perfect and the question to be answered is, did Ruby Goldstein stop Griffith vs. Paret III too late? First, let us look at other mitigating circumstances. Benny "Kid" Paret was a world champion. The words "world champion" really meant something in those days. At the time there were only nine weight divisions and nine champions—not 17 weight divisions and over 100 so-called world champions, as is the case today.

It was not uncommon for a ref to give a defending champ the benefit of the doubt, especially one with the proven ability to come back and win after being hurt. A striking example of this can be seen in the 11th, 12th, and 13th rounds of the sixth Jake LaMotta vs. Sugar Ray Robinson bout in 1951 for LaMotta's middleweight championship.

LaMotta, the sport's ultimate iron man, was exhausted and practically defenseless during those rounds. He took a horrific beating, absorbing dozens of unanswered blows to the head. Yet the referee, knowing LaMotta's reputation for durability and for turning defeat into victory at the last minute, let it go on far too long. If it were any other fighter taking that beating, the fight would have been stopped no later than the 12th round.

True to form, Benny "Kid" Paret nearly pulled off an upset when he dropped Emile hard with a perfect left hook in the sixth round of their final fight. Emile was badly hurt but made it to his feet at the count of eight. The bell rang seconds later.

Griffith recovered during the one-minute rest period and took back control of the fight, but there was no inkling of what was to come. Paret had been hurt several times after scoring the knockdown but always came back with a flurry and even managed to win the 11th round on one judge's scorecard as Griffith slowed down to conserve energy.

Back to Goldstein's decision: during Griffith's final vicious assault the referee did not "freeze," as some have suggested. He moved to stop the fight as soon as he was in position to see the extent of Paret's distress. For a few seconds the broad back of Griffith blocked Goldstein's view while Paret was trapped in the corner of the ring. In the few seconds it took to step around the near-maniacal Griffith and pull him off the stricken fighter, Griffith was able to get off an additional five or six damaging punches. The extent of the damage became obvious as the unconscious champion slowly sank to the floor. The speed and volume of Griffith's punches was just incredible.

Ill-fated Benny "Kid" Paret, trapped in a corner, was already unconscious when referee Ruby Goldstein intervened to stop the fight, March 24, 1962. *Associated Press*

Whether you believe the referee did or did not stop the fight in time is not the real issue in this particular case. What no one seemed to realize was how badly injured and vulnerable to further damage Paret's brain was after his destruction by Fullmer. Perhaps a thorough neurological exam might have turned up something, but that was never ordered or even suggested.

No one knows if stopping this fight a few seconds earlier would have made any difference. The fatal punch may have been landed before the final flurry. It could have been Griffith's right cross in the 12th round that staggered Paret and drove him into the corner. Or perhaps it occurred in an earlier round.

It is also possible that even if Paret had managed to avoid that final awful blizzard of 14 punches delivered in just five seconds, and had made it to the final bell, he might have collapsed into a coma in the dressing room. That is what had happened to a preliminary fighter named Jose Rigores just ten months earlier at New York's St. Nicholas Arena, and to Davey Moore, the featherweight champion of the world, after he was stopped in the tenth round of a title defense in Los Angeles against Sugar Ramos. Davey walked out of the ring to the dressing room under his own power, talked to reporters for a few moments, and then collapsed into a coma and died a few days later.

The Real Culprits

Although one cannot be sure when the fatal punch was landed, the bottom line is this: Paret was damaged goods going into his third fight with Emile Griffith. He should not have been allowed in the ring that night. The right time to have stopped the fight was before it ever began.

So who is to blame? The list of those who are most complicit begins with Paret's manager. Blame should also extend to the callous promoters. But the most complicit entity, and the one that bears the greatest responsibility for the tragedy, was the negligent New York State Athletic Commission, the government agency that oversees boxing in the state, conducts medical exams, and licenses everyone connected with the sport. Where was the oversight and concern the commission's own charter states is the very reason for its existence? Answer: there was no oversight or concern—just blatant negligence.

State-Sanctioned Mayhem

Both Paret's manager and the New York State Athletic Commission failed in their duty to protect a vulnerable fighter when he needed it most. Without adequate oversight and medical supervision, including suspending a boxer who sustained too much punishment, a violent contact sport such as boxing becomes nothing more than state-sanctioned mayhem.

If referee Ruby Goldstein shares any blame at all, it is way down on the list. Was the death of Paret his fault? Absolutely not. And to argue the point back and forth only serves to divert attention from the real culprits.

Benny "Kid" Paret was doomed before he ever stepped into the ring. When he heard the knock on the dressing room door summoning him to the Madison Square Garden ring for the final boxing match of his young life, the person knocking on the door might as well have been the warden of a prison summoning him to the execution chamber. All that was missing was a priest administering the last rites. For on the night of March 24, 1962, Benny "Kid" Paret was an abused fighter whose tortured brain and exhausted body was a ticking time bomb waiting to explode—if not in this fight, then the next. The fuse had already been lit, most probably in the Fullmer fight. The soon-to-be ex-champion was literally a dead man walking. Emile Griffith, the other victim in this tragic scenario, was the final straw.

Epilogue

Emile Griffith fought for 15 more years and had a legendary career that included winning the middleweight championship. He was a changed fighter after his tragic bout with Paret (see chapter 20). Thereafter he rarely tried to stop an opponent. In his next 80 fights he scored only 11 knockouts. He died in 2013 at a nursing home in Hempstead, New York.

Manny Alfaro continued to manage fighters for a few more years and then faded from the boxing scene.

Ruby Goldstein refereed one more fight after Griffith vs. Paret and then retired. An internal investigation conducted by the NYSAC cleared Goldstein of any wrongdoing. Unfortunately, the commission staff never addressed its own incompetence and negligence, nor did anyone else for that matter. Most outside criticism was directed at the violent nature of professional boxing itself. Perhaps that is where the real problem lies.

II
THE MYTH OF "THE THRILLA IN MANILA"

(September 30, 2012)

"The great enemy of truth is very often not the lie—deliberate, contrived and dishonest—but the myth—persistent, persuasive, and unrealistic. Too often we hold fast to the clichés of our forebears. We subject all facts to a prefabricated set of interpretations. We enjoy the comfort of opinion without the discomfort of thought."

—John F. Kennedy

There is an old saying, "Beauty is in the eye of the beholder." But can the same be said of a great prizefight? The answer to this question has much to do with how the beholder defines a great prizefight. Subjectivity of perception on the recollection of an event often produces different accounts of that event. In analyzing the third fight between Muhammad Ali and Joe Frazier I tried to be as dispassionate and objective as possible. This article produced more controversy and responses, both positive and negative, than any I have ever written. I present my case before you—judge for yourself.

Today is the 37th anniversary of the famous "Thrilla in Manila"—the third and final fight between archrivals Muhammad Ali and Joe Frazier. It was on this day in 1975 that Ali retained his heavyweight title with a 14th-round TKO of Frazier in Manila, the Philippines.

The platitudes for that fight continue to be repeated so often and with such conviction, in print, television, and on the internet, that people who've never seen even one round believe it to be the greatest heavyweight championship match of the 20th century.

Some have gone so far as to say it was the greatest fight of any weight division in the entire history of the sport! In 1997 *The Ring* magazine awarded it "Fight of the Century" honors in its all-time ratings. In 1999 ESPN's *SportsCentury* series ranked the fight as the fifth-greatest sports event of all time! The bandwagon was getting way too crowded. But there was still room for the resident boxing historian of a popular cable TV boxing program (no, not the fellow with hat and cigar) to jump on board. When asked "What fight would you show to a new fan to demonstrate boxing at its very best?" he unhesitatingly answered, "The third Ali vs. Frazier fight . . . it had everything."

These extreme statements and honorifics take in a lot of territory, especially when one considers all of the great prizefights that have taken place since the Marquis of Queensberry rules were introduced to boxing over 100 years ago.

I believe there are several reasons why Ali vs. Frazier III continues to maintain its lofty status, while other more deserving fights do not enjoy the same degree of notoriety. We can start with the words "The Thrilla in Manila." The catchy phrase originated with Ali and appeared on every poster and program, eventually becoming the fight's permanent identifying label. More than three decades after the fact, even people with absolutely no interest in the sport have a vague recollection that "The Thrilla in Manila" refers to an exciting boxing match that involved Muhammad Ali.

They might also remember that it was a particularly brutal match. But, if you have been around boxing long enough, you know it was no more brutal than countless other professional prizefights.

Now ask yourself this question: What if the fighters involved were not named Ali and Frazier but instead were two heavyweight contenders named "Smith" and "Jones"? Same fight, just different names. Would "The Thrilla" still be remembered today as a great fight?

I believe that anyone who witnessed the first Rocky Marciano vs. Jersey Joe Walcott title fight would call it great even if they did not know the names of the fighters. A great fight has to be recognized on its merits alone.

Here is a second point to ponder: Do you think we would still be lauding this fight in such glowing terms if it was Ali who was not allowed to come out for the 15th round and Frazier was the victor?

A Good, Tough Club Fight

To accurately evaluate "The Thrilla in Manila"—*based strictly on its merits as a prizefight*—is to come to the conclusion that it was no better or worse than a good, tough, club fight. Even from a historical perspective it lacked gravitas. For example, the Johnson vs. Jeffries "White Hope" fight and the second Dempsey vs. Tunney "Long Count" fight were not great, but their historical significance to the sport raised them to another level.

I can hear the cries of outrage emanating from the army of Ali loyalists who consider what I have just written as something akin to sacrilege, especially by those fans that came of age during his reign. That is understandable. Strong emotions coupled with blind hero worship and a follow-the-crowd mentality often cloud rational judgments.

But how does one justify naming "The Thrilla in Manila" as one of the greatest fights of the century when it was not even the best fight of the 1970s!

There were at least seven outstanding prizefights in the 1970s that, in my opinion, were better and more interesting than "The Thrilla." Topping the list is the first Ali vs. Frazier bout that took place four and a half years earlier and was superior in every way. The others were Sugar Ray Leonard vs. Wilfredo Benitez (welterweight); Carlos Monzon vs. Rodrigo Valdez I (middleweight); Roberto Duran vs. Esteban De Jesus (lightweight); Matthew Franklin vs. Yacqui Lopez I (light heavyweight); Alexis Arguello vs. Alfredo Escalera I (junior lightweight); Carlos Zarate vs. Alfonso Zamora (bantamweight).

My purpose is not to diminish the greatness of Ali—that is beyond question—but to set the record straight about a fight that has been distorted and misrepresented for decades mainly because it conveniently feeds into the legend and lore of the most famous boxer who ever lived.

A Reliable Litmus Test

My friend and fellow IBRO (International Boxing Research Organization) historian Bobby Franklin uses a simple litmus test to determine the quality quotient of a professional boxing match. "There are certain favorite movies I may come across when I'm channel surfing, such as the first *Godfather* movie, *Casablanca*, or *The Shawshank Redemption*," says Bobby.

Even though I've seen these movies a hundred times, no matter what part of the movie is being shown at the moment I just have to stop and watch it because I'm going to see something new in it and I'm going to enjoy it. And it's the same when I'm watching boxing.

If I go to the Classic Sports channel and they're showing fights, there are certain ones I'll stop at, but the "Thrilla in Manila" is not one of them. That's a fight you've seen it once and you know it. The lines are boring. It if were a movie it would be very boring. It's just two guys hitting each other so I don't go there again.

I agree with Bobby. I never tire of watching a great movie . . . or a great prizefight.

Revisiting "The Thrilla in Manila"

For those of you who may not have seen the fight, and to refresh the memory of those who have, let us time travel back to October 1, 1975, and take a ringside seat at the Araneta Coliseum in Quezon City, just a stone's throw from Manila, capital of the Philippines.

As the 27,000 fans in the sold-out indoor stadium cheered, and millions of people throughout the world watched via closed-circuit television, the two gladiators entered the arena amid much pomp and ceremony courtesy of the fighters' hosts, President Ferdinand Marcos and his shoe-happy wife Imelda.

The betting odds favored Ali at 8-to-5.

Weighing a solid 215½ pounds, the 5'11" Frazier was, as always, in excellent condition. Ali, at 6'3" and 224½ pounds, was a bit overweight.

One year earlier, Ali had regained the heavyweight championship from George Foreman weighing a trim 216 pounds. While the extra eight pounds Ali carried was intended to add power to his punches, it could also mean that he was not trained to the very peak of condition. If the latter was the case—as it proved to be—Muhammad would be in for a rough night unless he could take out Frazier in an early round.

Ali was quite confident that Joe Frazier was a spent fighter who was ripe for the taking. His assessment was not totally inaccurate. Frazier had definitely seen better days. He looked ragged and shopworn in his previous outing seven months earlier while scoring an eighth-round TKO against washed-up Jimmy Ellis. Five years earlier a prime Frazier had overwhelmed Ellis in just four rounds.

Although Ali didn't know it, Joe's vision in his left eye was impaired by a cataract. Years later his personal physician would admit that going into this fight Joe's vision in his left eye had deteriorated to 20/400, which is legally blind. Joe also had an arthritic left shoulder that had to be treated with cortisone before each fight. This information was kept quiet by Joe and his management team and only came to light when Frazier documented it in his 1996 autobiography.

A Little Less Smoke—a Little Less Float

But Ali himself is no longer the elusive "float like a butterfly, sting like a bee" speed demon of years past. He can only float and sting in spurts. In between these brief interludes of activity he will go into his "rope-a-dope" routine made famous in his title-winning fight against George Foreman a year earlier.

Both fighters have deteriorated since their first classic battle in 1971, but Frazier more so than Ali. In this fight the playing field is leveled as each man's weaknesses will be exploited by the other man's strengths.

To the untrained eye, "Smokin' Joe" looks as he always has, moving ever forward in that perpetual jiggle-and-bob style of his. Yet there are subtle differences. When he moves within punching range his hands do not fire off with the old piston-like rapidity. And his attempts to slip or weave under Ali's jab, which in the past were accomplished with rapid, fluid movements of his head and upper body, now appear stiff and ill timed. Most alarming of all is the fact that his bread-and-butter punch, the left hook, appears to have lost some of its explosive power *and accuracy*.

The fight starts as expected with Ali using his speed and mobility to avoid Frazier's rushes. But when Ali stops to punch, he plants his feet firmly on the canvas, putting the full weight of his body into his power shots. He is attempting to end the bout quickly and avoid a war of attrition. Ali appears very confident in these early rounds as he freely trades punches with Joe, taking liberties that he would not have dared four years earlier.

Ali knows he can score effectively if he stays away from the ropes and corners. But he cannot sustain an attack for more than a few seconds. The heat in the poorly air-conditioned arena is affecting both fighters, but it is Ali who tires first. It is only when Ali retreats to the ropes and goes into his defensive shell that Frazier begins to score with some degree of consistency. Yet even when he is able to break through the rope-a-dope defense, his punches, although damaging and hurtful, do not carry enough steam to stagger or knock down the champion.

The anticipation of a knockout is not always essential to establish a great fight, but the lack of it, particularly in a heavyweight championship, robs the event of an essential dramatic element.

Repetitive Patterns

Beginning in the fourth round, the tempo of the fight changes and a repetitive pattern begins to develop. Ali, as he fatigues, either grabs Frazier in a clinch or does his rope-a-dope thing with ever-increasing frequency. Over the course of the fight he initiates *no fewer than 95 clinches to Frazier's one.* This behavior on Ali's part seriously detracts from the overall quality of the fight.

It is Frazier who does all the work during those 14 minutes as he pounds on Ali's arms and torso. This is about as interesting as watching a boxer pound a heavy sandbag in the gym.

In his effort to conserve energy, Ali's stalling tactics become incessant, predictable, and eventually tiresome. It is not the type of activity one expects to see in a great fight.

"A Somber Brutality"

Despite these imperfections one aspect of the bout that is often lauded by the pundits is its brutality. The sight of Frazier relentlessly punching his stationary target while Ali, head down, gloves up, braces himself against the ropes, is indeed brutal to watch. It reminds one of the meat locker scene in the first *Rocky* movie. Except that Ali is only slightly more animated than a side of beef.

It is obvious Joe wants to inflict as much damage as he is capable of dishing out. His punches, especially the persistent attack on Ali's kidney's, midsection, and ribs, cause many ringsiders to wince. But the effort has about as much artistry as a day laborer slugging a concrete sidewalk with a sledgehammer. There is a crude and imprecise quality to Joe's attack, the

Muhammad Ali covers up while Joe Frazier pounds on his arms and torso. Ali initiated 95 clinches and spent a total of 14 minutes in "rope-a-dope" mode, October 1, 1975. *Associated Press*

aesthetics of which are further downgraded by Ali's submissive defensive posture. Where is the drama in this?

Brutality, by itself, is not enough to quantify a superior prizefight even though, in the right hands, it can have a singular, spellbinding artistry. Joe Louis's swift and precise one-round annihilation of Max Schmeling in 1938 is a perfect example. The same is true of Sugar Ray Robinson's studied demolition of Jake LaMotta in the final rounds of their sixth bout.

Not so for "The Thrilla in Manila."

Several years ago, while doing research for my first book, *The Arc of Boxing: The Rise and Decline of the Sweet Science*, I came across a newspaper report of a particularly brutal fight that took place at Yankee Stadium on June 27, 1951, between Jake LaMotta and light heavyweight contender Bob Murphy. The article was written for the *New York Post* by the late Jimmy Cannon, perhaps the greatest sportswriter of the 20th century. "The Bronx Bull" spent most of the fight up against the ropes absorbing a savage beating. In his description of the fight, Cannon used words that could have accurately described "The Thrilla in Manila":

> They fought with a somber brutality but their ferocity turned monotonous and became unexciting. It was as though the multitude in Yankee Stadium last night watched a man being slugged into a bloody daze by a thug using a salami as a blackjack.
>
> The fight racket was reduced to its bleakly savage essentials. . . . It was a graceless fight but a harmful one.[1]

Today hardly anyone remembers that fight because other than its "somber brutality" there was not much else to distinguish it from many other brutal prizefights.

Unlike his less discerning modern-day counterparts, Jimmy Cannon would not have been caught up in the exaggerated hyperbole of Ali vs. Frazier III. He had an exacting eye for the truth and X-ray vision for seeing past the layers of baloney and insipid commentary that too often attend this once great sport. He also had been watching and analyzing fights since the 1930s, so his frame of reference and perception reflected that experience.

Ali the Illusionist

Ali realizes he will lose the decision unless he can interrupt Frazier's attack with brief offensive displays. When the action moves away from the ropes he easily scores with quick combinations that excite the crowd. Joe's decline, as compared to his prime, is most apparent at these times. But the punches do not stop him or even slow him down.

After round three Ali abandons the attempt to knock out Joe and, except for his occasional flurry, reverts to survival mode. He no longer puts the full weight of his body into his blows. That would cause him to expend too much energy. More often than not he will fling out his arms, slapping with a half-open glove or, when he attempts an uppercut, hitting Joe with the underside (wrist) section of the glove. But no matter what he attempts he cannot hold Joe back for more than a few seconds.

From rounds 4 to 12 Ali seems less concerned with the accuracy and strength of his punches than he is with impressing the judges by conveying the illusion that he is in control when he opens up with a flurry of punches. He dances about the ring for a few seconds to arouse the crowd and to remind the judges of who he is, hoping this will negate his all-too-frequent rest stops.

Ali is a shrewd manipulator. It is a formula he knows well, and it comes in handy in other fights as his athletic skills deteriorate. His success in this regard is reflected by the official scoring. In a close contest that most observers (including the Associated Press) have dead even at the end of the 14th round, all three Filipino judges have Ali leading by a wide margin (8–5–1, 8–2–4, 9–3–2). The two *New York Times* sportswriters assigned to cover the fight have it just the opposite, with Frazier winning 8 of the first 13 rounds.

Predictable Ebb and Flow

Irrespective of the off-base scoring by the officials, there is a sloppy quality to the efforts of both men as they take their turns meting out punishment. It is this give-and-take aspect of the bout that many fans, still enthralled by the myth of "The Thrilla in Manila," love to refer to as the "ebb and flow" of a great fight.

"Ebb and flow" is indeed one of the hallmarks of a great prizefight. However, that sterling quality must contain a sense of uncertainty. In this fight the "ebb and flow" becomes all too predictable.

When a tiring Ali decides to "ebb" against the ropes, he allows Frazier to "flow" for up to a full minute without returning a meaningful counterpunch. When Ali is rested enough to come off the ropes and go on the offensive, he will "flow" back for 10 or 15 seconds with a few swift arm punches before returning to the relative safety of the rope-a-dope. Ali is ever mindful of the pace and his own dwindling energy reserves. He appears stymied by Frazier's seemingly limitless reserves of stamina, so he either clinches or retreats to the ropes where the routine will start all over again. His efforts are never sustained enough to turn the tide of battle and swing the momentum back to him.

Ali has underestimated Frazier and overestimated his own ability to hurt this madman who seems intent on making him suffer. He is now paying the price for not coming into the ring in the best possible condition. The rope-a-dope strategy that worked so well against the stamina challenged George Foreman is not having the same effect on Frazier.

Hot Dog or Beer, Anyone?

A great fight demands one's attention every second. By the middle rounds, with the pattern of the fight firmly established, and the possibility of a sudden ending very remote, a fan who understood what was really going on could have walked out to the concession stand for a hot dog and beer, returned to his seat several minutes later, and be unconcerned about having missed anything important.

Turning Point

After aggressively pursuing Ali throughout most of the fight, Frazier finally begins to slow down in the 12th round. He has dished out a lot of punishment, but he has also been pummeled. The oppressive heat and his relentless pace have used up most of his energy reserves. Joe's fuel tank is running low. His punches, especially the hook, are now being thrown in a wide arc—a sure sign of serious fatigue.

Ali senses an opportunity and knows he must come on strong—it's now or never. In the 13th round he digs deep into his own last resources of stamina and willpower. The tide of battle turns as Ali lands several sharp punches that close Joe's already damaged left eye (the one with the cataract). Making matters worse, Joe also sustains a cut over his right eye.

Now unable to see at all out of his left eye, Joe's posture changes. In attempting to locate the target for his hooks, he turns his body toward the left (trying to see out of his rapidly swelling right eye) and straightens up. This is a recipe for disaster because Frazier cannot abandon his crouch and weave or he will be unable to get under and away from the taller man's punches and then counter with his left hook. The exhausted, half-blind challenger becomes a sitting duck for Ali's accurate right crosses.

Ali, aware that less than three rounds remain if the fight goes the full distance, musters every last ounce of strength to come off the ropes and try to end the fight. He moves to center ring and plants his feet to put maximum leverage into his punches.

There now appears to be, finally, a decisive and dramatic turning point in the fight. Yet, even at this juncture, considering what has happened over the past dozen rounds (not to mention in their two previous fights), the excitement generated by Ali's sudden and sustained aggression is tinged, at least in this witness's eyes, with an emotion bordering on sadness.

As I watch these two former giants of the ring struggle and suffer, I cannot help but compare what they once were to what they have now become.

Unless you are hopelessly enthralled by the Ali mystique, it is not difficult to feel empathy for Joe Frazier at this point in the battle. He is so much the honest workman, always giving 120 percent effort, always trying his best with whatever weapons remain in his diminished arsenal. To slack off would be so out of character.

In the entire fight, except for one brief moment in the 14th round, Joe never seeks the refuge of a clinch, although no one would fault him if he did. The once durable fighting machine with the murderous left hook has, in this fight—even as he wins rounds—revealed himself to be a tarnished facsimile of the original. All this damaged warrior has left to battle with is his unconquerable fighting spirit. Beating up a tired old version of Joe Frazier is not the great accomplishment it's made out to be by Ali's army of frenzied sycophants.

The bell ending the 13th round is a welcome respite for both fighters.

Target Practice

Nothing much happens in the first two minutes of the 14th round as Frazier blindly charges and Ali clinches or retreats to the ropes as he gathers his resources for one last push.

With only one minute left in the round, Ali comes off the ropes and lands seven straight punches to Frazier's jaw without a return, but Ali cannot put him down. Frazier awkwardly lunges with a left hook that misses. Their mutual exhaustion is apparent to the wildly cheering audience.

About 20 seconds before the bell sounds, ending the round, Ali lands two perfect right crosses to Frazier's jaw, but stubborn old Joe still will not go down! He is like a battered car in a demolition derby after the doors, fender, and frame have been smashed to bits but whose motor simply will not quit.

Rounds 13 and 14 contain the only dramatic moments for this sad and unnecessary fight, during which time Ali takes target practice on Joe's head.

At the bell ending the 14th round, both depleted warriors walk slowly back to their corners, battered but unbowed.

Joe's trainer, Eddie Futch (who took over from the late Yank Durham two years earlier), realizes his fighter is virtually blind and cannot see the punches aimed at him. Three more minutes of repeated punishment to Joe's unprotected head could have dire consequences. Over Joe's fervent protests, Futch decides it is in the best interest of his fighter to call a halt. Muhammad Ali, slumped in his corner in a state of near collapse, is awarded the technical knockout victory.

Bottom Line: A Seriously Flawed Fight

To their everlasting credit both men displayed the fighting spirit and never surrender attitude that is the inner core of every great champion. No matter if you rooted for Ali or Frazier, it was this epic battle of wills that many impassioned fans focused on almost exclusively to the point of not knowing or caring about what else was taking place. But to say it was a great fight because of this battle of wills is to see only one aspect of a fight that, when viewed in its totality, was seriously flawed.

"The Thrilla in Manila" was damaged goods from the outset. It should never have happened. Until Ali began braying to the press that he wanted Joe one more time, the public was not clamoring to see them fight a third time. Why dishonor the memory of that first magnificent classic with another fight staged four and a half years later between two over-the-hill legends? There was nothing left to prove. Mike Casey, one of boxing's most astute and insightful historians, accurately described the fight as "a meeting of two decaying talents who were already treading a dangerous path when they clashed for the final time to beat the remaining resistance out of each other."[2]

Some scribes, trying I suppose to see some purpose in all of this, wrote that no one could question Ali's courage in a boxing ring after this fight. But why even ask the question? Ali had already proven his courage against the likes of Ken Norton and George Foreman, and in that unforgettable first bruising contest with Smokin' Joe.

In or out of shape, Ali took on all comers throughout his career, fearlessly welcoming the challenge of every major heavyweight contender and champion of the 1960s and '70s. Very few heavyweights of any era could make the same boast.

Joe Frazier's courage in a boxing ring had never been in doubt. He did not need this fight to prove anything, certainly not at this stage of his career. In fact, in many people's eyes he had already beaten Ali twice. (Their forgettable second bout in January 1974, when both were ex-champs, was a weak imitation of the first, minus the controversy and drama. Ali was gifted with a 12-round decision that many fans and sportswriters thought he lost.)

Joe would have done well to heed the advice of his friends and family who urged him to retire after his poor showing against Jimmy Ellis seven months earlier.

As for the most obvious excuse for staging this fight, that it provided a huge payday for both men, the price paid in exchange, in terms of physical damage, was far too great. Although it was an exhausted and drained Ali who famously said he felt "close to death" in the fight, it was really Joe Frazier who came out the worse for wear because he was already damaged and sick going into it.

The fight took plenty out of Ali too but not as much as people think. One year later he still had enough of the old skills, speed, and reflexes to eke out a close 15-round decision over top contender Ken Norton. (Most observers thought Norton won.) Ali was in shape for that one. At 34 years old it would have been the ideal time for him to retire and never take another punch to the head.

What really finished off Ali as an effective fighter was a bout that took place two years after "The Thrilla" in September 1977 (see chapter 3). Ali made the awful mistake of going into a fight with power-punching Earnie Shavers overconfident and out of shape. In a fight he could have easily won if in proper condition (his belly fat hung over his trunks), Ali allowed the stamina-challenged Shavers to control the pace of the fight. Ali's timing and conditioning were atrocious. He was tagged numerous times by Shavers's humongous brain-jarring right-hand punches.

Mesmerized boxing judges once again gifted "the Greatest" with another questionable 15-round decision. But the bout had taken a terrible toll on Ali's health. He was subjected to the worst and most sustained head beating of his career by the hardest-punching heavyweight in the world. That one fight caused more head trauma than all three Frazier bouts put together. Yet he continued to fight and train for another two years.

Separating Fact from Fiction

In the entire history of modern professional sports no athlete has generated as much controversy and has aroused as much partisan zeal as Muhammad Ali. The highly charged circumstances of the first Ali vs. Frazier fight in 1971 created a colossal drama that went far beyond the confines of a boxing ring as the divergent personalities and beliefs of each man became identified with different sides of the contentious political and social controversies of their era. Sides were taken and lines were drawn.

Four and a half years after that first and best Ali vs. Frazier bout, many of those same fans were still passionate about Muhammad Ali, strongly identifying with his struggles and triumphs both inside and outside of the ring. To these devoted fans, many whose interest in boxing began with the rise of Ali, the man was nothing short of a demigod.

The media, never a trustworthy source, was also enamored of the colorful champion and loved the story of his comeback from the brink of defeat in "The Thrilla." They helped to solidify the myth that it was the greatest heavyweight championship fight of all time.

Ali's win resulted in another ancillary benefit for the champ and his fans. The 1971 classic was pushed into the background even though "The Thrilla" did not come close to matching it in terms of quality, drama, or historical significance. What put "The Thrilla" over the top—and this is key—was that Ali had finally beaten his most persistent nemesis in a decisive manner. Thus "The Thrilla in Manila" became the most overrated boxing match in the history of the sport.

Boxing at Its Best

If I were to show a new boxing enthusiast a videotape of boxing at its best, I would not choose "The Thrilla in Manila." I would show a match that genuinely conveys the excitement and quality of a truly great prizefight. I might start with the aforementioned Marciano vs. Walcott title bout, or perhaps the amazing Archie Moore's light heavyweight title defense against Yvonne Durelle in 1958, or one of my personal favorites, Tony Canzoneri's 1933 defense of his featherweight crown against the fabulous Cuban Kid Chocolate.

As an appetizer I might show Joe Louis's knockout at the hands of Max Schmeling in 1936 and then follow it up with the incredible rematch two years later. Of course I would add Conn vs. Louis I to the list as well. Of more recent vintage is the first Alexis Arguello vs. Aaron Pryor war.

I would also have to include a performance by the greatest of the great—the incomparable Sugar Ray Robinson. His stunning and dramatic come-from-behind victory over England's Randy Turpin in 1951 speaks for itself. Want to see a great brawl minus the clinches? Check out both Carmen Basilio vs. Tony DeMarco fights of 1955. I could list many more. A new fan would not even have to be familiar with their names to appreciate the greatness of these fights.

Hopefully, in years to come, all of the above will still command the respect and attention they so justly deserve. The first Muhammad Ali vs. Joe Frazier fight of 1971 belongs in this elite company. "The Thrilla in Manila" does not.

12

GET IN LINE PACQUIAO–MARQUEZ IV:
BOXING'S TOP TEN ONE-PUNCH KOs

(January 2, 2013)

On December 8, 2012, boxing superstars Manny Pacquiao and Juan Manuel Marquez met for the fourth and final time. Their three previous bouts (one draw and two split decisions for Pacquiao) had been among the most exciting fights of the new century. Fifteen thousand fans in the Las Vegas MGM Grand Garden Arena and over 1 million pay-per-view customers anticipated another rousing give-and-take 12-round battle between these two evenly matched welterweights. Nobody expected the sudden ending that occurred with only seconds remaining in the sixth round when Marquez landed the punch that put Pacquiao down for the full count.

The shocking one-punch knockout of Manny Pacquiao by Juan Manuel Marquez brought back memories of other electrifying one-punch KOs. Following are my top ten choices for the most spectacular and dramatic one-punch endings. Preference is given to historically significant bouts between top-tier fighters.

1. 1957—Chicago Stadium, Chicago, IL—Sugar Ray Robinson KO 5 Gene Fullmer: Obvious choice for top spot. The perfect fighter throws the perfect punch. What other middleweight on the planet could take out the seemingly indestructible Fullmer with a single shot? Who else could be so supremely confident that he could do it? Only a fighter for the ages. Sugar Ray, 36 years old and a 3-to-1 underdog, is middle-

Sugar Ray Robinson, standing, has just landed the perfect punch. Gene Fullmer struggles unsuccessfully to beat the count, May 1, 1957. *Author's collection*

weight champion for the fourth time, having lost the title to Fullmer four months earlier. The Sugar Man is truly the one and only.

2. 1952—Municipal Stadium, Philadelphia, PA—Rocky Marciano KO 13 Jersey Joe Walcott: Perhaps the best heavyweight championship bout of all time. Has all the ingredients required of a truly great prizefight. Behind on points, Marciano nails Walcott with a devastating right and wins the title. A thrill fest from beginning to end.

3. 1897—Carson City Racetrack, Carson City, NV—Bob Fitzsimmons KO 14 James J. Corbett: The fight that introduced the words "solar plexus" to the vernacular courtesy of one of the game's all-time great punchers. Fitzsimmons wins the heavyweight championship and emphatically emphasizes the value of a well-placed body shot.

4. 1946—Yankee Stadium, New York, NY—Tony Zale KO 6 Rocky Graziano: Dead End kid Rocky Graziano is in the midst of an epic slugfest with the "Man of Steel" for the middleweight championship. Midway through round six a battered Zale lands his equalizer—a brutal right under Rocky's heart followed by a left hook to the jaw. But it is the body punch that does the real damage. Rocky, like Corbett 50 years earlier, has had the wind knocked out of his sails and is fully conscious while being counted out.

5. 1984—Caesars Palace, Las Vegas, NV—Tommy Hearns KO 2 Roberto Duran: "The Hit Man" meets "Hands of Stone." Fight fans couldn't believe what they were seeing. Duran is mugged and totally dominated by Hearns in a one-sided blowout. Dropped twice in the first round, Duran is still dazed by the onslaught of leather when he comes out for round two. With the round barely a minute old, Hearns lands two distracting left jabs to the stomach followed instantly by a thunderous right cross to the chin that renders Duran unconscious. The ref doesn't even bother to count. Hearns retains his junior middleweight title. Still mesmerizing to watch.

6. 1994—MGM Grand, Las Vegas, NV—George Foreman KO 10 Michael Moorer: After being shellacked for nine and a half rounds, the 45-year-old, 250-pound ex-champ, a 3-to-1 underdog, maneuvers 26-year-old Moorer into position for a humongous right-hand punch. Ten seconds later Big George is heavyweight champion, regaining the title he lost 20 years earlier. Baby boomers all across America rejoiced.

7. 1951—Forbes Field, Pittsburgh, PA—Jersey Joe Walcott KO 7 Ezzard Charles: Jersey Joe's fifth try for the title. He is 0-for-2 against "the Cincinnati Cobra." Few expect a different result. But an inspired Walcott feels destiny calling. Joe patiently waits for just the right moment to strike. In the seventh round he slips inside a Charles left jab and slams home a left hook to the point of the champion's unprotected chin. Call

it the Miracle at Forbes Field. Jersey Joe, at 37, is the new heavyweight champion of the world.

8. 2012—MGM Grand, Las Vegas, NV—Juan Manuel Marquez KO 6 Manny Pacquiao: After exchanging knockdowns, Manny is taking charge in the sixth round and Marquez is getting beaten up. Then, with seconds left in the round, Manny becomes careless as he pressures Marquez into a corner. Marquez lands a tremendous overhand right to Pacman's jaw. The power of the punch is increased by Manny's forward momentum. He is out cold before he hits the canvas. Certainly the most shocking knockout of the new century.

9. 1931—Chicago Stadium, Chicago, IL—Tony Canzoneri KO 3 Jackie Kid Berg: England's sensational "Whitechapel Windmill" seems unstoppable. Fighting like a miniature Harry Greb, Berg has already triumphed over Tony Canzoneri, Kid Chocolate, Billy Petrolle, Joe Glick (twice), and Mushy Callahan (for the junior welterweight title). In their first match, a year earlier, Berg gave Canzoneri one of the worst beatings of his career. This time it is all Canzoneri. In the third round he connects with a perfectly timed right cross to Berg's incoming chin. Berg falls forward unconscious and is counted out. As Manny Pacquiao can tell you—it happens.

10. 1968—Madison Square Garden, New York, NY—Bob Foster KO 4 Dick Tiger: 38-year-old light heavyweight champion Dick Tiger was past his peak but no one had ever come close to knocking him out. The end came with the suddenness of a lightning bolt. Foster's explosive left hook almost decapitates Tiger. The once indestructible iron man is knocked flat on his back. The old warrior makes a valiant effort to rise but cannot beat the count. Bob Foster has arrived.

Honorable Mention: Other Notable One-Punch KOs (in Chronological Order)

Bob Fitzsimmons KO 1 Peter Maher; James J. Jeffries KO 23 James J. Corbett; Jess Willard KO 26 Jack Johnson; Sam Langford KO 8 Fireman Jim Flynn; Sid Terris KO 1 Ruby Goldstein; Sugar Ray Robinson KO 3 Rocky Graziano; Rocky Marciano KO 6 Rex Layne; Bob Foster KO 4 Mike Quarry; Mike Weaver KO 15 John Tate; Evander Holyfield KO 3 Buster Douglas; Bernard Hopkins KO 9 Oscar De La Hoya.

Before he won the heavyweight championship in 1919, Jack Dempsey took out highly ranked contender Fred Fulton with one punch. The fight lasted 18 seconds, including the count. Two of Joe Louis's one-punch KOs were filmed: Lee Ramage KO 2 and Al Ettore KO 5. I have no doubt that scattered among flyweight champion Jimmy Wilde's 98 KOs were plenty of one-punch endings. "The Mighty Atom" may have been the greatest pound-for-pound puncher of them all. Speaking of superpunchers, Sugar Ray Robinson (108 KOs) and Archie Moore (131 KOs) had their share of one-punch knockouts, but few were filmed. In a televised 1951 bout, Moore's unusual power and accuracy was on display when he flattened heavyweight Embrel Davidson in the first round. Moore was outweighed by 35 pounds.

13
FOUL PLAY IN PHILLY
(April 30, 2014)

Heavyweight champion Jersey Joe Walcott was a battle-hardened cagey veteran with over 20 years' experience as a professional boxer. Although he was now 38 years old, Walcott still possessed the speed and reflexes of a much younger athlete. In 1952 he put his precious title on the line against a hard-punching undefeated young contender named Rocky Marciano. The 29-year-old challenger, a slight betting favorite, had scored 37 knockouts in 42 fights. Jersey Joe was confident he could defeat his less experienced opponent. Up for grabs was the richest prize in sports—the heavyweight championship of the world. But with the stakes so high not everyone, as we shall see, was willing to play by the rules.

On September 23, 1952, in Philadelphia's Municipal Stadium, Jersey Joe Walcott defended his heavyweight crown against challenger Rocky Marciano. During the seventh round of a thrilling fight a caustic substance got into Marciano's eyes. He returned to his corner blinking and squinting. "There's something in my eyes, they're burning."[1] Freddie Brown, one of the best corner men in the business, sponged Rocky's eyes with copious amounts of water, giving the challenger some relief. But the burning began again in the eighth round. At the bell Rocky returned to his corner in obvious distress, telling his trainer Charley Goldman, "My eyes are getting worse. Do something, I can't see." Goldman and Freddie Brown continued to douse his eyes. Al Weill, Marciano's volatile manager, was beside himself. Leaving the corner, he approached referee Charley Daggert and pleaded with him to investigate Walcott's gloves and shoulders. The referee waved him back to the corner.

If there was something illegal going on in Walcott's corner, Weill's complaining must have gotten someone's attention because by the end of the tenth round Rocky's eyes had cleared and his vision returned to normal.

After 12 brutal rounds Walcott was ahead in the scoring. Unless Rocky could win by a knockout he would lose the decision. Less than a minute into the 13th round Marciano connected with a devastating right cross to Walcott's chin, and one of the greatest heavyweight title fights of all time came to a sudden and dramatic ending.

Was there foul play in Philly? The kinescope of the closed-circuit telecast lends credence to the belief that Walcott's gloves were doctored. At the end of the sixth round the camera shifts to Walcott's corner, and

Rocky Marciano lands a right to heavyweight champion Jersey Joe Walcott's jaw, September 23, 1952. During the fight Marciano complained of a caustic substance that got into his eyes. *Getty Images / Bettman*

if you watch closely, you can see Felix Bocchicchio, Walcott's manager, rubbing Walcott's left and right gloves as if he is applying something. Was this just a nervous reaction? I think not. The action looks too deliberate. After the eighth round the camera again follows Walcott to his corner. As soon as he sits down we see Bocchicchio leaning through the ropes, and he again rubs Walcott's right glove for at least six seconds in a circular motion before the camera moves over to Rocky's corner. (My personal kinescope copy clearly shows this, but for some reason it has been cut from the version available on YouTube.) Just before the bell rings to begin the ninth round the camera moves back to Walcott's corner, and we again see his manager quickly rub Walcott's gloves and then wipe his hands on the fighter's stomach and trunks, as if trying to remove something. This part *is* included on the current YouTube version. Could the substance just be Vaseline? It's doubtful. There is no reason to apply Vaseline to a fighter's gloves in the midst of a fight.

Rocky Marciano always believed that Jersey Joe's manager had rubbed a hot, irritant salve—perhaps a capsicum ointment—on Walcott's gloves and upper body. Rocky had good reason to suspect foul play. Felix Bocchicchio had resurrected Jersey Joe's career and put him on the road to the championship, but he was also a well-known gambler and an organized crime figure in Philadelphia and New Jersey with a rap sheet dating back to 1925.[2] Rocky never believed Walcott was aware of anything illegal going on in his corner. "He was too wrapped up in the fight [to notice]," Marciano said. "He was too great a champ to go along with something like that. They wouldn't tell him. But somebody did it, because I know what was happening to my eyes." Peter Marciano, Rocky's brother: "Rocky believed he was blinded intentionally until the day he died. He spoke of it often."[3] After he retired as undefeated champion, Rocky accused Bocchicchio of rubbing the substance on Walcott's gloves and upper body in a story published in the *Saturday Evening Post* in October 1956. Walcott's manager sued for libel. A Pennsylvania jury believed the allegations and found in favor of the *Post*.[4]

Now let's jump ahead to February 25, 1964. The scene is the Miami Beach Auditorium. Cassius Clay, a 7-to-1 underdog, is about to challenge heavyweight champion Sonny Liston. It's not Philadelphia, but it might as well be. In Liston's corner his principal seconds are two men whose home base just happens to be the City of Brotherly Love: Joe Polino, a well-known trainer and corner man, and former heavyweight contender Willie Reddish, Sonny's chief trainer.

As the fourth round came to a close it was apparent that the odds did not reflect what was taking place in the ring. The challenger appeared quite capable of pulling off a huge upset. But near the end of the round Clay looked pained and began to blink furiously. He returned to his corner in an agitated state. "Cut the gloves off!" screamed young Cassius, whose eyes felt like they were burning up. A caustic substance of unknown origin had somehow gotten into Clay's eyes just as he seemed to be taking charge of the fight. The very capable and experienced Angelo Dundee, Clay's trainer and chief second, kept a cool head. He sponged the stricken fighter's eyes in an attempt to wash away whatever was causing the problem. At the bell to begin the fifth round rang, Clay was still complaining. "I can't see. We're going home." Dundee refused. "No way," he shouted. "Get in there and fight. If you can't see, keep away from him until your eyes clear. This is the big one! Nobody walks away from the heavyweight championship."[5]

Dundee pushed him out of the corner.

Even though he was fighting half blind, Clay incredibly was able to survive the round despite Liston's efforts to render him unconscious. Swaying and shifting like an Indian rubber man, Clay instinctively avoided most of Liston's punches. It was an amazing display by an extraordinarily talented 22-year-old athlete.

In the following round, with his vision improved, Clay dominated Liston, landing dozens of unanswered punches. The exhausted and demoralized champion returned to his corner at the end of the sixth round a tired and beaten fighter. Claiming an injured shoulder, he told his seconds he could not go on. Cassius Clay—soon to be renamed Muhammad Ali—became the 22nd heavyweight champion of the world.

Conclusion: There is strong reason to believe that someone in Liston's corner tried the same illegal methods used in the Marciano-Walcott fight to influence the outcome by temporarily blinding Clay. When asked his opinion, Angelo Dundee, ever the diplomat, said that a substance used to treat Liston's cut under his eye must have accidentally gotten into Clay's eyes. But wouldn't it have gotten into Liston's eyes as well, and why would anyone choose to treat an eye cut with a caustic substance in the first place?

Two days after the fight heavyweight contender Eddie Machen told reporters, "The same thing happened to me when I fought Liston in 1960. I thought my eyes would burn out of my head, and Liston seemed to know it would happen." He theorized that Liston's handlers would rub medication on his shoulders, which would then be transferred to his opponent's forehead during clinches and drip into the eyes. "Clay did the worst thing when he started screaming and let Liston know it had worked," said Machen. "Clay panicked. I didn't do that. I'm more of a seasoned pro, and I hid it from Liston."[6]

Years later Joe Polino, Liston's assistant trainer, told *Philadelphia Daily News* reporter Jack McKinney what actually happened.

According to Polino, in between the third and fourth rounds, Sonny had told him to "juice the gloves." Polino said they were always ready to do that if Sonny was in real danger of losing. He admitted they had done it in Liston's fights with Eddie Machen and Cleveland Williams. He said it was a stinging solution but did not specify what was in it.

According to McKinney, "Polino told me that he put the stuff on the gloves at Sonny's express instructions and then threw the stuff under the ring apron as far as he could." McKinney also added, "Joe himself felt so conflicted over this. He'd been sucked into it, but he knew if he ever came clean he would never work again."[7]

In each of the above scenarios the heavyweight champion of the world was facing defeat. It appears that desperate and illegal measures were taken by someone in the champion's corner to influence the outcome. The other common denominator is that both Walcott and Liston were handled by Philadelphia boxing people. Philadelphia was home base for Blinky Palermo, the notorious fight fixer and longtime godfather of the city's boxing scene. Blinky operated freely in Philly but was banned in New York State. This is not to say that he was involved in either incident (in fact he was in jail in 1964), just that Philadelphia was no stranger to boxing scandal considering who had been in charge for many years. Fight fans with long memories remember the notorious incident involving Harold Johnson, who claimed he was drugged after someone had given him a "poisoned orange" just before he stepped into a Philadelphia ring to face Cuban heavyweight Julio Mederos in 1955. Johnson, the betting favorite, was stopped in the second round. Professional boxing was suspended in Philadelphia for six months following the incident.

Perhaps because Marciano defeated Walcott to win the title the matter was not pursued by Weill or anyone else. There was no investigation by Pennsylvania boxing officials into the possibility that Walcott's gloves were doctored. Florida officials were even more lax in the aftermath of the Clay-Liston bout. Florida didn't even have a state boxing commission. Instead, local municipalities (in this case Miami Beach) ran the show. The only investigation that took place concerned the veracity of Liston's claim that he injured his shoulder, which may have been bogus or exaggerated, but could not be proven.

Both Rocky Marciano and the fighter then known as Cassius Clay were destined for greatness. The nefarious attempts to alter the course of boxing history failed because Clay's amazing speed and reflexes and uncanny athletic instincts enabled him to survive the fifth round. The attempt to foil Marciano was also unsuccessful because of the Rock's almost superhuman toughness and determination. For three full rounds Marciano could barely see the target in front of him yet he kept attacking in his relentless way, bringing the fight to Walcott despite taking punches that would have stopped most heavyweights in their tracks. On that night it would have taken more than the two fists of a mortal being, let alone a "caustic" solution, to defeat the indestructible "Brockton Blockbuster."

14
FIGHTS OF THE CENTURY: THEN . . . AND NOW

(May 17, 2015)

"Even as he disrobes himself ceremoniously in the ring the great boxer must disrobe himself of both reason and instinct's caution as he prepares to fight."

—Gerald Early

The recent Floyd Mayweather Jr. vs. Manny Pacquiao superfight on May 2, 2015, was only the fifth boxing match in 109 years to be billed as "The Fight of the Century." The previous century had seen four such matches, with the great boxing promoter George L. "Tex" Rickard responsible for three of them. Tex invented the phrase in 1906 to publicize the Joe Gans vs. "Battling" Nelson lightweight title fight. He made good use of it twice more over the next 15 years for the Jack Johnson vs. James J. Jeffries and Jack Dempsey vs. Georges Carpentier heavyweight title fights. Of course logic would dictate that there could be only one "Fight of the Century," but whoever said the business of boxing was logical? The last fight prior to Pacquiao and Mayweather to be labeled a "Fight of the Century" was the Joe Frazier vs. Muhammad Ali heavyweight championship in 1971.

Of the five contests mentioned above, only two managed to actually live up to the tremendous prefight buildup. Despite the huge social and political ramifications of the 1910 heavyweight championship bout between Johnson and Jeffries, the actual fight was a dud. Johnson, still in his prime, easily dominated the previously undefeated former champion (who was making an ill-advised comeback after a five-year layoff) before stopping him in the 15th round.

The Dempsey vs. Carpentier extravaganza of 1921 was also hugely significant but for different reasons. Over 90,000 fans—the largest crowd to ever attend a sporting event—watched Dempsey flatten the overmatched Frenchman in less than four rounds. Dempsey vs. Carpentier will never make anyone's all-time list of great fights, but its importance to the economic and cultural side of boxing was monumental. For the first time in history a sporting event had drawn over $1 million in paid admissions. It was also the first time a championship match was broadcast over the radio. The fight jump-started the golden age of sports in America and transformed professional boxing into popular entertainment for a mass audience.

As anyone who saw it will attest, the first Ali vs. Frazier fight more than lived up to its prefight hype. Like Johnson vs. Jeffries 61 years earlier, the event was intertwined with the social and political issues of the times. But unlike that fight it was an intense and exciting struggle between two undefeated heavyweight champions that brought out the best in each man. The combined worldwide audience (live and at theaters showing the fight on closed-circuit television in America or telecast for free via satellite throughout the rest of the world) was estimated at over 300 million people. Madison Square Garden, the venue for the fight, priced ringside tickets at $150. The cheapest balcony seat was only $20. (The wildly inflated ticket prices in Las Vegas for Pacquiao vs. Mayweather ranged from $1,500 to $10,000.)

So which "Fight of the Century" deserves top honors? I think a very strong case can be made for the 1906 duel between Gans and Nelson, arguably one of the most incredible and disturbing boxing matches ever staged.

The battle between "the Old Master" and "the Durable Dane" for the lightweight championship of the world was a fight for the ages. It took place in Goldfield, Nevada, a mining boomtown located halfway between Reno and Las Vegas. The town's financial bigwigs, flush with money, decided that some kind of spectacular public attraction would draw further attention and generate additional infusions of cash into Goldfield's mining stock. (Much of what they sold turned out to be worthless mining properties, but that's another story.) A committee of distinguished citizens was formed to come up with proposals. One suggestion was that a giant hole be dug along the main street and filled with free beer. Another idea was to stage a camel race. Enter Tex Rickard, cattle rancher, gambling hall impresario, and promoter extraordinaire. Rickard had already made and lost several fortunes. Sensing an opportunity, he proposed an all-star boxing match between two of the world's best boxers—lightweight champion Joe Gans and his number one challenger "Battling" Nelson. The idea was immediately accepted.

Joe Gans, the first African American boxing champion, won the lightweight championship in 1902. Dubbed "the Old Master" because of his extraordinary skill, he had already cleaned out the lightweight division and was forced to take on welterweights and middleweights to keep active. The only serious challenger to his title was a boxing brute named Oscar Matthew "Battling" Nelson of Chicago, by way of Denmark. Nelson's other nickname was "the Durable Dane." He was the type of fighter who thrived on fights beyond 15 rounds. Nelson was a rough customer with a reputation as a dirty fighter. He seemed impervious to punishment, and his stamina and relentless style was legendary. His trademark punch was a short left hook aimed at the liver, with thumb and forefinger extended to provide greater penetration. Nelson claimed the "White lightweight championship" and was confident he could defeat Gans in a "fight to the finish"—meaning a fight with no time limit. Such a fight could not end in a decision but would continue indefinitely until one of the contestants was either knocked out, quit, or was disqualified.

Fights to the finish, a staple of the bare-knuckle era, were not uncommon in early turn-of-the-century gloved fights, especially in the western states. A bout limited to 15 or 20 three-minute rounds would favor Gans. A fight to the finish against iron man Nelson was another matter. Gans, in need of cash and having run out of challengers who would agree to fight him, consented to a finish fight. He was confident he could knock out Nelson.

Nelson's almost superhuman ability to absorb punishment and his endless reserves of stamina was fascinating to some people. Among the curious was Columbia University's rowing coach Dr. Walter B. Peet. He examined the Durable Dane for his endurance and found Nelson's heartbeat to be only 47 beats per minute compared to 72 for the average person. As the good doctor explained it, such a low heartbeat was only found in the "colder blooded animals which survived the days of antiquity and the cold of the Ice Age." Further consultation with surgeons and the curator

Lightweight champion Joe Gans, circa 1900. "The Old Master" is still rated as one of the greatest boxers of all time. *Stanley Weston Archive*

of the American Museum of Natural History concluded that measurements of Nelson's head revealed "the thickest skull bones of any human being since Neanderthal man."[1] It seemed obvious that "Battling" Nelson would have the advantage in a fight to the finish.

Nelson threatened to pull out of the fight several times unless he received the lion's share of the purse. Gans, in desperate need of a decent payday, agreed to accept a $10,000 guarantee while Nelson, the challenger, was to receive $20,000. The fight was scheduled for Labor Day, September 3, 1906. (Ever the showman, Rickard displayed the entire $30,000 purse in $20 gold pieces in full view through a window of a bank in Goldfield.)

Aware of Gans's precarious financial condition and how much he wanted the fight, Nelson's manager made the unprecedented demand that he weigh in three times on the day of the fight (at noon, 1:30, and 3:00 p.m.) while wearing his trunks, gloves, and shoes. It was a blatant attempt to weaken the champion. Gans would have to weigh no more than 133 pounds or else forfeit $5,000 of his purse. The great fighter, confident of victory, agreed to all of the demands.

On the day of the fight, Gans was quoted in his hometown paper, the *Baltimore Sun*: "I have given in on every point just to secure this match. I am betting everything I can get my hands on, and I have got to win. I will have the Dane chopped to pieces and asleep inside of 15 rounds." Nelson told the same paper, "I am going to give Gans an awful beating, and I think he will be begging for mercy long before the twentieth round is reached. I will let Gans wear himself out, and then I'll come through and get him. Watch me. There will be crepe in Coontown on Labor Day while the Danish descendants are celebrating."[2] A week before the fight all hotel rooms were sold out. Late arrivals slept on the ground. Many of the 200 Pullman cars that had been chartered to transport fight fans served as hotel rooms.

The 24-year-old Nelson had 70 pro fights under his belt. Gans, eight years older, was a veteran of 187 fights. Both weighed in at 132¼ pounds. Gans was favored at odds of 10-to-7.

They entered the ring shortly after 3:00 p.m. Some 8,000 fans filled the wooden arena built especially for the fight. Gate receipts of $76,000 set a new world record for title fights. Among the ringside spectators were a U.S. senator, various mining tycoons, stars of the vaudeville stage, and the son of President Theodore Roosevelt. Before the fight began, several telegrams sent by prominent individuals were read to the crowd, including one from Joe's mother imploring her son to "bring home the bacon," words that have since entered the American lexicon.[3]

In one last attempt to further undermine Gans's chances, Nelson's manager, Billy Nolan, argued that Gans should have weighed in wearing bandages on his fists. Gans responded that he would fight without taping his hands. It was a decision he would regret after breaking his right hand on Nelson's head in the 32nd round.

For security purposes, Rickard had arranged for 300 deputy sheriffs, their open vests displaying holstered pistols, to maintain order. To forestall any shenanigans by his crooked manager, Gans announced to the crowd that he had instructed referee George Siler to ignore any attempt by his corner to throw in the towel no matter his condition. Nelson told the referee to do the same for him. By mutual agreement only the referee would have the authority to stop the fight. The crowd, evenly divided in their sentiments, cheered both fighters.

Gans (right) and Battling Nelson, "the Durable Dane," pose for the cameras before the start of their historic 42-round battle, September 3, 1906. *Author's collection*

111

As expected, Gans dominated the early rounds by easily outboxing Nelson. His accurate and powerful punches drew blood from Nelson's nose, mouth, and ears. Despite the punishment, Nelson kept coming forward. Gans was the division's hardest puncher, but no matter how many times he landed, Nelson rarely broke ground. The crazed Dane kept boring in, attempting to place his head against Gans's chest and deliver body blows at close range. More often than not, utilizing his superb footwork, jab, and counterpunching skills, Gans was able to keep most of the action at long range, even managing to knock down his rock-jawed challenger twice for short counts. In desperation Nelson began butting Gans. Gans protested to the referee. Warnings were issued but no action was taken.

The pace of the fight was relentless. During the minute rest between rounds, each man's seconds waved huge towels in an attempt to offer their fighter some relief from the sweltering desert heat. Finally, in the tenth round, Nelson bloodied Gans's mouth with a series of punches. After 15 rounds of fighting Gans had lost, at most, two rounds. The pace finally began to slow after the 20th round. There was more wrestling and clinching as the fighters sought to grab a few moments respite before beginning another assault.

By the 30th round, both gladiators were showing signs of exhaustion. They had fought under the broiling Nevada sun the equivalent of two grueling 15-round title bouts. Nelson, although bleeding profusely and with his left eye closed, was still the aggressor and was now landing more often. At one point, after missing a swing, he fell through the ropes, whereupon Gans, a consummate sportsman, reached down to help him back into the ring. Nelson responded by kicking him in the shins.

As the bout passed the two-hour mark, there was an increase in stalling and wrestling. Even the fans were showing signs of exhaustion. At the bell signaling the start of the 40th round, the crowd was in awe of the fact that both warriors were still standing.

As described in *Joe Gans: A Biography of the First African American World Boxing Champion*, authors Colleen Aycock and Mark Scott attempt to understand the mental state of the fighters as the bell rang for the 41st round:

It is quite possible that both Gans and Nelson are in a state of clinical delirium at this point, but their bodies are trained to fight on with or without their minds. Dehydrated, battered and bloody, the gladiators may or may not really know where they are.[4]

Nelson totters like a bull the picador has struck with forty lances. Gans the matador has been gored, fouled, and kicked, but is still waiting to deliver the *coup de grace*, a blow that will come at the beginning of the 42nd round that almost decapitates Nelson.[5]

And so it finally ends. The iron man was at the end of his tether and on the verge of finally taking the count. Suddenly he struck Gans with a low blow. Was the punch deliberate? Very likely Nelson sought to foul out instead of suffering the humiliation of a knockout defeat. Gans sank to the floor and was unable to continue. Intentional or not, the foul blow was obvious to everyone in the arena and the referee had no choice but to disqualify Nelson and award the bout to Gans. No one objected to the disqualification.

Gans was carried out of the ring but not before announcing to the crowd that he would meet Nelson again in two weeks to prove he could win without being fouled. A cascade of boos and derision descended upon Nelson. He quickly retreated to his dressing room.

The much-anticipated rematch would not take place for another two years. It would not carry the label of "Fight of the Century." By that time Gans, his resistance compromised by his struggle to make weight for their first marathon fight, had contracted tuberculosis. Gans fought the last two years of his career while slowly dying. The man acknowledged to be one of the ten greatest boxers of all time (some say the greatest) passed away in 1910 at the age of 35. His record showed only 12 losses in 196 fights, including 100 wins by knockout.

Battling Nelson, surely one of the toughest and dirtiest fighters who ever lived, would go on to win the lightweight title and defeat the disease-ravaged Gans in two subsequent bouts. But he paid an awful price for his shock-absorbing style of fighting. The Durable Dane eventually lost his mind and ended his last days in an insane asylum while still training for a comeback.

IS FLOYD MAYWEATHER JR. AN ALL-TIME GREAT BOXER? THE EXPERTS WEIGH IN

(September 7, 2015)

Fight fans have always enjoyed comparing and analyzing the merits of the best boxers from different eras. Debates still rage as to the winner of imaginary contests between Jack Dempsey and Joe Louis, or Muhammad Ali and Mike Tyson, and hundreds of other dream matches. In recent times many fans compared Floyd Mayweather Jr. very favorably to some of the all-time greats. Are they right?

If the modern era of professional boxing had begun in the 1980s, instead of the 1890s, there is no question that Floyd Mayweather Jr. would rank among the top ten greatest boxers of all time. But the modern era of professional boxing began over 100 years ago. That is a lot of boxers to consider! Most historians agree the sport's true golden age, in terms of the numbers of quality boxers competing at the same time, occurred from the 1920s to the 1950s. Floyd Mayweather Jr. turned pro in 1996. Over the past 18 and a half years he is undefeated in 48 fights. Yes, his amazing speed, reflexes, and keen sense of anticipation have enabled Floyd to win titles in five weight divisions—but could he have attained that same level of success if matched against the best fighters of decades past?

Before I go any further, let me establish some ground rules. I do not measure a contemporary fighter's alleged greatness by the number of title belts he possesses or his won-lost statistics. The out-of-control title inflation that has plagued the sport in recent decades and the huge number of undefeated records (unprecedented in the history of the sport) built on inferior opposition should deemphasize those factors. Far more important is an accurate analysis of the fighter's technical skills while at the same time taking into account the quality of his competition.

Send In the Clowns

Prior to the 1970s, before an alphabet soup of competing "sanctioning organizations" wrecked boxing's traditional infrastructure by anointing their own set of champions and contenders (often based on payoffs and corrupt relationships with powerful promoters), the boxing establishment recognized, at most, ten world champions in ten weight divisions (the traditional eight and at various times two "junior divisions"). That was the self-imposed general rule for more than half a century. It wasn't a perfect system (after all, this is boxing), but for the most part it worked. Boxing fans could easily identify the ten champions and the top ten contenders within each weight division, all of whom were rated according to merit. Today, thanks to the greed of the quasi-official sanctioning groups (their racket is extorting "sanctioning fees" from every fighter who competes for one of their cheesy title belts) there are over 100 "world champions." Even dedicated fight fans would be hard pressed to name more than half a dozen. In order to multiply the number of champions—thereby generating more fees—these boxing parasites created seven additional weight divisions. There are now about 100 world champions and 680 "top ten" contenders in 17 weight divisions listed among the four major sanctioning groups. In other words, there are far more opportunities to win a championship than ever before—and also to defend it against a challenger plucked from the thinnest talent pool the sport has ever known.

Floyd Mayweather Jr. has taken advantage of and benefited from the absurdity by often cherry-picking challengers who he surmised would present less of a threat. Against such limited opposition Floyd's technical flaws are obscured by his extraordinary speed and athleticism. But on the few occasions when he defended his title against a capable opponent, these flaws were exposed.

Moment of Truth

Although Manny Pacquiao was among the two or three best opponents that Mayweather had ever faced, their recent megabout came at least five

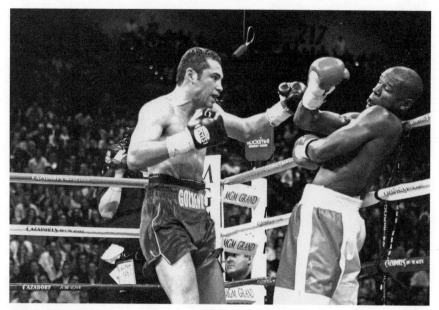

Floyd Mayweather Jr. (right) edged out Oscar De La Hoya to win a close decision, May 5, 2007. *AP/Kevork Djansezian*

years too late. Both fighters were past their prime. Mayweather won a very close decision, but their fairly tame encounter failed to provide the answers we seek. It was his bout with Oscar De La Hoya eight years earlier (May 5, 2007), when Floyd was at his absolute best, that does provide the answer.

Oscar De La Hoya was the first opponent Mayweather encountered in his prime who was at or near his level. Oscar was slightly past his own prime and had fought but once in the previous 20 months, but he was still one of the best boxers in the world. The result was a very close split-decision victory for Mayweather. Shortly after that bout, I interviewed several boxing experts and asked for their thoughts on Mayweather. The following are excerpts from those interviews.[1]

Weighing In

Teddy Atlas (One of the sport's greatest trainers and currently a ringside analyst for ESPN.):

> In the old days there were fighters who were good defensively, but the difference was they had the attitude, and the wherewithal, to go and find

a way to create an offense that would make it possible to take control of the opponent in a more meaningful way, in a more dominant way, and in a much more productive way.

Even a recent fighter like Sugar Ray Leonard, who I think was a terrific fighter, would find a way to be aggressive and get to his opponent while at the same time maintaining a responsible defense. He would not just find a way to do enough to just get by.

In his fight against Oscar De La Hoya, there didn't seem to be an ability shown to you by Mayweather to create another way to get to him—other than when De La Hoya made it easy for him and just opened the door for him by walking in with no jab and not offering up the answers and the resistance that he should have. The only offense that was created by Mayweather was actually given to him by his opponent.

Boxing means using your head, using geometry, using the science of angles, the science of adjustments. And all you have to do is make it a kind of landscape where the other guy can't use what he has. You fight in a place where speed doesn't come into play. You use your reach to keep your opponent at a certain distance where you can time him. Timing can always get the better of speed when it's used properly and understood properly. You time your opponent and keep him at the end of your punches. And if you use your reach properly you are not giving him anything to counter. Whenever De La Hoya used his left jab this "great" fighter Mayweather looked like he had no answers. But when Oscar didn't use his jab and just walked in it looked like Oscar had the problem.

When De La Hoya forced Mayweather to the ropes he flailed away instead of placing his punches in the right way. You would expect a fighter at that level to find the right places and to know what the right places were, and where they were. De La Hoya threw his punches almost in a hopeful way. Real top guys don't throw in a hopeful way. They throw their punches in a defined way—in a way that their experience and judgment tells them they need to throw.

You cannot get intoxicated to the point where you are comparing Floyd Mayweather Jr. to the greatest fighters of all time. I'm not taking anything away from Floyd, but I think it's insulting to the great fighters and to the great history of the sport to make that comparison.

Mike Capriano Jr. (Former trainer and manager. Saw his first pro fight in 1938. During the 1950s was head coach for the Camp Lejeune Marine Corps boxing team that won a record number of service championships.):

I think the critics have a misunderstanding of the difference between speed of movement and speed of attack. Those fast and elusive old-time boxers we saw always were involved in maintaining the attack. They were always looking for spots to land effective punches. They weren't runners doing nothing and then jumping in and throwing a flurry of punches. They were different.

Ali never ran away like Mayweather. Ali was fast but he was moving left to right and looking to hit you with punches. Sugar Ray Robinson was also extremely fast. He was up on the soles of his feet bouncing and moving left to right. But he wasn't running here and running there. He was interested in making contact with his punches. And Robinson was a very hard puncher.

Mayweather just wants to punch and run. But against those old time welterweight and middleweight fighters you are not going to do that because they're going to keep you on the ropes and hit you with clean punches. He could run all he wants but sooner or later he has to come in to make contact with his opponent and then those guys are going to tie him up and grab him, push him into the corner, push him up against the ropes and start ripping punches up.

When De La Hoya had Mayweather on the ropes he was unable to hurt him or keep him there. You've got to be able to slide and move in. De La Hoya doesn't know how to do that. He doesn't know how to move under punches. He's in that crouch but he doesn't bend under and really get down. He's slapping Mayweather 100 times with that left hand when he's got him on the ropes and it's ineffective.

What De La Hoya should have done when he had Mayweather on the ropes was to stay right in his middle. He should have had his head right in the middle of his chest. You then take a step back to get leverage and throw an uppercut or hook. De La Hoya did not know how to keep him on the ropes.

Neither fighter landed any terrific punches; no right cross combinations or left hooks underneath and over . . . real punches that dug in. They also did not appear to know how to step in with their punches.

This fight wasn't any kind of test that establishes the credibility of greatness. They both looked like a pair of ordinary ten round fighters. They traveled the distance well but, as I've said, they are not getting hit by guys that are going to hurt you. The better old timers would feel their opponent out for a couple of rounds and then, all of a sudden, "bing, bang" you'd see some dynamite punches coming in.

Carmen Basilio would have beaten both De La Hoya and May-weather. They are not in Emile Griffith's class either. And how about Kid Gavilan? I mean Gavilan's going to fire punches that make a difference. And he's strong and he's pushing you. Gavilan would have Mayweather on the run, up against the ropes. He'd be throwing that bolo and other shots and he's hurting Mayweather. It's a different kind of fight.

Fighters like Joey Archer and Billy Graham are going to box May-weather. They'd have that left hand out in front and throwing combination punches. They are going to box him. And when Mayweather jumps in to deliver his quick punches he's not going to hit anybody because they're going to tie him up and put him back out there. It's going to be a boxing match. The old pros are looking at him and arranging for where they're going to attack and they're setting him up.

The old timers came to fight. He could do all the running, but they wouldn't get caught up in his evasive movements. Mayweather has speed, but it is not combined with cleverness. They'd just wait until he's in position where they could hit him. He's going to have to fight sometime. The referee is going to tell him "look, you've got to engage this guy." We've seen fighters run all night and people began booing and carrying on. So he can run around but when he fights a superior pro you'd see a different fight. You won't see it today because no one knows how to do that. Fighters like Fritzie Zivic gave people college educations. There's no one around like that today.

Tony Arnold (Amateur and professional boxer 1949–1957. Former archivist for one of boxing's largest film libraries.):

What did Mayweather do with his speed? He made De La Hoya chase him. That's all. He didn't use his speed like a Willie Pep to maneuver around an opponent's defenses and hit him with sharp combinations and then move out of the way. I'm talking about using speed in a clever way. Mayweather just used his speed to keep himself from getting hit. And that's supposed to be a great? There was no real display of skill or strategy.

Mayweather's jab is so tentative and ineffective I can't even call it a jab. His right foot was already going back as he threw it. He was backing off because he's very cautious and he was worried about a counterpunch. The jab was just keeping distance between him and De La Hoya. It wasn't being used to outbox De La Hoya, it wasn't controlling the fight and it wasn't even a good defensive move because he wasn't able to do anything. He just jabbed and backed off. But that tentative jab was enough to keep De La Hoya at long range for much of the fight.

Mayweather's strategy was to hit De La Hoya with quick potshots and dance away and just pile up enough points to stay ahead, which he barely did. I mean the fight was practically even as far as I'm concerned. Mayweather did not set anything up. He didn't make De La Hoya miss and then counter. He was relying on his speed and luck to land punches. They were just flailing at each other. I didn't see any smart combinations. I did not see any good calculating counterpunching. I never saw either fighter throw a two or three-punch combination. There was no taking advantage of mistakes. There was no looking for opportunities. I don't think they would have known an opportunity if it fell on them. Mayweather and De La Hoya are not thinking fighters with the skill or experience to know what to look for.

Mayweather is quicker than the other guy, he throws faster punches, he maneuvers around, but he doesn't show any real skills. I didn't see any real feinting or good head movement. I never saw him slip and counter. Not once. I didn't see any skill in that area at all. He's got so many flaws.

Bill Goodman (Licensed cornerman with the New York Athletic Commission 1957–1966. A student of the boxing scene for over 60 years.):

Floyd Mayweather Jr. has a great deal of natural ability but it hasn't been brought out the way it was with the fighters of years ago. I don't think he jabs enough. And he doesn't take advantage of opportunities. He ducks and slips punches but instead of taking advantage of what he just did he lets it go by. He doesn't follow up. He makes some pretty moves, and looks nice doing it, but nothing happens. He doesn't fire. Mayweather throws one left hand and he stops punching. He doesn't follow it up with 2–3–4 left jabs like they did years ago. Consequently, he doesn't get a barrage going, he doesn't get any momentum.

Mayweather is very fast, but he does not compare to those better welterweights that were around years ago. How can you compare him to a guy like Tommy Bell from the 1940s? It's night and day. Of course someone who doesn't know Tommy Bell would see a number of losses on his record and not be impressed. But look at who he fought! Bell fought anybody and everybody. Like most fighters he stayed around a lot longer than he should have, but in his prime he would have licked both Mayweather and De La Hoya with one hand tied behind his back.

Even a guy like Gil Turner, who was a 1950s welterweight contender, wouldn't have any trouble with either Mayweather or De La Hoya. Isaac Logart and Gene Burton wouldn't have any problem with them either. Not only were these contenders well educated; they put their education to use. They fought frequently and kept busy—and they were better fighters.

They talk about Mayweather's speed, but he isn't as fast and as skillful as Bernie Docusen who fought Sugar Ray Robinson for the title in 1948 and gave him plenty of trouble. Would you say Mayweather's going to give Ray Robinson as a welterweight plenty of trouble?

There's no comparison. But you go and tell that to a young boxing fan today and they think you're a psycho.

What these authentic boxing experts are saying (and I emphasize the word "*authentic*") is that Floyd Mayweather Jr., despite his obvious talent, is not in the same league as the best champions and contenders of previous decades. To the untrained eye, Mayweather appears to be a great fighter because his dazzling speed is more than enough to dominate second- and third-rate opponents. But when faced with an opponent he could not totally dominate with his speed, Floyd's stylistic flaws were revealed.

Part of the problem many people have in evaluating the quality of today's champions is that since the 1990s, the line separating the skills of top amateur and top professional boxers has become blurred. Most of today's champions have extensive amateur backgrounds. But they are not exposed to the same type of professional apprenticeship common to fighters of the past. The majority win a title belt before their 20th pro contest and have fought less than 150 rounds. The averages years ago were 40 to 70 fights and about 400 rounds. (Floyd Mayweather Jr. had only 16 fights and 64 rounds of professional experience at the time he won his first title in 2001.)

There is no chance to gain the kind of bout-to-bout education and experience that empowered the early greats. This is why there remains a hint of lingering amateurism in the fighting styles of most of today's champions. They do not need to master the finer points of professional boxing technique because the competition does not demand it. In addition, their trainers do not have enough knowledge or background to teach the old moves. Body punching, feinting, drawing a lead to set up a counterpunch, proper use of the left jab, bobbing and weaving, infighting, timing, and mobile footwork are among the lost boxing arts. These days an athlete with superior speed and size rules the roost because no one has the experience, training, and know-how to effectively counter those purely physical qualities.

It is right that Mayweather owns the "pound-for-pound best" title because in a pugilistic population lacking both seasoning and ring savvy, fighters with superior athletic prowess automatically rise to the top—and Floyd just happens to be the most physically gifted fighter. But at age 38 Floyd's legs have lost their spring, his speed is a smidgen slower, and his endurance is not what it once was. Without the sophisticated skill set of a seasoned old pro to fall back on (think Archie Moore, Emile Griffith, and Roberto Duran), Floyd, like Roy Jones Jr. before him, will soon be vulnerable against even those second-rate opponents he used to chew up and spit out. Is Andre Berto that opponent? (They are scheduled to fight on September 12 [2015].) Again, Floyd has chosen wisely from the weakest of the herd. On paper a Berto victory looks nearly impossible. Once very promising, the 31-year-old with a 30–3 record is now damaged goods because of steroid use and ill-advised weight training that have diminished his speed and punch. Nevertheless, against an aging fighter anything is possible and don't think Floyd doesn't know it. If he is unable to score an early KO, an attempt will be made to steal rounds and score points with occasional flurries. At this point in his career, pacing is very important. Don't be surprised if Floyd fails to impress.[2]

Summing Up

There is no denying the fact that Floyd Mayweather Jr. is a very good fighter. His whippet speed and finely honed fistic instincts might have stymied some of the ring greats from boxing's golden age—but not for long. They would have made the necessary adjustments. If Floyd was born 50 years earlier he might have developed the ring generalship and cleverness that is missing from his otherwise impressive repertoire. Those qualities would have been an absolute necessity if he were to compete successfully against the top fighters of the past. But even then, Floyd's success would not have been guaranteed in that fierce competitive jungle. What is certain is that without these added dimensions Floyd would not have been able to establish a legitimate claim to greatness.

16

BOXING'S TEN GREATEST QUOTES

(October 25, 2015)

No other sport has produced more memorable quotes or phrases than boxing. I am not referring to the many clever and colorful (and sometimes outrageous) statements uttered over the years by various boxing personalities. Mike Tyson's obscene rants that included such gems as "I want to eat his children" or "I try to push the [nose] bone into the brain" do not qualify for this list. The winning quotes are those that have withstood the test of time and entered into the American lexicon. The following quotes fit those criteria. They have been used by journalists, politicians, and people in all walks of life. Yet how many are aware that they emanate from the world of boxing? I've saved the best for last, so counting back from ten to one, here they are:

10. "I Shoulda Stood in Bed"—Joe Jacobs (1935)

Joe Jacobs was the prototype of the fast-talking, cigar-chomping fight manager. Sportswriters loved him as he was always quick with a memorable quote delivered in a staccato New York accent. As described by author David Margolick, Jacobs was "the quintessential Broadway guy, a Damon Runyon character from whom even Damon Runyon, then writing a sports column for the Hearst newspapers, could pick up some pointers."[1] As a "Broadway guy," Joe invariably slept late, but one of the few times he broke with tradition was when he got out of a sickbed to attend the 1935 World Series between the Tigers and Cubs on a wet, cold day in Detroit when the temperature was near freezing. When a reporter asked him about the experience, he famously complained, "I shoulda stood in bed," which is New Yorkese for "stayed in bed." Shakespeare could not have said it any better.

9. "I'll Moida Da Bum"—Tony Galento

The squat 5'9", 235-pound New Jerseyite with the sledgehammer left hook was one of the most colorful fighters of any era. "Two Ton" Tony was a crude, beer-guzzling brawler who often used these words to describe what he would do to a future opponent. He said it most often when referring to heavyweight champion Joe Louis, whom he challenged for the title in 1939. In an unusual fit of pique, Louis, angered by Tony's incessant prefight trash talk, decided to punish him. Galento, a stubborn foe, did his best and even managed to drop Louis in the third round. After taking a short count, Louis got up even angrier and battered Galento into a bloody hulk before knocking him out in the next round.

8. "We Wuz Robbed"—Joe Jacobs (1932)

Another gem from the irrepressible Joe Jacobs who regularly butchered the King's English. He spoke the immortal words after heavyweight champion Max Schmeling (whom he managed) lost a controversial decision to Jack Sharkey.

7. "Only in America"—Don King (1975)

The phrase was appropriated by King in the early '70s. But a more accurate phrasing should be "Only in Boxing." For only in the unregulated "red-light district" of sports could a convicted killer and diabolically clever sociopath run roughshod over an entire sport and bring it down to his level.

6. "The Bigger They Are the Harder They Fall"—Bob Fitzsimmons (1902)

The actual quote is: "The bigger they come the harder they fall." It has been attributed to former heavyweight champion Robert Fitzsimmons in an interview in 1902, but it probably goes back further than that. Fitzsimmons (heavyweight champion 1897–1899) was one of the hardest punchers of all time. He weighed about 167 pounds in his prime and often beat heavier men, including a 300-pound opponent he flattened in the first round.

5. "Honey, I Forgot to Duck"—Jack Dempsey (1926)

President Ronald Reagan was being wheeled into the operating room shortly after taking a bullet in the 1981 assassination attempt on his life. Still conscious, and amazingly maintaining his sense of humor, he looked up at his wife, Nancy, and told her: "Honey, I forgot to duck." The president was referencing the line Jack Dempsey used to explain his defeat to his wife after he lost the heavyweight championship to Gene Tunney in 1926. Reagan was only 15 years old at the time, but the phrase obviously made an impression on the young sports fan and future president of the United States.

4. "We Will Win Because We Are on God's Side"—Joe Louis (1942)

Heavyweight champion Joe Louis, who had recently enlisted in the still segregated army, spoke these words at a March 1942 war bond rally in front of 18,000 people in Madison Square Garden. The great man's words became a popular slogan and made their way into songs and posters.

3. "He Can Run but He Can't Hide"—Joe Louis (1946)

Joe's public comments were as compact and on target as his punches. He could say more in a few words than most people say in 100. On the eve of Joe's rematch with Billy Conn, a reporter asked him if his lighter and faster opponent's speed would be a problem. Louis's answer was prescient. He knocked Conn out in the eighth round.

2. "Float like a Butterfly, Sting like a Bee"—Cassius Clay (1963)

He did and he could!

1. "I Coulda Been a Contender" —Marlon Brando (1954)

One of the most famous movie quotes of all time was spoken by actor Marlon Brando in his role as the anguished ex-pug Terry Malloy in the classic movie *On the Waterfront.* The words originated from an actual conversation screenwriter Budd Schulberg had with Roger Donoghue, a once promising welterweight who quit the ring after killing an opponent. Donoghue was hired to instruct Brando how to move and act like a former professional boxer. When Schulberg asked Donoghue if he could have been a champion, the fighter replied, "Well, I could have been a contender."[2]

17

DEMPSEY'S ARM AND THE STATE OF MODERN BOXING

(December 23, 2015)

In this chapter I purposely focused on former heavyweight champion (1919–1926) Jack Dempsey's impressive muscular development to juxtapose the wrong approach taken by too many of today's trainers who attempt to increase a boxer's punching power with the type of weight training that does more harm than good.

Heavyweight champion Jack Dempsey's punching power was legendary. At a body weight of about 190 pounds, the "Manassa Mauler's" punches could drop opponents who outweighed him by 50 or more pounds. His left hook was often compared to the kick of a mule. The astonishing muscularity of Dempsey's left arm, as revealed in this fascinating photo, is a sight to behold and bespeaks of an awesome destructive force.

Dempsey's impressive muscular development was achieved naturally, without benefit of weight machines, supplements, or steroids. It was the result of genetics combined with years of hard manual labor, and countless hours spent in gymnasiums training, sparring, and fighting. His body was perfectly suited for the demands of his sport. Unfortunately, many of today's boxers mistakenly believe that enhancing their muscularity by lifting weights (20 to 100 pounds, or more) and targeting specific muscle groups will improve their punching power and overall athleticism. But such irresponsible training techniques do not take into account that a properly trained boxer's muscles are highly refined and uniquely suited for his sport, just as a ballet dancer's muscles are highly refined and uniquely

Jack Dempsey, right, in the peak of condition, trains for an upcoming bout, circa 1920. *Author's collection*

suited for his activity. Old-school trainers understood that. As far as they were concerned, adding weight lifting to an elite boxer's training routine was akin to pouring sand into the gas tank of a Cadillac.

If It Ain't Broke, Don't Fix It

Prior to the 1980s, barbells or weight machines were never seen in a boxing gym. "If it ain't broke, don't fix it" should apply to boxing. Former heavyweight champion Joe Frazier said it best: "We teach old school boxing training. We train fighters the way Louis and Dempsey and Henry Armstrong trained, and Willie Pep and Jack Johnson and Rocky Marciano, and all the other great fighters in history. Those guys were some of the best to ever fight, and if it was good enough for them it's good enough for us too."[1]

Today's boxers are not helping themselves by turning to fads that are not scientifically proven and serve no useful purpose. Any exercise or training routine that compromises the speed or reaction time of the boxer—be it hand speed or leg speed—should be eliminated. Gennady Golovkin and Sergey Kovalev, two of the sport's hardest punchers, are not overly muscled. To their credit (or the credit of their trainers), it is obvious they do not incorporate weight lifting into their training routines. Hopefully it will stay that way.

Competent boxing trainers—the few that are left—are not close-minded. They are open to new ideas, provided they result in improvement to the boxer. Sadly, most of the people currently training and managing boxers have no idea what's broken and what isn't. As a result, they are incapable of showing the boxer anything that would school him in the finer points of technique. So they spend hours having the fighter perform useless "punch pad" routines or hire a strength and fitness coach from another sport and think it will make the boxer stronger and add power to his punches. They are evidently not aware that for a boxer, strength and power are not synonymous.

Compensating for a Lack of Knowledge

Many so-called trainers accept these unproven methods as a way to compensate for their lack of knowledge. Instead of concentrating on improving a boxer's balance, timing, and defensive and offensive techniques (which most are incapable of doing), they concentrate on conditioning. But it's all a load of crap. Legendary trainers Ray Arcel, Jack Blackburn, Charley Goldman, and Angelo Dundee would never have tolerated such nonsense. As Teddy Atlas says, "Without the fighter or his management realizing it, they are undermining their own fighter. Instead of making him accountable in the areas that he needs to improve, they go looking for shortcuts."[2] Some of these new age boxer-training routines are not just silly (you can see them on YouTube) but also damaging.

Over the past 20 years too many fighters have been victims of wrong-headed training techniques. The list includes Tim Bradley, whose career was practically ruined by strength coaches who had no idea how to condition a boxer. Fortunately, he fired his trainers and brought in Teddy Atlas, who retooled his style and banned weight training. But a lot of damage had already been done. Another victim was Jeff Lacy, once one of boxing's hottest prospects. Lacy made the mistake of hiring a strength coach who decided this already very strong athlete needed to bulk up. His career quickly went downhill. Sporting oversized pecs and huge biceps, Lacy became stiff and slow, and was no longer able to throw a straight punch. He was easy prey for the swift-moving Joe Calzaghe, a fighter whose natural speed was never compromised by unnecessary weight training.

The late Emanuel Steward, who trained dozens of world champions, was also disdainful of the new methods. In 2008 I interviewed Steward for my book *The Arc of Boxing*. Current trainers should heed his sage advice:

> Many weight trainers and conditioners confuse the training techniques needed for boxing with the strength training needed for football and other physical sports in which strength training has been utilized for many years. I am very upset with having these strength coaches involved with professional boxers. Fighters like Michael Grant and Frank Bruno are so tight they can't get their punches off normally. And after about five or six rounds their muscles become fatigued. A fighter also takes a chance tearing his muscles by weight lifting . . . look at Tommy Hearns, Bob Foster, Joe Louis and all those great punchers. They are usually rangy guys. Even Foreman was a loose, naturally strong kid. They didn't have these tightly muscled builds that came from lifting weights.[3]

Of Mountain Lions and Bears

Compare Dempsey's lean but muscular physique to the overly muscled anatomy of the recently dethroned Wladimir Klitschko. Who has the better build for boxing? Is it the slow-moving, somewhat muscle-bound 6'6", 245-pound Klitschko or the 6'1", 192-pound Dempsey, whose trip-hammer punches were delivered with the speed of a fast middleweight? The answer should be obvious, irrespective of the fact that Klitschko is exactly the same height and weight of Jess Willard, whom Dempsey destroyed in three brutal rounds to win the title. I have no doubt that Dempsey's superior speed and punching power would be the deciding factor in achieving the same result against Klitschko.

I find the argument that today's giant heavyweights would be too big for Dempsey, Louis, and Marciano ludicrous to the extreme. At 190 pounds both Jack Dempsey and Rocky Marciano could deliver a higher volume of power punches with greater speed and accuracy than any dreadnought—past or present. And they did it without becoming exhausted. No 250-pound slab of beef has ever matched the combination of speed, stamina, *and power* of a hard-punching quality heavyweight in the 190-to 210-pound range. Is a mountain lion too small to take on a bear that outweighs it by hundreds of pounds? If you think so, then I suggest tuning into cable television's *National Geographic Wild* for a reality check. What could a strength coach do for a mountain lion? Speed, cunning, strength, and courage will determine the winner.

Survival of the Fittest

A smaller but faster and smarter heavyweight will often prevail over an opponent possessing only superior size and strength. Any fighter who weighs between 190 and 210 pounds is big enough to handle a super-sized heavyweight, providing he has the wherewithal and boxing smarts to know how to counter superior size and strength. In a battle between heavyweights, survival of the fittest does not necessarily mean survival of the biggest. At least that's the way it used to be. But things are different today because the current era of supersized heavyweights exists in tandem with the era of supermediocrity. So, when taking into account today's extremely thin and inadequate talent pool, size does matter.

If you remove the top talent from any group of performing artists, those residing at the bottom of the barrel will rise up and take their place. But if you cannot tell who is good and who isn't, then you won't be able to tell the difference. That is what has happened to boxing over the past two decades as the sport continued its descent into ignorance and stupidity—at every level. Today the heavyweight division is so devoid of talent that what used to be found floating at the bottom of the barrel has now risen to the top.

I am still reeling from the experience of watching that awful exhibition (I cannot call it a fight) between Klitschko and Tyson Fury. I actually found myself yelling in disgust and disbelief at the TV screen. Over the past half century I have seen some horrendous matches, but this one was in a class by itself because someone had the gall to call it a fight for "the heavyweight championship." The overall incompetence, amateurishness, and lack of fighting spirit of both contestants was astounding. I could not believe what I was seeing. That was the last straw for me. I figuratively threw in the towel on my once favorite sport. To be honest, I really don't care if I never see another contemporary boxing match again.

18

A WORLD OF PROFESSIONAL AMATEURS

(September 1, 2018)

It's been said that boxing is a reflection of the society and culture that surrounds it. Unfortunately, boxing's current landscape appears to validate that statement.

On August 4, 2018, I watched an HBO boxing doubleheader featuring two light heavyweight title fights: Sergey Kovalev vs. Eleider Alvarez and Dmitry Bivol vs. Isaac Chilemba. The bouts confirmed to me that the art of boxing, as I knew it, is dead and unlikely to be revived anytime soon.

It's not so much what I saw but what I didn't see. As in so many other televised contests, the sophisticated boxing skills that were once so common among the top echelon of professional fighters 50 or more years ago are absent from today's champions and contenders. In the title fights mentioned above, fewer than a dozen body punches were exchanged and there was virtually no infighting. There were no double jabs or combinations and no feints, ducking, parrying, or weaving under punches. Footwork was in two directions—forward and back. Absent was lateral movement or circling an opponent. Other than occasionally stepping back out of range to avoid a punch, defense was limited to the usual gloves in front of the face while standing still and waiting to be hit. No attempt was made to slip a punch and counter. Every round was a repeat of the previous because the fighters did not have the experience, training, or ring savvy to know how to change tactics.

With few exceptions, the majority of today's top professional boxers all fight the same way. There is very little variety in their fighting styles. Even several years after turning pro it is basically the same style they used as amateurs. In the past that would have been perceived as a weakness when competing against an experienced professional. Today the difference between the best amateur boxers and the best professional boxers is negligible. And that is why, in boxing's current culture and climate, it is impossible to produce a world champion who merits comparison to the greatest boxers of the 1920s to the 1970s.

One of the sport's current stars is the former two-time Olympic gold medalist (2008 and 2012) Vasyl Lomachenko. This extremely talented boxer won his first title in 2014 in only his third professional fight. Over the next four years he added two more division titles to his impressive resume. But we will never know how great Vasyl can become because the talent pool in the lighter weight divisions lacks depth. Where are the great fighters to test him? Answer: there are none.

Lomachenko is a rare commodity. He reminds us of the very promising professional prospects who often caught our attention during boxing's golden age. But even if he had been competing during the last vestiges of that era—the 1960s and 1970s—his rise to the top would not have been as rapid or as easy. And there would be no guarantees he would ever win a title. Despite his amazing amateur record he would not have been ready this early in his career (less than a dozen professional fights in four and a half years) for the likes of Sugar Ramos, Vicente Saldivar, Carlos Ortiz, Nicolino Locche, Roberto Duran, or Aaron Pryor.

What makes Lomachenko stand out today is his use of extreme speed of punches combined with rapid and constantly shifting footwork that he uses to confuse and befuddle second-rate opponents. This used to be known as "stick-and-move" strategy. It is rarely seen today. I'm grateful to Lomachenko for reviving it. Hopefully it will catch on. After all, a target swiftly moving to and fro is always more difficult to hit than a stationary one. It is a simple concept that doesn't seem to have penetrated today's boxers or their trainers. The best way to neutralize a constantly moving target is to either keep your opponent preoccupied with a busy left jab, make him miss, and then counter, or cut off the ring while applying unrelenting pressure. Luckily for Lomachenko there are no outstanding pressure fighters today in the mold of a prime Manny Pacquiao or Julio

Cesar Chavez. Another was Ray "Boom Boom" Mancini who gave the great Alexis Arguello trouble for 13 rounds. Ray wasn't ready to take on Arguello, but if we were to replace Arguello with Lomachenko, I think the result would be a win for Boom Boom.

Forty years ago another gifted professional, Wilfred Benitez, won the junior welterweight title from the great Antonio Cervantes in his 26th professional fight. It is the same title Lomachenko won by stopping Jorge Linares in the tenth round on May 12, 2018. It was Loma's 12th pro fight. Linares had a decent amount of professional experience, but at best he is a slightly better than average boxer. Yet by using an effective jab and quick counters he was able to keep the fight even through nine rounds. Now what do you think would happen if we were to replace Linares with a prime Antonio Cervantes or Wilfred Benitez?

Perhaps a boxer with as much natural talent as Lomachenko may have adapted if he had come along 50 or more years ago. But it's impossible to say. In years past there were so many terrific prospects who faltered when it came time to make the leap from great prospect to great boxer.

I don't say this to demean the current crop of world champions. (At last count there were over 100 spread over 17 weight divisions!) The best of them possess an abundance of natural talent, are in excellent physical condition, have extensive amateur experience, and usually put forth a tremendous effort. It is not their fault that after turning pro they do not receive the type of quality training and competition that would have a positive impact in improving their boxing technique.

A major reason for the lack of refined skills is the shortage of qualified teacher-trainers who understand and can teach the finer points of boxing technique. Nevertheless, despite these drawbacks, I think it is important to make comparisons between today's best and those of decades past if only to gain perspective and to inform and enlighten us as to what it truly means to be a great boxer.

Among today's fighters there are a few who are not of the cookie-cutter variety. Lomachenko, Terence Crawford, and Gennady Golovkin are in this category. They are pleasing to watch because they are capable of performing at a higher level than the sea of mediocrity that surrounds them. They bring back memories similar to the type of young talent we used to see years ago. Golovkin is the most "old school" of the three. But an accurate appraisal of their current level of overall skill and experience indicates they are not as well rounded and seasoned as the top contenders and champions of boxing's golden past. Through no fault of their own they will never be tested in the same way the best fighters of the 1920s to 1970s were tested. They will never experience the type of brutal competition their counterparts in decades past had to contend with while trying to hold on to a title or a top ten rating.

Let's return to the four fighters mentioned at the beginning of this chapter, all of whom are either current or former light heavyweight champions. How would they have fared against the best light heavyweight champions of the 1970s and early 1980s? (Comparisons to golden oldies like Loughran, Rosenbloom, Lewis, Conn, Moore, or Johnson are unnecessary because the answer is too obvious.) Does anyone who has seen the following boxers actually believe today's champions could defeat Bob Foster, Matthew Saad Muhammad, Victor Galindez, John Conteh, or Michael Spinks? And what about Richie Kates, Jerry "the Bull" Martin, Yacqui Lopez, Eddie Mustafa Muhammed, Jorge Ahumada, Dwight Braxton, Marvin Johnson, and Eddie Davis? These 1970s-era light heavyweights did not build up their records fighting second- and third-rate opponents, as is the norm today. They did not avoid the hard fights.

All of the above proved to be tough and seasoned professionals capable of giving any great boxer of the past a competitive fight. Aside from the quality of their training and the seasoning they acquired over the course of their careers these accomplished professionals possessed another very important weapon: psychological toughness. A fighter who could combine that type of resilience with superior boxing skills was very, very tough to beat.

Of the four light heavyweights who headlined the HBO show, the best of the lot is Alvarez, who won his portion of the title by stopping Kovalev in the seventh round. He did very well considering he hadn't fought in over a year. (Long layoffs and inactivity is another feature of the current boxing scene.) I am impressed by Alvarez but also saddened. He is extremely talented, well schooled in basic boxing technique, and very determined. Had he been more active (only four fights in the last two years), he could have eclipsed Andre Ward as the star of the division. But at the age of 34 and with only 23 pro fights in 11 years the former amateur champion will never have the opportunity to realize his full potential.

Another example of unrealized professional talent is Dmitry Bivol. As a successful amateur boxer he engaged in nearly 300 fights, winning a slew of regional titles before turning pro in 2014. Three years later Dmitry won a portion of the world light heavyweight title in only his 12th professional fight. As an amateur he performed at the highest level. Using those same amateur skills, he has attained great success in a very short time as a pro. Dmitry won't be required to improve much beyond his current skill level because the line that once separated top amateur boxers from top professional boxers has become blurred. In his most recent bout he won a dreary 12-round decision against a second-rate opponent whose purpose was just to survive the 12 rounds and collect his payday. It would be nice if the four current champs were to engage in a tournament to determine who is best—but don't hold your breath waiting for that to happen.

Forty years ago, Dmitry Bivol would be labeled a hot prospect and maybe in line for a semifinal in Madison Square Garden. But as good as he is, Dmitry would not be ready to challenge a prime Victor Galindez, the reigning world light heavyweight champion. At that time 300 amateur fights and 14 pro wins (88 rounds) didn't make you ready to challenge an outstanding professional boxer whose record showed over 50 pro bouts and 485 rounds.

And what of Kovalev—the once mighty "Krusher"? In 2017 he put up a stirring but losing effort against a very good Andre Ward. That decision could have just as well gone to Kovalev. It was that close. His return bout with Ward seven months later ended in controversy and left many fans puzzled. Slightly ahead on points, the Krusher took several borderline shots to the midsection. He reacted by draping himself over the ropes. The referee awarded the TKO win to Ward. In his recent bout against Alvarez he was also ahead on points. Kovalev tried hard for a KO in rounds five and six but couldn't put Alvarez away. That futile effort, and his opponent's stubborn resistance, appeared to dampen Kovalev's fighting spirit. He came out for the seventh round looking tired and discouraged. Carrying his left hand dangerously low and moving slowly, Kovalev was knocked down by a solid right cross.

What surprised me was that Kovalev, after arising from the first knockdown, did not appear to know what to do. But a quick review of his record explained why. In nine years Kovalev had fought only 143 professional rounds. Seventeen of his 28 knockout victims never made it past the second round. A seasoned pro who is knocked down or hurt would have known how to tie up his opponent in a clinch or bob and weave his way out of trouble, or at least make the attempt. Kovalev, used to knocking out inferior opposition, didn't know what to do when the situation was reversed and it was he who was in trouble. He remained an open target and was quickly dropped twice more before the referee stopped the fight.

Part III
INTERVIEWS

There are several common threads that run through the following interviews. All five of these extraordinary athletes are tremendously proud of what they have accomplished as boxers, and rightfully so. They also exhibit traits that I have noticed in virtually every great fighter I have ever interviewed. They are courteous, intelligent, self-aware, and alert. All have a deep appreciation and respect for the art of boxing, especially the importance of the jab and their ability to "hit and not get hit." It is obvious to me that these men used boxing not only as a vehicle to show off their prodigious talent, but also to express something much deeper within themselves. Under different circumstances they could have achieved success in a myriad of other professions, but they heard the siren call of the gladiator and, for better or worse, could not refuse.

19

ARCHIE MOORE

(Interviewed on February 26, 1983)

In 1983 I had the great good fortune to meet and interview the legendary Archie Moore. The former light heavyweight champion (1952–1962) had amassed one of the greatest records in boxing history. After a long and arduous 17-year campaign, "the Old Mongoose" (Archie's colorful nickname) finally won the championship in his 177th professional fight. He fought from 1935 to 1963 and retired with an outstanding 186–23–10 won-lost-draw record (including one no contest). It is safe to say his extraordinary number of knockout victories—131—will never be eclipsed.

Archie was in New York City to present an award to one of his former opponents, Charley Burley. Burley was just one of at least a score of genuinely great boxers whom Moore fought during his illustrious career. Many of the names in that record read like an entire Hall of Fame roster: Cassius Clay (Moore made it a point to say that he never fought Muhammad Ali since the future heavyweight champion had not yet changed his name at the time they fought), Rocky Marciano, Ezzard Charles, Charley Burley, Jimmy Bivins, Holman Williams, Bert Lytell, Lloyd Marshall, Harold Johnson, Eddie Booker, Teddy Yarosz, Joey Maxim, and "Bobo" Olson, to name a few. If Archie Moore were fighting today, he would be heavyweight champion after already having won both the middleweight and light heavyweight titles.

Although his formal education ended in high school, Archie never stopped learning. He was a worldly individual and full of the wisdom of life experiences. He possessed an analytical mind and was intensely curious about a wide range of topics. Mostly self-educated, Archie was, without question, one of the most remarkable, charismatic, and accomplished characters I have ever met.

As author Joyce Carol Oates has so accurately stated: "The brilliant boxer is an artist, albeit in an art not readily comprehensible, or palatable, to most observers."[1] Archie was an artist in the truest sense of the word. On September 21, 1955, the near-40-year-old Moore challenged Rocky Marciano for the heavyweight championship of the world. Although knocked out in the ninth round, Moore put up a rousing fight, even dropping Rocky hard in the second round for a short count. This is how the *New York Times* reported it the following day: "Moore . . . gave an exhibition of boxing skill that, even in defeat, was almost as thrilling and moving as the display of awesome power that eventually brought the victory to Rocky."[2] When this sport was still worth our time and attention, Archie Moore's name stood out like a brilliant shining star.

Three legendary boxers and one excited author, 1983. Left to right: Archie Moore, Mike Silver, Sandy Saddler (former featherweight champion), and Charley Burley (uncrowned welter- and middleweight champion). *Author's collection*

Interview

Mike Silver: Archie, you are in New York to honor one of your former opponents, the great Charley Burley. So I think it's appropriate to begin with him. You lost a unanimous ten-round decision to Burley and were knocked down four times. What happened?

Archie Moore: Charley Burley had a very deceptive style of fighting. He just tricked me. He tricked me because we both boxed similar, but whereas mine was an apparent forward movement Burley's was a continuous serpentine movement. He was like a threshing machine going back and forth. His body would sometimes lean over towards you and he'd pull it back just in time. Hitting him solid was almost impossible. But what made him so dangerous was that he could punch from any angle. He was never off balance although he appeared to be off balance on many occasions.

Mike: You had one of the longest careers of any boxer who ever lived. You fought in four separate decades—the 1930s to the 1960s. What was the secret of your boxing longevity?

Archie: Well, I knew how to fight. I was also a master of pace. It was very important to know how to force pace and set a pace. As a result very few people could make me fight out of my system of fighting. Eddie Booker, Lloyd Marshall, and Charley Burley made me fight out of my system. In my winding-up years Marciano was one, as was Durelle. I had to fight out of my system to get back into that fight. Another boxer I had trouble with was Jimmy Bivins. Jimmy knocked me out the first time we met because he had such a deceptive reach. Although he was no taller than I was [5'11"], his arms touched below his knees. When he pulled his arms up they looked no longer than mine, but when he reached them out he hit me with the hook.

Mike: Well, you obviously learned from your mistake because you defeated Bivins four times after that. Looking over your amazing record I noticed that the great Ezzard Charles defeated you three times during your prime fighting years. Did Ezzard make you fight out of your system of fighting?

Archie: No . . . no. He just outfought me. Ezzard was always in superb condition. He was a nice stand-up fighter and an expert boxer. Whereas he was not a terrific puncher, but he was a good puncher with both hands.

Mike: Archie, you are acknowledged to be one of boxing's all-time knockout artists. Are great punchers born, or can a boxer increase power by perfecting such things as balance, leverage, and timing?

Archie: Those ingredients you just mentioned are conclusive; all are an admixture as such as you just described, especially timing.

Mike: Who were some of the great punchers Archie Moore fought?

Archie: Charley Burley was a terrific puncher, although to look at him you would not know it. His build fooled everybody. Burley's legs were skinny, he was not extra wide of shoulder, he was small in weight, and his height was the same as mine. But that man could get more leverage into a punch than anyone I ever fought. Another great puncher was Curtis "Hatchetman" Sheppard, who once missed a punch to the jaw and broke a man's collarbone. Lloyd Marshall was the snappiest hitter of them all. He could knock you out with either hand. Ron Richards was a tough hitter. Marciano was a very hard puncher—a bludgeoning type of hitter—super conditioned by Charley Goldman. He was 100 percent aggression. There were others, but I'd have to look at the record because I forget.

Mike: Archie, I think it's fair to say that since you were still fighting at an age when most other boxers were long retired, you had to utilize every advantage, mental, physical, and psychological, in order to maintain your edge over much younger opponents. Can you give an example?

Archie: In 1955 I fought Nino Valdes in Las Vegas, Nevada. At the time Nino was the top ranked heavyweight. He was 6'4" tall and weighed about 215 pounds. It was a 15-round bout and the winner was promised a bout with Marciano for the heavyweight title. The fight was staged at an outdoor arena in the late afternoon. As the sun began to settle on the west side of the ring, I was sitting in my corner facing the sun and noticed that Nino was sitting with his back to the sun. The bell rings, and I move to maneuver and before any activity starts I've already got my head under his chin and I'm muscling this big guy around. I face him into the sun and I keep turning him to the sun. He's trying to get back around and I keep cutting him off. I'm always maneuvering him back to face the sun, which was very bright. And all the while I keep spearing him with the left hand and keep twisting and twisting and turning him, and try as he could, he could never make me turn into the sun. The sun was of course bothering him and I kept thumping him with the left jab. Hard stiff, stiff jabs. Pretty soon his eyes began to lump up. One eye closed up completely and the other was closing fast. By this time the sun was going down and the fight was coming to a close. I won 14 out of 15 rounds.

Mike: What does Archie Moore think of today's boxers?

Archie: I think modern-day fighters do not get proper basic training. Boxing is based on disciplined training and disciplined repetition. Do you know the best friend a fighter has when coming up? [*Archie points to a large floor-length mirror.*] A very important part of training is practicing your moves in front of the mirror. But most fighters never come in contact with the mirror until they start to jump rope. Since they skip rope in front of a mirror, why don't they shadowbox in front of a mirror? You can do that at home. You go through the motions. You learn how to duck. I can see where I'm going to hit my opponent. Am I at the right distance from him? I can hit him over the heart. I can hit him in his liver. I can step aside and hit him in the kidney. Go over the top, whatever.

Mike: After your victories over Joey Maxim for the title, you defended it against Harold Johnson. This was your fifth meeting with Johnson, who you already had outpointed three times. In this fight you were behind on points when you knocked Harold out in the 14th round.

Archie: Harold Johnson was a great fighter. A picture book boxer. I was just his nemesis the same way that Ezzard Charles was my nemesis. Joey Maxim was a difficult boxer to fight because he knew so much about defense. Joe was 99 percent defense. And Joe was very durable and tough.

Mike: What are the ingredients that go into making a successful prize-fighter, and what advice would you offer to a young boxer asking for guidance and direction?

Archie: The first ingredient is discipline. Discipline and desire. It is said that desire is the candle of intent and motivation is the match that lights it, and that candle must be kept burning. Once you make up your mind to go all the way to the top in boxing, first of all, go and get the best qualified instructor to teach you the things you need to know. It should be someone you like, someone that you can deal with, and someone you can listen to and obey. It should also be someone that you have trust in. Otherwise, somewhere down the line you're going to have a breakup, a mix-up, or an argument and you lose a friend. Because the person who is your instructor, your trainer, your teacher, he's closer to you than your father.

Mike: The number of expert boxing instructors, as compared to years ago, has diminished. What can be done about that?

Archie: As far as the area of improving the skills of boxers is concerned, I have developed a whole new system of teaching the basic boxing techniques. It is a new and revolutionary technique. I taught it to George Foreman and we went down to Jamaica and won the title with it. I thought George had untapped reservoirs of strength and it was up to me to channel it.

Mike: Can you describe your revolutionary system and how it works?

Archie: I could readily describe it but I prefer not to at this time.

Mike: OK. Let's change the subject. Who in your opinion was the greatest pound-for-pound boxer you have ever seen?

[*Author's note*: Archie did not answer immediately, taking about ten seconds to consider his answer.]

Archie: Henry Armstrong. Here is a man who won the featherweight, lightweight, and welterweight titles all in the same year, and the men he beat to win those titles were great fighters in their own right.

Mike: What about Sugar Ray Robinson?

Archie: When Ray was active there was nobody any smoother. Watching Ray fight was like drinking a nice . . . soft . . . drink. I enjoyed watching Ray Robinson fight because I appreciate beauty in athletics. I enjoyed watching Oscar Robertson move on the basketball court, Jim Brown on a football field, Andretti in an automobile, Willie the Shoe ride the horses. Everybody had their way of doing things with skill. These are skilled men and there's nothing I like better than skill. When a guy does something, and does it well, I admire that. There's never been anybody more grace-ful, skillful with a rope than Ray and I've seen some awfully good rope skippers. I would rather see Ray Robinson punch a speed bag than watch the average guy go out and fight a six-round fight. Ray was a skillful man; he was a game man. In his time there was nobody more beautiful than he was, although there were one or two guys that might have beaten Ray in their time. I would like for someone to say, personally, that I think Charley Burley could have beaten Ray in Ray's best time. But people hate to go out on a limb.

Mike: Is there anything about your boxing life you would have changed or done differently?

Archie: I'd have liked to have made some money and have more financial gain out of boxing. You see, a boxer's wish is to be independent. This is a profession. I like to be without obligations to other people but I was obligated. But I was mindful of whom I borrowed money from and I was careful not to get mixed up with people who would be embarrassing to you at a time when they wanted to collect.

Mike: Thank you, Archie. I very much appreciate your taking the time to do this interview.

Archie: You are welcome. I enjoyed it.

20

EMILE GRIFFITH

(Interviewed on January 10, 1998)

Emile Griffith was born February 3, 1938, in the U.S. Virgin Islands. He moved to New York City when he was 16. In 1958, two months after winning the New York Golden Gloves 147-pound Open Championship, he turned pro. Throughout his entire career he was managed by Howard Albert and Gil Clancy, who also trained Emile.

Over the next 19 years Emile Griffith established a legendary boxing career that included winning both the welterweight and middleweight championships. He fought more main events (24) in both the old and new Madison Square Gardens than any other boxer. Among his 112 opponents are some of the most formidable champions and contenders of the past century: Carlos Monzon, Luis Rodriguez, Jose Napoles, Dick Tiger, Nino Benvenuti, Rubin "Hurricane" Carter, Benny "Kid" Paret, Alan Minter, Florentino Fernandez, Denny Moyer, Joey Archer, Jorge Fernandez, Gaspar Ortega, Stanley "Kitten" Hayward, and many others.

Griffith won the welterweight title on April 2, 1961, when he knocked out Cuba's Benny "Kid" Paret in the 13th round. Six months later he lost the title back to Paret on a close decision that most observers thought Griffith deserved to win.

Their third fight for the championship, on March 24, 1962, at Madison Square Garden, was nationally televised (as were the previous two). At the weigh-in that morning Paret decided to unnerve Griffith, perhaps to gain a psychological edge. While Griffith was on the scale Paret made a lewd gesture and in front of boxing officials and other people called him *maricón*, derogatory Spanish slang for "faggot." Griffith, rumored to be bisexual, was infuriated and had to be restrained from attacking him on the spot.

That evening, except for the sixth round when Paret floored him for an eight count and he was saved by the bell, Griffith was in control and ahead on points. Then, in the 12th round, Griffith staggered Paret with a right to the head and drove him across the ring and into a corner. There was no escape. In five seconds Griffith landed 14 rapid-fire punches to Paret's head. The last several punches were delivered when Paret was already unconscious and being held up by the ropes. As referee Ruby Goldstein pulled Griffith off his stricken opponent, Paret slid slowly to the canvas. The unconscious fighter was carried from the ring on a stretcher and rushed to a hospital where he underwent emergency brain surgery. He never regained consciousness and died ten days later.

Some people blamed the referee for not stepping in sooner to stop the fight. But the truth is Paret should never have been allowed to fight that night. It was later determined that he was still suffering from the aftereffects of a terrible beating he took just three months earlier in an attempt to defeat Gene Fullmer for the middleweight championship (see chapter 10: "Don't Blame Ruby").

Outside of the ring Emile Griffith was an ebullient, fun loving, and sensitive individual who smiled often and loved to interact with his fans. The tragedy devastated him. He considered retirement but then decided to go on with his career and continued to fight for the next 15 years. But it was obvious the Paret tragedy had affected his fighting style. Terrified of killing another opponent, he was never as aggressive and preferred to use his consummate boxing skills to outpoint opponents rather than go for the knockout. From the Paret bout to his retirement in 1977, Griffith fought 80 bouts but only scored 12 knockouts. Some of his greatest performances occurred during that time. He won the middleweight title by unanimous decision from Dick Tiger in 1966. The following year he lost and then regained the title from Nino Benvenuti. In 1973, at the age of 35, he lost a very close decision to middleweight champion Carlos Monzon that most fans (including this writer) thought Griffith deserved to win.

Like many boxers before him, Griffith continued to fight past his prime. His superb defensive skills kept him from taking a beating, but in the final three years of his career (1974–1977), he won only eight of his 18 bouts.

Ever since the ugly incident with Paret at the weigh-in, the gossipmongers have speculated about Griffith's sexual orientation. For his thousands of fans that is irrelevant. All that mattered were his accomplishments as a boxer and his character as a man. But, in 2005, perhaps to put the matter to rest once and for all, Griffith told *Sports Illustrated*, "I like men and women both. But I don't like that word: homosexual, gay, or faggot. I don't know what I am. I love men and women the same, but if you ask me which is better . . . I like women."[1]

The widespread publicity and criticism that accompanied the Paret fight became the basis of the 2005 documentary *Ring of Fire: The Emile Griffith Story*. In the final scene Griffith is introduced to Benny Paret's son, who was an infant when his father died. Benny Paret Jr. embraces Griffith and tells him he is forgiven. In addition to the documentary, two stage plays and an opera based on Griffith's story have premiered since 2013.

In retirement, Emile worked as a prison guard and also trained other boxers, including world champions Wilfred Benitez and Juan Laporte. In the final years of his life the legendary boxer suffered from dementia puglistica. He died on July 23, 2013, at a nursing home in Hempstead, New York.

Emile Griffith in 1998. The former welterweight and middleweight champion holds the all-time record for main events at Madison Square Garden. *Photo by Herb Cohen, author's collection*

Interview

Mike Silver: Were there any fighters you looked up to when you were young?

Emile Griffith: I tried to fight like Floyd Patterson, who was heavyweight champion when I first began to box. I used to have the same hairstyle, with that peak in the front, like Floyd. I tried to fight like him. When I was getting ready for the Golden Gloves I used to look at Sugar Ray Robinson on TV.

Mike: You fought every top welterweight and middleweight of the 1960s and 1970s. Who was your toughest opponent?

Emile: Guy by the name of "Hurricane" Carter. Oh, that was some night.

Mike: What happened in that fight?

Emile: Well, I think it was in the first round he put my lights out.

Mike: Carter was one of only two opponents who stopped you. Was he the hardest puncher you ever fought?

Emile: No, I fought a guy named Florentino Fernandez also. And I fought a guy by the name of Dick Tiger. Those three were the toughest guys I fought. Don't forget I'm a welter, 147 pounds, and these guys are 160 pounds I'm fighting.

Mike: You won a ten-round decision over Florentino Fernandez in 1960. What was your strategy in that fight?

Emile: Hit and run. Hit and run. After that fight I was so sore. I had to sit in a tub of hot water filled with Epsom salts. I didn't want to get out.

Mike: Of the three [Carter, Fernandez, Tiger], who gave you the toughest fight?

Emile: That's a good question. Hmmm . . . I would say Dick Tiger.

Mike: Why?

Emile: Because he was there every time, punching on me all the time.

Mike: In defense of your welterweight title you defeated such outstanding boxers as Ralph Dupas, Jorge Fernandez, Luis Rodriguez, and Jose Stable. Eventually you ran out of challengers so you moved up a weight class and fought Dick Tiger for the middleweight title.

Emile: Dick Tiger and I used to spar together all the time. I knew his style a little but I wasn't sure I wanted to fight him. When Clancy first told me I was going to fight him I said, "You go fight him yourself, not me!" I knew he was very strong and could hit.

Mike: What was your strategy in that fight?

Emile: My strategy was to box him all the time. I was never a puncher. I was a boxer. I could box all day and night.

Mike: But you dropped him.

Emile: It was a lucky shot.

Mike: Could you describe your boxing style?

Emile: I was a boxer. My jab was the most important punch to me. Use that left hand all the time . . . keep the man off guard.

Mike: Why is the jab so important in boxing?

Emile: Well, it's not just important to me. It's important to all those guys who ever want to use it. You just can't go and throw right hands all the time. You set up the opponent before you throw the right hand. Show him the left until he gets tired of seeing it and then throw the right hand.

Mike: You train fighters today. What do you teach a beginner?

Emile: First thing I teach is footwork. Without footwork and movement you've got nothing. You have to get in your roadwork. Then I teach the way to use your hands in there. It's not trying to knock the guy out. Just try to keep him away from you. You use the jab, jab, and then right hand . . . it tells you when you want to go.

Mike: Would you let your son box?

Emile: To tell the truth, I'd be the first one to put him in there. Why? Because I was there and I know if he sees me going to the gym every day he will want to be there. And I wouldn't stop him. I would encourage him to box. Boxing is my life. I love the sport. If it wasn't for boxing I would never be here, where I am today.

Mike: Would you say the Tiger fight was your best performance ever? Or is there one fight in particular that stands out where you could say, "I think I was at my best in this particular fight"?

Emile: I think my best fight was when I was fighting for the welterweight title.

Mike: Would that be against Luis Rodriguez?

Emile: [*Slightly annoyed*] Now you know which guy it is—may he rest in peace.

Mike: Oh, Benny "Kid" Paret.

Emile: He was a wonderful fighter. While I was fighting him he had me thinking all the time. He had a good style. He was always up in my face all the time. Every time I looked to do something, if I didn't do it I got hit. If I turned around I got hit.

Mike: After the tragic ending of your third fight with Paret, you wanted to quit boxing.

Emile: After that I didn't want to be a fighter then.

Mike: What made you change your mind?

Emile: What really made me start fighting again was my little friends, my little buddies in the gym. The kids would come by and say, "Champ, are you going to fight again?" I'd say, "Yes, I'm going to fight again." That's why I started to fight again.

Mike: Your style of fighting also changed to some degree after the Paret tragedy. You rarely went for a knockout and were content to use your outstanding boxing skills to outpoint your opponents, whereas before you were knocking out some good fighters. You seemed satisfied to do just what you had to do in order to win without trying for a knockout.

Emile: That's true. It did change my style. I didn't have that fighter in-stinct in me anymore. I just went in the ring to win the fight and not get hit, to block punches, and keep the guy away from me.

Mike: Was there one opponent that you consider the smartest or the trickiest?

Emile: He [Paret] was very tricky. He reminded me a little bit of Luis Rodriguez.

Mike: Speaking of Rodriguez, he seemed to be able to beat everybody except you. You won three of your four fights with him. All were close decisions but he always had trouble with you. Why is that?

Emile: That's because I wouldn't let him fight his fight against me.

Mike: How did you do that?

Emile: I was on him all the time. I just kept staying close and punch all the time. Luis was a very good fighter. They used to call him another Kid Gavilan. Clancy would say to me, "Always keep the pressure on him. Punch first. Don't give him time to get off first." If he gets off first I'm in trouble.

Mike: You also fought another all-time great fighter—Jose Napoles.

Emile: That was a good fight.

Mike: Napoles won the 15-round decision. You were 31 years old and still in your prime but he clearly outpointed you. What was the problem with Jose?

Emile: Well, like you say, I was getting older and I thought it was never going to end. But he was a good fighter and I won't use that as an excuse. He beat me and it was a good fight.

Mike: If you had a chance to fight Napoles again, do you think, looking back, you might have changed your strategy or done something differently

Emile: Well, I can say yes now because I never did have a rematch. But like I say, he was the better man. I have no excuse; he beat me fair. It was just one of those nights, I guess. Sometimes you get that motion and that drive and you're right because you want to be. That night you feel you can beat the world. And maybe that *is* your night. Other nights you feel you'll beat the world and you can't do it.

Mike: You once told me that Napoles had an extra step that bothered you.

Emile: Maybe he had an extra step, or whatever, but that night he was good.

Mike: Who would have won in a fight between Napoles and Luis Rodriguez?

Emile: I think I would say Luis Rodriguez.

Mike: Why?

Emile: Because of the way he moved his hands. He had fast hands. I'm not saying that because I defeated him.

Mike: After you won the middleweight title from Dick Tiger you had two successful defenses against Joey Archer.

Emile: That was fun.

Mike: Why was that fun?

Emile: [*Laughs*] The reason why I say it was fun fighting Joey Archer is because we were like two boxers trying to outsmart each other. He's doing something to me this round and I come back the next round and do the same things back to him. It was like a chess game. But Joey was a very good young man.

Mike: You fought so many great fighters, Emile. Another name that stands out is Carlos Monzon. You had two fights with Monzon for the middleweight title. He stopped you in the 14th round in the first fight. Two years later, at the age of 35, you fought him again and lost a controversial 15-round decision that many people thought you won.

Emile: Well, I felt I won that fight.

Mike: Did you take him too lightly the first time?

Emile: No. I never take any of my opponents lightly. When I hear that bell it's either him or me.

Mike: What did you do differently in the second fight?

Emile: Well, I kept him busy. I was punching more, throwing more punches and I was doing what I didn't do in the first fight. When I fight an opponent the second time, or the first time, I try to enjoy myself while I'm doing it. And when I enjoy myself while I'm doing it the fight seems to be easier for me and better to me.

Mike: How do you rate Monzon as a fighter?

Emile: He was a very good champion.

Mike: How does he compare to some of the great fighters you fought in your prime?

Emile: I compare him with the others very favorably. He could punch, he could box, and he hit very hard too.

Mike: How would he have done against Dick Tiger?

Emile: Monzon was taller and had a longer reach but Tiger would hold his own.

Mike: Do you think Monzon would have beaten Joey Archer?

Emile: That's a good fight. Both of them fight about the same. But I don't think he would have beaten Joey.

Mike: Looking back on your career if you could fight one opponent again, using a different strategy, is there a certain opponent you would have fought differently, or would like another shot at?

Emile: I would like Rubin "Hurricane" Carter again.

Mike: Why?

Emile: Why? Because he caught me off guard and he knocked me out.

Mike: The very first time I saw you fight was your national television debut when you won a ten-round split decision against the veteran welterweight contender Gaspar Ortega in Madison Square Garden.

Emile: That first fight with Gaspar Ortega was a lesson for me. I enjoyed the fight with him. I respected the man. The reason I respected him was because he knew more about the sport than I did.

Mike: You had three title fights with Nino Benvenuti. How good was Benvenuti compared to the others you fought?

Emile: Benvenuti was a very good, smart boxer. He knew what he was doing.

Mike: Who was better, Benvenuti or Archer?

Emile: I would say Benvenuti because he hit harder.

Mike: What about Benvenuti and Dick Tiger?

Emile: Well, to tell you the truth, Tiger didn't really hit me and hurt me or anything like that. But Benvenuti was a little sneaky; he'd get in there, do damage, and run like hell—excuse the French [*laughs*].

Mike: You became very friendly with Benvenuti after you retired.

Emile: Nino invited me to Italy. Everyone there was happy to see me. He said to me, "You are going to be godfather to my son." I said, "No, I'm going home." He said, "Either you become godfather or I'm not putting you on the plane." I said, "OK." A very nice man.

Mike: Near the end of your career you defeated three top Philadelphia boxers, Stanley "Kitten" Hayward, Gypsy Joe Harris, and Benny Briscoe.

Emile: I fought Hayward the first time in the Garden. He beat me. I trained very hard for the rematch. I went back to his hometown and beat him. They said to him after the fight, "That isn't the same Griffith you beat in New York," 'cause that's how good I whipped his butt down there. He wanted more and he got more! I was a different person when I fought him in his hometown.

Mike: Any thoughts about Gypsy Joe?

Emile: I liked Gypsy. He's my friend. They all said his eye was bad when he fought me. But the doctor gave him permission to fight me. So what are they trying to say? I didn't know that he was hurt with his eye. So I don't know what they are talking about.

Mike: Benny Briscoe?

Emile: Benny was a good man. Not as hard a puncher as Tiger. I never gave him a chance to land a punch on me.

Mike: Where do you put Briscoe compared to Monzon or Benvenuti, or some of the other guys?

Emile: For me he's not in the same class with those guys. He was flashy and everything but he wasn't in the same class.

Mike: Any regrets about your career?

Emile: No regrets at all. I love boxing. Baseball was my first love but then I tried boxing and fell in love with it. There is good and bad to it. I didn't do anything in the ring that someone before me didn't do. Do you understand what I'm saying? Whatever happened to me in the ring, I didn't do it that somebody else didn't do ahead of me. So I don't know why they're making all this big brouhaha about me. The only reason all these things happened was because of these names that show no respect for people. If they got respect for you, OK. You'd do it too if you had to.

Mike: How is your health?

Emile: No complaints.

Mike: If you could change anything about your career what would you change?

Emile: I would have held on to my money. I did not hold on to it. At the time I had many mouths to feed; matter of fact, I still do.

Mike: You were nearly 40 years old when you decided to retire. You fought for 19 years and had 112 professional fights. In your last fight you lost a ten-round decision to future middleweight champion Alan Minter.

Emile: I thought if Archie Moore could do it I could do it. But Father Time said, "Champ, you can only go so far now." After the Minter fight, the Irishman [Gil Clancy] told me to retire. Not that I wanted to, but I felt I just had to. Some fighters don't want to quit. I think the boxing commissions should set a special time for a fighter to retire because some of them don't want to quit and if things are bad now why make it worse than what it is. So I think they should make a time they have to retire.

21

CARLOS ORTIZ

(Interviewed on February 11, 1998)

C arlos Ortiz rates as one of the great lightweight champions of the 20th century. A savvy and seasoned professional, he used consummate boxing skills to defeat the best lightweight boxers of his era. The list includes Joe Brown, Ismael Laguna, Duilio Loi, Sugar Ramos, Kenny Lane, Battling Torres, Flash Elorde, Paolo Rossi, Doug Vaillant, Dave Charnley, Johnny Busso, Cisco Andrade, and Len Matthews.

Carlos was born in Ponce, Puerto Rico, on September 9, 1936. Eight years later he moved to New York City. A local Boys Club provided his introduction to boxing. From 1948 to 1954 he fought in amateur boxing tournaments throughout the city. He turned pro at 18 with a first-round knockout of Harry Bell at the historic St. Nicholas Arena in New York City.

Carlos was undefeated in his first 27 professional fights before losing a split decision to Johnny Busso. He defeated Busso in a return bout. After outpointing England's Dave Charnley, he lost his second fight on a split decision to Kenny Lane. A dramatic victory over Len Matthews earned him a rematch with Lane for the vacant junior welterweight title. A cut over Lane's eye forced a stoppage after the second round. He defended the title, successfully winning a split decision over Italy's Duilio Loi in San Francisco. The return bout was staged in Loi's hometown of Milan. Ortiz lost the title to Loi on another split decision. Their third bout eight months later resulted in another close win for Loi.

After failing to regain the crown, Carlos decided to focus his energy on winning the more prestigious lightweight championship held by Joe "Old Bones" Brown. On April 21, 1962, Ortiz, an 8-to-5 underdog, won a unanimous decision over Brown. He defended the title successfully four times, including a victory over Kenny Lane, before losing a decision to Panama's Ismael Laguna in 1965. Ortiz won back the crown from Laguna and, in a masterful boxing performance, won a unanimous decision over Laguna for the second time.

On June 29, 1968, after eight years as lightweight champion and ten successful defenses, Ortiz lost the lightweight championship to the Dominican Republic's Carlos Teo Cruz. Two years later he launched a comeback at the age of 36. After winning nine fights, he was stopped for the first and only time in 70 fights by Scotland's former world champion, Ken Buchanan. Ortiz did not come out for the seventh round. Age and the wear and tear of a 17-year boxing career had finally caught up with him. But his reputation did not suffer. He had already established his credentials as one of boxing's most respected and revered champions. Carlos currently resides in the Bronx with his wife, Maria.

Carlos Ortiz in 1998. Experts rank Ortiz as one of the greatest lightweight champions of the 20th century. *Photo by Herb Cohen, author's collection*

Interview

Mike Silver: How did you get started in boxing?

Carlos Ortiz: I got into a fight one summer in the pool on 23rd Street and East River Drive, New York City. I got into trouble. I hit a kid and they called the cops. They almost arrested me. The cop said to me, "We're not going to put you in jail now, but if you don't go over to the PAL [Police Athletic League] and join the program we're going to put you in jail." I thought he was kidding but I got scared. And that's exactly what I did. At the time I was going to the Madison Square Boys Club, which was a couple of blocks away from where I used to live. I was about 10 or 11 years old. When I joined the PAL I was 12. The cop said, "You better join some organization that will keep you out of the street and behave yourself." I took that cop up on his request. So that was my beginning in boxing.

Mike: Was there an attraction to boxing? What kept you interested in the sport?

Carlos: The competition. I loved boxing because it was a competition sport. You had to be the best to stay there and that really got to me. Every time I did it I tried to do it better and better and better.

Mike: Did you take to it right away? Were you good at it?

Carlos: It was like I was born with a pair of gloves. I remember I heard this boy punching the bag and the noise mesmerized me. It was the most beautiful noise I have ever seen. I asked him if he would teach me how to punch the light bag and he did. And I learned it very fast. I had that knack, you know. I guess I had natural ability for a fighter. It was fantastic the way I caught on to it.

Mike: What was the toughest thing in boxing to get the hang of? Was there anything in particular that you found difficult to master, even though you were a natural, as you say?

Carlos: The most difficult part of boxing for me was trying to dodge a punch coming at you maybe a thousand miles per hour when it's like two feet away from you. You have to dodge it without getting hit and I always wondered how in the world these guys could do that. When I first started boxing I paid more attention to dodging or slipping a punch without it hitting your face. It was tough at first but it didn't take me long before I learned it pretty good.

Mike: Was it a matter of getting the timing down?

Carlos: It was a matter of timing . . . and speed. It also has a lot to do with your leg position, your body position, the position that you take while you're in front of your opponent. It has a lot to do with everything. There are so many things that you have to look out for, it's incredible.

Mike: How many amateur fights did you have?

Carlos: I don't really know how many amateur fights I had in my whole career because I fought from when I was 10 years old and then when I turned pro at 18, that's eight years. And throughout those eight years I was fighting in the Boys Club, then I fought in the PAL, then I fought in CYO, et cetera, et cetera. So I would assume I had 75, 80, 100 fights, I don't know.

Mike: How is amateur boxing different than the pros?

Carlos: It's the difference between night and day. Professional boxing is tough. Once you get into the pro ranks you're going to learn the pro moves, because they're not the same as the amateur moves. You have good fighters in the pros. You come up against guys who know how to fight, and if you don't learn how to fight you're through. A professional fighter is going to do the utmost to survive, to win. So you've got to be careful. You have to know what you're doing. You have to study what you're doing. And the fights are longer in the pros—four, six, eight, ten rounds. You get to the championship level it used to be 15 rounds. So you really had to get adapted to it and you had to get ready for each and every fight.

Mike: What motivated you to succeed?

Carlos: I had to work hard because I was afraid of losing. I worked hard because I loved the sport. I loved to train. I loved boxing and the more I did it, the more I loved it. The more I loved it, the harder I worked at it. And the harder I worked at it, the more successful I was.

Mike: Of all your 70 professional opponents who was the toughest?

Carlos: All of my 70 opponents were tough. Now who was the smartest? And who was in the best of condition? That's a different story. Johnny Busso, from the East Side, beat me in 1958 and broke my string of 27 straight victories. He was tough.

Mike: What made him tough?

Carlos: What made him tough was that he was in the same league as I was. He came up at the same time and we both were striving for the same thing.

Mike: You beat Busso by unanimous decision in the rematch. Three months later you lost your second fight to a clever southpaw named Kenny Lane. You defeated him in two subsequent rematches.

Carlos: Oh yeah! A smart and experienced fighter, that's Kenny Lane. He was, I would say, the second smartest fighter that I ever fought. Besides being smart he was a southpaw. Nobody, in my time, wanted to fight a southpaw. I fought eight southpaws and they were the hardest guys to fight. Kenny Lane was great. Almost no one beat him but the champion and me.

Mike: In 1959 you fought Philadelphia lightweight Len Matthews. At the time he was one of the hottest prospects in the country and a very dangerous puncher. Matthews had knocked out 13 of 18 opponents.

Carlos: [*Exclaims*] Ah! What a fight! What a fight! This is one of the fights I cherish the most because Len Matthews was a *killer*. He was knocking everybody out. When I made the fight people were surprised that I agreed to fight him in Philadelphia, his hometown. And when they heard about it, they said I was crazy, that I had gone out of my mind. Why did I do this? Why fight Len Matthews in his own hometown when he could have come over to New York City and fight me here? But in New York City they were not offering me the same money they offered me to fight him in Philadelphia.

Mike: Were you confident you could beat Matthews?

Carlos: Len Matthews is a good fighter but I didn't think anyone could beat me whether I fight him here or I fight him in Philadelphia, or in China. It was one of the greatest fights that I ever encountered. I mean it was a gem. Len Matthews hit me once with a left hook between my eyes and nose that numbed my whole face. I couldn't feel my face for approximately a minute and a half. When the round ended—I believe it was the fifth round—I ran to the corner because I couldn't feel my face. I sat on the stool and I asked my handler whether my face was still there [*laughs*]. And he said, "What do you mean?" I said, "I can't feel it. Is it still there, is my nose still there?" They said, "Yeah everything is fine." They put an ice bag on my face for a few seconds and I got a little bit of feeling back. Then I came out for the sixth round and I pummeled Len Matthews.

Mike: What were you thinking when you came out for the sixth round?

Carlos: I said I better take care of him now because otherwise he's going to take care of me. This kid's a good puncher and he's liable to get in a lucky one and hurt me. That sixth round was one of the greatest rounds that I've ever had. I hit him with an uppercut that ricocheted from the stomach to the chin and I got him up against the ropes and I must have hit him a hundred shots to the face. Too bad the referee didn't want to stop the fight. They thought I was going to get tired and then he was going to come back and regain his strength and knock me out. But I fooled them. I was in the best shape. I wasn't going to get tired. They made a mistake and I knocked him out. They stopped the fight in the sixth round and boy that was a thriller. It was beautiful.

Mike: I've seen a film of your fight with Len Matthews. Right from the beginning you did not fight your normal long-range type of fight. You kept the fight at very close quarters. Why?

Carlos: Right. It was all set up that way. Len Matthews was a long-range puncher. If he kept you at arm's length he would knock your head right off. We didn't know how good he was inside. So my strategy was to fight him inside at the beginning and not let him get off those straight right-hand punches and terrific left hooks that he used to throw. When I started the inside fighting it worked for me and it kept on working, although he still was dangerous because he hit me on the nose and numbed my face up. He had the power, but the thing was he was not a polished professional fighter, I think. He was a good club fighter. If you fought him he'd knock you bowlegged. I didn't fight him. I outsmarted him. Like I did Joe Brown. I outsmarted him. I fought him different than anybody else.

Mike: Was Matthews the hardest puncher you ever fought?

Carlos: Well, I fought like ten good punchers. Joe Brown was a deadly puncher. Matthews was a strong, sharp hitter. Battling Torres, Sugar Ramos, those guys were devastating. Battling Torres, he was like a sledge-hammer. Every time he hit you you felt it.

Mike: In 1960 you defended your junior welterweight title against Battling Torres. He was undefeated in 31 fights and had knocked out 24 opponents. What was your strategy?

Carlos: My strategy in beating Battling Torres was not to get scared [*laughs*], because when I went to LA they kept talking about this Mexican like he's some kind of brute. He's been knocking everybody out. He knocked out Johnny Busso in two rounds. I was really a little bit worried. I didn't know what the heck I'd gotten myself into. Good thing I saw him training in the gym. Once I saw him all the jitters went out of me. When I got into the ring it was easy. I outsmarted him. He was a good puncher and that's all I had to be careful about. Once I got away from his punch everything else was easy.

Mike: Tell me why you felt you could beat Torres after you saw him in the gym.

Carlos: Look, a fighter could be strong. He could have the greatest punch in the game but without experience it's not going to do you much good if you don't know how to use it. All I had to do was see an opponent for two or three minutes sparring in the gym and I know if this guy is going to give me trouble, or he's not going to give me any problems. Once I saw this kid I said that he would be taken care of and he wasn't going to be a problem to me.

Mike: In 1962, seven years after turning pro, you finally won the light-weight title from Joe Brown, an outstanding boxer, and one of the best of the post–World War II lightweight champions. He was making his 12th title defense. You were an 8-to-5 underdog. Many experts thought it would be a tough fight for you but you won an easy 15-round decision.

Carlos: I learned a lot from him. Although I beat Joe Brown very easily that doesn't mean he was easy to fight. I beat him easily only because I did my homework. In order for you to beat him you had to outguess him. You could not outpunch him, you could not outbox him, and you could not outdo him in anything because he was that good. I mean, you had to be lucky. And I think that I was a little bit lucky. The way that I fought him had a lot to do with me beating him for 15 rounds.

Mike: Joe Brown's nickname was "Old Bones." He was 36 years old at the time and had been champion for six years. Despite his age he was still considered one of the best fighters in the world. Yet you beat him so easily that people actually thought the fight might have been fixed. But it was not fixed and you were able to win at least 13 of the 15 rounds. How did you do it?

Carlos: Well, see, I fooled Joe Brown. I put out a story before the fight that I was going to go out and beat Joe Brown to a pulp right away. I was going to outmaul him and outfight him and concentrate on a body attack. But I fooled him. It was the other way around. I came out with a jab. He was not expecting a jab. He was expecting me to go out and throw combinations and press him all the time. I didn't do that. Every single second that I was there I was jabbing him. I was confusing him with my left jab. I was going in and out. And that confused him. He never thought about me doing that kind of a fight. So he was always on an edge. He was never set up to throw his punches because I never let him set up.

Mike: By your own admission, after you retired from boxing in 1972 you had some rough times. The money wasn't there after a while, and you had personal problems. How did you overcome these problems, and what brought you out of that situation?

Carlos: I had my problems. I went into boxing not because I wanted to get rich. I've never been a materialistic individual. I like to have money but being rich was never life to me. When I came into boxing I became rich. I became very popular. I had more than what I could handle. That was my problem. I did not know how to handle everything and I let it get out of hand. And because of that I got into financial trouble, family trouble, and so forth. But that served as a lesson to me. I'm not glad those things happened but it was a lesson that I had to learn, and I guess it was good for me because I got through those problems and I came out well, I came out strong, I came out much smarter. And people love me today for what I am, not for what I was. In my time of glory I was loved by people because of my fame, because of my money. Today I'm happy. I may not have what I had in those days but I tell you one thing, I'm the happiest guy in the world today. I cherish my life, I value my life and boy am I going to live it up the way it is.

Mike: How do you maintain your positive outlook?

Carlos: I maintain my position by just being satisfied with what I have, with what comes my way, with what I've earned myself. I am no longer trying to be what I am not. I know what I am today. I'm Carlos Ortiz. I'm still the lightweight champion of the world. I believe that people today acknowledge me more than before because of my attitude and my way of living. And I'm going to stay the way I'm living today and I hope that everything comes my way, the way I want it.

Mike: You've been more fortunate than some of your former opponents. Battling Torres was shot and killed at the age of 31. Doug Vaillant committed suicide. Others have had drug and alcohol problems. Do you have any idea as to why you were able to land on your feet and they were not?

Carlos: I learned a great lesson from a great organization, which is AA [Alcoholics Anonymous]. You have to value your life. At one point in life you have to come to the realization that there is nothing more valuable than your life here on earth. When I came to that realization, that good living doesn't have to be bad living, I woke up. I saw the light, like they say. And I kept on doing the good things that they told me to do and up to now everything has come out roses, like they say.

Mike: I'm going to give you the names of some of your best opponents. Just give a comment or two about what you thought of each one.

Carlos: OK.

Mike: Duilio Loi.

Carlos: Very European fighter.

Mike: What does that mean?

Carlos: A defensive fighter. He was a smart boxer. You throw the punches and he would slip and throw a couple of punches and the crowd in Milan was for him all the time. Just because he made you miss they were going crazy so he wins the round right there.

Mike: Was he the smartest fighter you ever fought?

Carlos: No. A good fighter is not used to a fighter running away from you, and that's what he used to do all the time, run, run, run.

Mike: Doug Vaillant.

Carlos: A fairly good fighter. I wouldn't say one of the best but he was my first title defense that I fought and I knocked him out. He was a light puncher. I wouldn't call him one of the best.

Mike: Paolo Rossi.

Carlos: Very dangerous son of a gun. You had to watch out for him every second of the fight. If you were not careful he would hit you with that left hook or that overhand right and knock you out. So I had to be on my toes all the time.

Mike: I remember that fight. You boxed him as carefully as you boxed Joe Brown.

Carlos: That was the only way to box him.

Mike: Flash Elorde.

Carlos: Very good southpaw. I wouldn't want to say he's one of the greatest that I fought but he was one of the good ones. But I was lucky because I could fight left handers like I fought right handers. I had no problem at all fighting left handers. He didn't give me any trouble at all. I knocked him out twice in the 14th round, I think. I was too strong for him. He was like a small lightweight.

Mike: Nicolino Locche.

Carlos: [*Laughs*] Oh, don't mention him! Lucky for me it was one of those nontitle fights. I went all the way to Argentina, his hometown, to fight him. The most difficult fighter I ever fought in my whole life. He didn't want to get hit, and he didn't want to hit me. The fight was a stinkeroo. He was always on the defensive. I'm trying to make a fight out of it and he's running. And just because he ran the crowd's cheering him and I couldn't understand it. Why? So at the end of the ten rounds they called it a draw. And I was glad with that.

Mike: In 1965 you traveled to Panama and lost the lightweight title to a speed demon named Ismael Laguna.

Carlos: That son of a gun [*laughs*]! He's one of the greatest fighters that I ever fought. He punched the heck out of me in that first fight in Panama. Boy did he surprise me! I mean he looked three times faster than when I saw him in the gym. And he punched three times faster. He didn't knock me out because of my experience.

Mike: You regained your title by beating him in the rematch in Puerto Rico. And then in the rubber match, in New York, you won again by unanimous decision. What had changed?

Carlos: I had already fought him so I knew what he was all about and I adjusted. The problem with the first fight was my anxiety to knock this kid out. I didn't think he had any business being in the same ring with me. What happened to me was that I got too careless in that first fight. The second fight I went in knowing that this man could actually beat me if I was not careful again. I started the fight nice and cool. I didn't go out and try to knock him out like I did in Panama. If you try to knock out a fast guy like him you're never going to hit him because you are not going to ever be in position to put your punches together and have any effect on him because he's always moving, and by the time you get set he's gone. So you have to have a different style.

Mike: Laguna was known for his speed and left jab, but you actually outjabbed him.

Carlos: You can't beat any good fighter without a left jab. The left jab is the most important punch that you have. Without it you are not going to beat a savvy fighter. I've always had a good jab. I've always had a good everything. But it just happened that Laguna couldn't beat me no how because I was too smart. The type of fighter that I am Laguna could never beat because he could not cope with intelligence in the ring.

Mike: So the left jab was key to winning the fight?

Carlos: It's a three-way combination: it's the intelligence, the movement, and the punching. You have to combine them together. If you don't combine them together you are going to make the fight harder. It just happened when I fought him in Puerto Rico and in New York I put all those things together at the same time, and it seemed very easy but that's the way it is when you do things right. I was also able to reach his chin with my right cross. Laguna used to have the same problem that I had. He used to step back with his left hand down. I had the same habit of pulling back with my head up and my left hand down. That's how Sugar Ramos knocked me down. Every time I would crowd Laguna a little bit he used to go back with his head high and I'd throw my overhand right and clip him right away every time. I would say that was one of the best fights that I ever had.

Mike: After six years as champion, and 12 successful defenses, you lost the title to Carlos Teo Cruz. He was tough and strong but certainly not up to your level as a boxer. It was a big upset, as I recall.

Carlos: That was one of the most difficult moments in my whole career. Thirteen years in the pros, 60 fights. To have to lose to a fighter like that was the hardest thing for me to accept, you know. There's a long story behind that. I didn't want to fight Teo Cruz in the first place. I told my manager that it was time for me to retire. I was going to take a long layoff and wait until they forced me to fight so I could call it a career without having to fight again. It so happened that my manager made a mistake and I paid for it. That's the last fight I ever wanted. He signed the contract and once he signed for it I didn't want to call it off. I went into the fight reluctantly and because of that I think that I didn't train right, I didn't feel right. I was not in the right situation, the right feeling, and I lost the fight.

Mike: You had one more fight after losing the title and then retired. But two years later, in 1971, at the age of 35, you returned to the ring and won nine fights over ordinary opposition. Then, a year into your comeback, you fought former champion Ken Buchanan. What happened?

Carlos: Disaster. I didn't want to fight Buchanan. I wasn't supposed to fight Buchanan. I made a contract to fight Roberto Duran in Madison

Square Garden. [Duran had beaten Buchanan for the title three months earlier.] Roberto Duran called the fight off about two weeks before. Then Madison Square Garden came to me and said, "Carlos, we've got to do something about the show. We have a substitute if you want to fight Buchanan." They said, "You are the only one who can save it by fighting him. You can do us a favor by fighting him and we can see if we can get Duran back some other time." I wasn't training for Buchanan. I didn't have my heart set on Buchanan. I wanted to fight Duran. I wasn't training for a speedster like Buchanan. I was winning the fight up to that last round. [*Author's note*: Buchanan was ahead on the judges' scorecards.] I finished the sixth round and I sat down. All of a sudden something's happening to my system, something which never happened before. I couldn't take a deep breath. I couldn't breathe right and when I felt this I had to decide within a minute the fate of my life, you know. And I decided that I was not going to go out there and get knocked out by a powder puffer like Buchanan and be embarrassed. So I said I'm going to stay in my corner, on my stool, and call it a career because I'm not going to endanger my life just because I want it one more time. So I stayed in the corner even though I was winning the fight. I stayed in the corner and decided that was it.

Mike: How do you think you would have done against Roberto Duran? How would you have fought him?

Carlos: I would have knocked him out. This is the one person that I wanted to fight. It's the reason why I made my comeback—to fight for the lightweight title. When I made my comeback I said I'm going to fight until I get a chance at the champion. When I got that opportunity that was great. But when Duran skipped that was the end of my career.

Mike: You felt you could have knocked out Duran even though you were 36 years old and past your prime?

Carlos: Well, that was the only reason why I wanted the fight because I knew within my heart, within myself, that I could have beaten Duran and everybody else knew about it too. Madison Square Garden agreed with me too, so that's why we went into it.

Mike: In 1972 Roberto Duran was only 21 years old and although a very formidable fighter he was still a work in progress and had not yet reached his prime. Could you have beaten Roberto Duran in your prime against his prime?

Carlos: I could have beaten anybody. Of course, I could have beaten Duran anytime.

Mike: How would you have beaten him?

Carlos: Just the same way I beat everybody else, with my knowledge, my left hand, my boxing ability, and my boxing skills. I don't want to sound like a Cassius Clay but I mean I was one of the greatest lightweights that ever lived.

Mike: Do you think Roberto Duran was a great lightweight?

Carlos: He was great. He was terrific. But that's not to say I couldn't beat him.

Mike: What do you think is missing from today's fighters compared to those of your generation, or before?

Carlos: A big problem today is that the good fighters don't want to fight the good fighters. Champions don't want to fight champions. The champions don't have any pride. If you want to be number one you've got to be number one all over. You've got to fight everybody—number one, number two, number three, number four, number five. You've got to fight all those guys to be considered number one if you really want to be considered number one. In the second place, who's the champion today? There are so many champions. So that's another problem. And there are too many weight divisions. Only five pounds divides all these weight divisions. I could have been champion of ten divisions if that would have been the case in my time. In my time there was a pride of being champion—one champion of everybody.

Mike: Do you think today's fighters are not as skilled as the fighters of your day or before?

Carlos: No. And that is not to say that they don't have the ability. It's that they can't develop because there are not as many fighters today compared to my time. In my time you could get the fights, you had the action, and you could get the experience. How in the world are you going to get good if you don't fight? In order to get good, in order to get that experience you have to get into that ring and battle it out all the time; if not, forget it.

Mike: Do you think fighters get hit too much today?

Carlos: Of course. You're going to get hit if you don't know how to duck, if you don't know how to defend yourself. And in order for you to learn all those things you've got to fight. You can't be champion with having 12 fights, 20 fights, 25 fights; that's not a champ. By the time I had 27 fights I was just a possibility. They used to call me a *possibility.* Today I'm a champion of the world. Not that I'm knocking anybody. I'm just saying that today it's easier.

Mike: Many of today's fighters seem to train differently than fighters of years ago. There is a lot of training with weights. In your day did you lift weights and what do you think of weight training for boxers?

Carlos: I never lifted a weight in my whole life. Weight training is no good for fighters. A fighter is supposed to have loose muscles, a loose body. With a tight body you cannot get your punches out fast enough, you cannot combine them together because your body is tight. You used to see fighters with muscles, but different type of muscles that were fighting muscles, not weight lifting muscles, which is what certain fighters of today have. They think that they're going to get strength out of that. No they don't. You don't get boxing strength from lifting weights.

Mike: Do you think the old-time great lightweight champs such as Benny Leonard, Henry Armstrong, Barney Ross, Jimmy McLarnin, Tony Canzoneri, Ike Williams, Beau Jack, Jimmy Carter, Joe Brown, and others are forgotten and not appreciated today.

Carlos: They are not appreciated at all today. Most of the people don't even know who they are. They don't know what kind of fighters they are. They're gone by the wayside, as they say. They're forgotten.

Mike: Why is that?

Carlos: Because people don't pay attention. They don't want to know about the past. They just want to know about the present.

Mike: Is there anything you would change about your boxing career if you had it to do over again?

Carlos: I wouldn't have fought Buchanan [*laughs*].

Mike: What advice could you offer a young boxer today who is just about to turn pro? What would you say to him if you could get him alone for five minutes to give him some advice?

Carlos: You better make sure that you want to give your dedicated attention to boxing. And you better make sure you work your butt off, because if you don't you're in trouble, kid, and it's best for you to stay home and go to work five days a week.

Mike: Would you let your own son box?

Carlos: Yeah, why not? If he did what he's supposed to do, if he worked the same way I worked and did the same things I did.

Mike: As you know, many fighters come out of the sport damaged. How come you ended up in much better condition than most?

Carlos: Well, I'm a smarter fighter in the ring. A lot of people have the wrong misconception about boxing. Boxing is to hit and not get hit. And if you go into the ring with that thought in your mind you'll be OK. But don't go out there and try to impress the public by showing them how much you can take or how hard a punch you can take. That's not the case in boxing. Boxing is I hit you, you don't hit me, over and over again. It's a skill that you apply.

Mike: Most fighters wind up with no money. Is there any way that fighters can be helped from being taken advantage of, or of being more capable with their finances?

Carlos: I have no advice to give. It's up to the individual to decide his own fate as far as the money is concerned. Get somebody who knows about it and let them take care of it if you don't know how to take care of it.

Mike: What do you think of Oscar De La Hoya?

Carlos: He's a possibility. In my time he would have been a possibility.

Mike: If he fought in your time do you think he would have been a better fighter?

Carlos: He could become a better fighter if he was in my time. I don't know about being champion, but as far as learning, because the kid likes to fight, I think he enjoys fighting, but he has to learn a lot more.

Mike: Has there ever been an occasion where you've had to use your fists outside of the ring?

Carlos: I have never lifted up my hands towards defense of myself outside since I retired.

Mike: Not since that episode in the pool.

Carlos: [*Laughs*] Not since that episode.

22

TED LOWRY

(Interviewed on March 12, 2003)

"Tiger" Ted Lowry was born on October 27, 1919. Ted's mother, a Canadian Indian from Nova Scotia, was a nurse; his father worked in the post office. Ted grew up in New Haven, Connecticut, and when he was 13 the family moved to Portland, Maine. In high school he was a star athlete, winning letters in four sports. He became a professional boxer in 1939 at age 19. Ted's main claim to fame is that he is the only fighter to go the ten-round distance twice against future heavyweight champion Rocky Marciano. At the time of their first fight, the 26-year-old "Brockton Blockbuster" had knocked out 19 of his first 20 opponents.

Lowry nearly handed Marciano the only loss of his career. In the early rounds he battered Rocky, and once it looked like the referee might stop the fight. Rocky came on in the middle rounds, but many in the audience thought he hadn't done enough to win. In fact, the reporter for the *Providence Journal* scored the fight for Lowry, six rounds to four. Even the majority Italian American crowd booed loudly when they heard the unanimous decision announced for Marciano. Commenting on his inability to knock out Lowry, Rocky said, "I think Lowry would have gone the distance if we had fought a hundred times. I could never get used to his style of fighting."[1]

From 1939 to 1955 (minus two years for military service) Ted Lowry engaged in 148 professional bouts and was stopped only three times. His opponents included some of the world's greatest boxers.

"Tiger" Ted Lowry averaged a fight a month for 12 years. He is the only fighter to go the ten-round distance twice with future heavyweight champion Rocky Marciano. *Author's collection*

While serving in the army during World War II, Lowry boxed a three-round exhibition with legendary world heavyweight champion Joe Louis, who was visiting the camps for boxing exhibitions to entertain the soldiers. The sparring session with the great Louis made a profound impression on Ted, which he discusses in the interview. Shortly after that exhibition he volunteered and was accepted into the elite 555th "Triple Nickel" Parachute Infantry Battalion, the first all-black airborne unit of the U.S. Army.

Ted was very proud of his service and was hoping to take part in the D-day invasion. Though combat ready, the unit never made it overseas. The armed forces were still segregated, and some high-ranking officials were reluctant to have highly trained black paratroopers coming into contact with racist white elements of the time. Instead the 555th was transferred to the West Coast when it was learned that the Japanese were floating thousands of balloons 30 feet in diameter filled with fragmentation and incendiary bombs across the Pacific Ocean. The balloons followed the jet stream and were intended to start forest fires in the northwestern states. Among the hundreds that made it across the ocean, a dozen exploded and started fires. On May 5, 1945, one of the bombs detonated and killed six people picnicking in the Oregon woods.

The battalion's assignment was to put out the fires. "We were trained to put out the fires," said Lowry, "but our primary job was to disarm the incendiary bombs. The drop zones were dangerous. We had very little experience disarming the bombs." During the summer of 1945 they answered some 36 fire calls with more than 1,200 individual jumps. All of this was kept secret at the time, so as not to cause panic in the homeland. The information was finally declassified in the 1990s.

But their status as elite troops did not prevent Lowry and his fellow soldiers from experiencing racism while stationed at an army base in Mineral Springs, Texas. There was a German prisoner-of-war camp located on the base. Several prisoners who were classified as trustees were allowed to ride into town in the front of a public bus to pick up food and cigarettes, while black uniformed U.S. soldiers like Lowry were forced to sit in the back. In an interview with journalist Bob Mladinich, Lowry recalled the incident: "They [the German POWs] probably shot some of our boys and they were laughing at us. I couldn't believe what I was seeing. It made no sense."[2]

After the war ended, he was shipped back to Fort Bragg and honorably discharged with the rank of staff sergeant.

Lowry's boxing career had commenced four years before he entered the service. By the time he fought Marciano in 1949, he had established a solid reputation as a tough and ringwise veteran boxer. At 5'10" tall and weighing about 180 pounds in his prime, Ted was a compact and powerfully built boxer who routinely fought opponents who outweighed him by 20 or more pounds. When he retired, his record showed 70 wins (46 by knockout), 68 losses (three by knockout), and ten draws. However, cold statistics cannot tell the entire story. In 1948 Lowry gave a prime Archie Moore all he could handle for ten rounds. He also outboxed light heavyweight champion Joey Maxim in a nontitle bout (Ted was robbed of a decision he should have won), lost a split decision to the great Tiger Jack Fox, and drew with rated heavyweight contenders Eddie Blunt, Lee Oma, Bernie Reynolds, and Lee Savold. Those fights are proof that "Tiger" Ted Lowry was capable of holding his own with some of the era's best fighters. So how do we explain those 68 losses?

The reasons have much to do with the difficulties faced by a talented black fighter not having the right connections and contacts. Before he entered the army in 1943, his record showed a respectable 45 wins (32 by knockout), 15 losses, and six draws. He had been fighting ten-round main events less than a year after his pro debut. Some of those losses were to more experienced ring veterans like Lee Q. Murray (twice), Young

Gene Buffalo, Eddie Peirce (twice), Vince Pimpinella, and Coley Welch. His excellent defensive skills and durability were already in evidence as no one was able to stop him. With the right management and connections, Ted was fully capable of moving up to contender status or a world championship.

Unfortunately, Ted never did acquire those connections. At some point during his career he realized a title shot was never going to happen, even if he achieved a top ten rating. This intelligent athlete knew the cards were stacked against him. A decision had to be made. He decided to accept reality and do what was necessary to provide for his wife and young children.

Lowry knew that a reliable journeyman boxer willing to take on anyone would enjoy a steady income win or lose. Fighting mostly in the New England club circuit, he would often take fights on short notice, subbing for other boxers who had pulled out of a show. It didn't matter to him who or where he fought as long as he kept busy and made a decent living. Lowry, as he proved time and again, could go the distance with anybody. Promoters and managers appreciated that he was capable of testing and extending an up-and-coming opponent without destroying him. Such fighters were a necessary ingredient in every future champion's education.

In order to maintain his busy schedule, Ted had to avoid taking punishment that might force him to cancel a future fight scheduled in one or two weeks. His defensive style, often unappreciated, would cost him decisions. There was also nothing to be gained by flattening a local hero and scaring off future opponents. But he could, when necessary, land the heavy artillery, as his 46 KO victories attest. If an opponent he was taking it easy with got out of line, he would bang him a couple of times and put him back in line. Promoters loved him. A quality journeyman boxer with a good chin was always in demand as long as he could be counted upon to give a good showing and last the distance.

Ted lost count of the number of hometown decisions that went against him. At least half of those 68 losses could just as well have gone the other way. He took those losses in stride and accepted them as the cost of keeping busy and earning a steady income. Winning was important, but not as important as staying active and available for the next payday. But on those occasions when Ted was matched against a top contender and he had nothing to lose and everything to gain, he became what he always could have become and let loose with the full measure of his talent. That was the case in his bout with Archie Moore and his 1952 nontitle go with light heavyweight champion Joey Maxim. Maxim was scheduled to defend his title against the great Sugar Ray Robinson. There was no way the powers in charge would allow Ted Lowry to get the decision and put a damper on that big fight. After the bout, Jack "Doc" Kearns, manager of Maxim, promised Lowry a title shot that never materialized.

Discouraged and thinking about retirement, Ted did not fight again for six months. Over the next two and a half years he fought only six times, winning four and losing two. He finally hung up his gloves for good in 1955 at the age of 35.

Although he never got the breaks that would have led to a title shot, Ted was not a bitter man. He always maintained a positive attitude toward life and considered his faith and a loving family and friends as his greatest treasure. In fact, I found him to be one of the finest persons I have ever met, in or out of boxing, and was proud to call him my friend.

Upon his retirement from boxing, he worked for several years as a prison guard before starting his own construction company. Ted also worked as a trainer and counselor for the Norwalk, Connecticut, Police Athletic League, mentoring the youth of Norwalk and keeping them off the street. He received numerous honors for his community service. His 80th birthday, on October 27, 1999, was named "Ted Lowry Day" in Norwalk. He was inducted into the Connecticut Boxing Hall of Fame in 2008. At the time of this interview he was putting the finishing touches to his autobiography, *God's in My Corner: A Portrait of an American Boxer.*[3]

If a prime Ted Lowry were fighting today I have no doubt he could easily whip the current cruiserweight, light heavyweight, and heavyweight champions—whoever they are—on consecutive weeks. That is both a commentary on his talent and the quality of today's champions.

Interview

Mike Silver: Despite having had 148 professional fights, you do not appear to show any neurological deficiencies so common among ex-fighters. At 83 your speech is clear, you are articulate, your memory is remarkable, and you look 20 years younger. How do you explain this?

Ted Lowry: Well, I knew how to fight. I was fortunate to have a very good trainer. His name was Roy Brooks. He was from Panama. I would say he was a scholar. He studied boxing. Roy was a former New England featherweight champion back in the 1920s. Jack Johnson [the former heavyweight champion] had trained him. He taught me to catch the punches, like Johnson, in my hand, on my gloves, on my arms. I very seldom took a solid punch. When I got hit and got dropped it was an accidental punch. Most of the punches I saw coming.

Mike: What was the most important lesson he imparted to you?

Ted: My trainer would tell me stance was the most important thing. Next thing to a jab is your stance. I fought in a slight crouch—bend at the knees a little. It allowed me to slip punches, and get under punches, also made my jab a little longer. He said anybody can go out there and throw punches, but not everybody knows what to look for, or how to block a punch, or how to get out of the way of a punch. When I was training he used to have featherweights in the ring with me and they'd be throwing fast punches and I'd have to block them. That's how I became so sharp at avoiding punches and not getting hit. I had a good defense and a good pair of eyes. I think out of 148 professional fights I was dropped twice but I was never knocked out. My trainer gave me the confidence that I needed, and I had a lot of help from Joe Louis.

Mike: What kind of help did you get from Joe Louis?

Ted: I boxed a three-round exhibition with heavyweight champion Joe Louis when he visited my army base in 1943. When I didn't get knocked down and I didn't get hurt all the fear that I might have had went out the window. I didn't care who I fought. I just felt like I could go with anybody. And from then on I started fighting heavyweights. I probably had it easier with the heavyweights because they were slower; they sent you a telegram when they were going to throw a punch.

Mike: That must have been quite an experience for a young boxer like yourself to get in the ring with the great Joe Louis. What were your thoughts and what happened in the exhibition?

Ted: I knew he had a terrific jab and I knew he had a powerful right hand, but I knew that before I got in the ring with him. When I got in the ring with him and we started working out I noticed that he carried his left hand low. That was the same thing Schmeling saw. I decide I'm going to let him know his left hand is low so I reach over and throw a right hand over the top of his jab and hit him slightly on the jaw. I jumped back and started smiling and threw my hands up to let him know I wasn't being smart. But he misunderstood me. He closed one eye and he started shuffling towards me. From then on every time he got me in the corner he would just throw punches. He wasn't supposed to hurt me, you know, but I could hear the wind as those punches went by—whoosh . . . whoosh . . . whoosh. I was ducking, slipping, doing everything so as not to get hit. I know now what he wanted to do. He just wanted to knock me down, and then he would have been satisfied. But it was my post and I couldn't afford to get knocked down. I would have had to hear about it every day. They asked Joe afterwards who was the best fighter he fought during his exhibition tour of the army bases. He said the one he fought in Camp Polk, Louisiana, was going to go a long way. That was me. What he said did a lot for my ego. Joe was strong. When he tied me up he lifted me right up off the floor. It might sound like a boast but he did not hit me, I blocked everything.

Mike: You had excellent defensive skills. But in reports of your fights it appears you did not often clinch or tie up an opponent to avoid punishment.

Ted: There wasn't a lot of holding in my fights. I would only tie you up when it was necessary. If I was in a corner or on the ropes I would tie you up to keep from getting hit, or I would spin you around and push you away. I always moved in behind a jab. Jab . . . jab . . . jab. I was protected at all times. I was the type of fighter that kept going forward all the time. I had a terrific right uppercut and left uppercut, and a nice left hook. I could knock you out with either hand—the left or the right. I was that powerful. I hit you with the full weight of my body. If I weighed 174 pounds that's what I used to hit you with. If you just swing an arm you've only got about 40 or 45 pounds behind the punch.

Mike: You fought middleweights, light heavyweights, and heavyweights. In your opinion which is the toughest weight division in boxing?

Ted: Middleweight. Because they could punch, they could box, move around, they're lighter on their feet and they could hit you like a light heavyweight.

Mike: In which weight division did you prefer to fight?

Ted: Light heavyweight. I stood a better chance of knocking them out. The big fellas, the heavyweights, were always bigger than I was. I could never get a good shot. I would have to loop a punch to reach their chins and that wasn't my style.

Mike: During your prime you rarely weighed more than 180 pounds yet often fought heavyweights who outweighed you by 20 to 50 pounds.

Ted: That's true. I weighed 174 pounds when I fought Eddie Blunt in 1942. Eddie was my first big opponent. He weighed about 230 pounds when I fought him. Do you remember Eddie Blunt? He was a heavyweight contender. I dropped him in New Bedford with a right hand. He got up and said, "Nice punch, kid." He could have pushed me around but he didn't. He was a clean fighter. [*Author's note*: Their ten-round bout was a draw.]

Mike: By the time you fought Eddie Blunt you were already a veteran of 61 professional fights.

Ted: It takes something to be a fighter, let me tell you. And it takes a lot of fights before you become an exceptionally good fighter. You've got to have more concentration in boxing. It's different training than for football or baseball. Definitely boxing is tougher than any other sport. It takes more out of you and you've got to be dedicated. You can really get hurt if you don't take care of yourself.

Mike: It appears that you took good care of yourself.

Ted: I never went into the ring out of shape. I'd do five miles of roadwork. I worked hard at it. I'd be out jogging and then I'd pick it up. I would sprint and run, about 100 yards apart, mix up the speed, because that's the way you fight. In some rounds you punch more than others. But I would not run uphill—too much a strain on your heart.

Mike: You are now coaching amateur fighters. When you teach a young fighter what do you emphasize?

Ted: Aside from proper stance and balance, I always emphasize defense. I really do. I've coached 176 amateur boxers and I've never had one get hurt. That's because I teach defense. I teach them the jab, teach them to block, teach them to slip, teach them to duck, teach them to get out of the way of a punch. I try to show them what to expect. If you know what to expect you don't get hit. I was taught well and I try to do the same for the amateur boxers I train.

Mike: What's your opinion of Mike Tyson?

Ted: People rave about Tyson. I never thought he was a good fighter, and I've noticed that he's never been able to get out of the way of a jab. I always thought that anybody with a good jab and a nice right hand behind it would beat him.

Mike: How would you have fought Mike Tyson?

Ted: I'd strictly jab him. I would go forward . . . jab . . . jab . . . jab. I'd fight him with jabs and I would beat him with jabs and throw a right cross and so forth and so on. He is not able to get out of the way of a jab. A good stiff jab . . . swell him up . . . puff up his eyes and everything and go to work on him.

Mike: But you said you walked into fighters. To walk into Tyson would be disastrous.

Ted: Not with the jab in front of me. I know he's throwing punches but don't forget, I block, I slip. I don't just walk in with my head up in the air. I'm covered when I go in there, but I'm not walking in unless I stick that left hand out first.

Mike: How would you fight Roy Jones Jr.?

Ted: I would have to do the same thing. I would slap the jab at him. But he would be moving around, so I'd have to follow him around. I'd have to corner him, cut the ring off on him. That's how I'd have to fight him. If you've got him don't let him go.

Mike: The current heavyweight champion is Lennox Lewis, who is 6'5" tall and weighs about 250 pounds. In his last title defense he knocked out Mike Tyson using the same strategy you just outlined. How would you have fought Lennox Lewis?

Ted: Lennox would have been tough because he had that long leg and you've got to get by that leg to get in there. But I personally would have jabbed at him to make him jab at me and then I'd slip inside. You'd have to fight him on the inside. But you would have trouble getting on the inside, because of the long legs and his body was way back there and then he throws that overhand right. But that's the way I would fight him. I would have to go to him, make him punch at me and slip on the inside and work on the body.

Mike: At your weight of 182 pounds and him weighing about 250, wouldn't that be too much for you?

Ted: You've got to wear him down. You've got to be punching in the body.

Mike: Do you think you could beat Lennox Lewis?

Ted: I've got to say yes. But I think what I would have to do is probably outsmart him. I would throw overhand rights with him and I would have to work on the body, get on the inside. There is no way in the world I could stay away from him because his arms are too long, he'd be able to tear me up, so I would always have to stay in close. I'd have to stay on him.

Mike: What about the fact that he was seven inches taller than you?

Ted: That's why I'd have to stay inside. I would make him jab first, catch his jab, and at the same time jab him back. That would make my jab as long as his. I'd always be able to reach him. I would get inside and under-neath and once I got him on the ropes I would keep him there. You got to work on the stomach in order to wear him down and bring his guard down. Because standing right up there you couldn't just hit him with a straight right hand; it would have to be an overhand right. You'd have to shoot that jab, and slip on the inside and shoot the right hand over the top of his jab. I used to do that a lot. That's what I used to hit Joey Maxim with. I hit him with 23 of them. He couldn't get out of the way. He'd jab, I'd slip on the inside and throw the right hand over that jab.

Mike: In 1948 you lost a ten-round decision to future light heavyweight champion Archie Moore. At the time Moore was the number one con-tender. As reported in the *Baltimore Sun* [August 3, 1948] you were com-petitive with one of boxing's all-time greats: "The fight started as if Moore would be able to coast to victory, but when Lowry became thoroughly warmed up Archie had his hands full. Lowry took Moore's best punches, and answered by tossing leather right back."[4]

Ted: Archie was smart. He was a thinking fighter. Archie knew what he was doing every time he threw a punch. He watched his opponent and he saw the openings and he'd set you up. He knew how to set you up. In other words, he might jab here and he'll watch the way you block. If he threw a right hand at you and you raise your hand he knew he could catch you underneath here. He was smart. He'd watch you like a hawk. It was always frightening the way he looked at you. He never took his eyes off you. I'll never forget how he caught me with that hook in the first round. I started jabbing him and realized "Oh, I can hit him!" I jabbed again, and I hit him again. He was catching everything I threw. I jabbed again and hit him again. Then, all of a sudden, he weaves underneath and wham! He weaved under my jab beautifully and hit me with that left hook. I can feel it now. It turned me all the way around. Almost broke my jaw.

Mike: So do you rank Archie Moore as the cleverest fighter you fought?

Ted: Yes.

Mike: Any other comparable to him in boxing ability?

Ted: Joey Maxim. He was smart. Joey didn't have the punching power but he was a very smart boxer. Very good at boxing. [*Author's note*: Ted Lowry lost a disputed ten-round decision to light heavyweight champion Maxim in a 1952 nontitle fight.]

Mike: Who was hardest puncher you ever faced?

Ted: Archie Moore.

Mike: What do you think about today's fighters?

Ted: The good fighters were getting out of it in the 1950s. Before that, when there wasn't that much work around, everybody was a fighter. I'm not trying to sound boastful but I feel I can beat the fighters I watch today. They are not taught right. They are taught how to throw a hook but they are not taught how to throw a hook with power. They teach the jab, but they don't teach you to step in with the jab. Nobody today has a hard jab.

You never see anybody these days jab a person and bust an opponent's head open, or bust the eyes open. It takes maybe three or four jabs to swell a man's eye. In my day you could do it with one punch, because you were moving in and hitting him with the weight of your body.

Mike: How would today's best boxers do against the best of your day?

Ted: I would say that the fighters of my time would be too much for the fighters of today. You take fellas like Ezzard Charles, Archie Moore, Jersey Joe Walcott—they were smart fighters, and they had punching power. They were good boxers. They knew how to move in, they punched hard, and they could take a punch. When you tried to hit them they'd ride with the punches. They didn't take the punches solid. They were going away when the punches were coming. I was taught, and I know they were taught, that when an opponent threw a left hand you knew what to look for next. If he threw a right hand you knew what to look for next.

Mike: I think part of the problem is a lack of quality trainers today.

Ted: As I said before, I was lucky to have a great trainer. He stayed with me for most of my career. A lot of fighters today are quick to change trainers, especially after a loss. That might be justified in some cases but it's preferable to stay with the trainer who taught you from the beginning. He knows his fighter, what he can do and what he cannot do. If a new trainer comes in, he doesn't know what his fighter can do. If he tells him in the middle of a fight to "double up with the right" or "throw a left to the stomach and follow with a left to the face and then a right cross and hook" or another combination, the fighter may not be able do it and the trainer doesn't even know it. Fights are won and lost in the corner. If you've got a smart trainer he's paying attention to your opponent and letting you know what you can do. You don't tell your fighter, "You're getting hit with the right." The trainer should be telling you what you could hit your opponent with. You tell him, "You've got to move left, or right, or move this way."

Mike: Are there any boxers today who impress you?

Ted: I watched Roy Jones Jr. against Ruiz the other night on television. I thought he [Jones] did some nice things. He counterpunched. His jab was snappy. He moved around nicely. I like the way he moved around.

I thought I saw the makings of a good fighter, one that probably would have gone a long way in my day.

Mike: But he wasn't up against much.

Ted: True, but he still did some nice things. I don't know if he could do those things if he fought a better fighter.

Mike: It was Jones's first bout against a heavyweight. All his previous bouts were against middleweights or light heavyweights.

Ted: Very few heavyweights are good boxers. Mostly they rely on their strength and punching power. I got to give credit to Muhammad Ali. He was a good boxer and he moved around. I didn't think much of his punching power, but he was a good boxer. But there again, there was nobody out there at that time that I thought was in his class.

Mike: What would have happened in a Joe Louis vs. Muhammad Ali fight? Who would have won?

Ted: I think Joe Louis would have knocked him out. But if Ali could run he would have outboxed Joe. The only reason I say "if Ali could run" is because Joe was the type who stayed right on you and it would be hard for Ali to outbox him, and if Joe hit him . . . it would be terrible. Joe Louis did not back up. He was always dangerous with the left hand or right hand, it made no difference.

Mike: Do you think Muhammad Ali was a great fighter?

Ted: No. He moved too much for me. But he was a good boxer. Good boxer. But I don't think that at the time he was fighting the top-notch fighters were around. There was nobody there for him to fight. He was the best of what they had. But if he had come along when I came along there were so many good fighters out there—good fighters who never got a chance to fight on top because they didn't have the right connections. I, for one, you might say. I fought all those fights and never got a chance to fight a champion in the Garden, where I should have fought them. Just imagine the money I would have if I'd have fought all those top-notch fighters in the Garden. I fought them in small clubs. If I'd have fought them in the Garden I might have two or three fights with them. If it was a close exciting fight they probably would have had a rematch. Just think of the money I missed.

Mike: Are you saying that Muhammad Ali would have had a much tougher time had he fought in your era?

Ted: Yes, yes, definitely so. They had heavyweights that never really got a chance.

Mike: Would one of those heavyweights have been Lee Q. Murray? At the time you fought him, in 1949, Murray had wins over Jimmy Bivins, Curtis Sheppard, and Turkey Thompson. Nobody remembers him today but he was a feared puncher with 43 knockouts in 60 wins. You fought him three times, losing two by decision and one by technical knockout. He was one of only three fighters to stop you. Tell me about Lee Q. Murray.

Ted: Lee Q. Murray was a terrific right-hand puncher. Long legs, long arms. Tough to get close to him. Lee Q. Murray would have knocked out Lennox Lewis. He would have beat, I guess, every heavyweight you got out there now. Rocky would have given him a good fight but Lee Q. would have beat him.

Mike: He would have beaten Rocky Marciano?

Ted: Yes. He really would. That's just my opinion.

Mike: As long as we are on the subject let's talk about Rocky Marciano. You lost a controversial ten-round decision to Rocky in 1949, three years before he won the heavyweight championship. At the time you had over 100 fights. Rocky was an undefeated young tyro with 19 KOs in 20 fights.

Ted: Rocky was a good man, a good well-conditioned fighter. He took a good punch and could punch. But—I hate to say this—he wasn't smart. I hope you understand what I'm saying when I say "smart," as far as boxing is concerned. A boxer has to be able to move around, move in, move out, slip, duck, bob, and weave. I didn't bob and weave, you know. But I did slip and I did duck. You've got to know how to use your head. They taught him to throw a jab, a left hook, and a right hand and one of those punches generally was going to hit you because a man can't block everything. I don't care who it is, you can't block everything. You're going to get hit with something. They just told him, "You just throw them punches and you'll catch him."

Mike: Compare the punching power of Joe Louis to the punching power of Rocky Marciano, if you can.

Ted: Rocky was the type of person if he hit you on your arm it would hurt. But Joe's punches traveled only about six inches. Louis was sharper. His punches were sharper. And he'd punch you with his body. He hit you beautifully. Pick you right up off the floor.

Mike: Would you say Louis had the harder punch?

Ted: I would say so. See, Rocky sent you a letter when he was going to punch. He swung from way out here. He hit hard but a smart fighter had no business getting hit by Rocky because he would send you a letter when he's gonna punch.

Mike: But, as you pointed out, Rocky kept throwing punches. He never tired. If he didn't knock you out right away he would eventually wear you down.

Ted: Yes he would because he would stay on you. I think Rocky would have beat Lennox Lewis. I think he would have beat Muhammad Ali. I think he would have beaten all those fighters at that time because he was in good condition, he was confident, and he would just keep going on, keep moving right in, walking in. The only one who might have given him a little trouble was Larry Holmes because he had that left hand.

Mike: When you fought Marciano the first time did you think he was just another fighter?

Ted: To be truthful, that's what I thought. I really underestimated him. I thought they were picking his fights so I never really gave him the respect that I should have given him.

Mike: When you fought him the second time a year later, Rocky had won nine more fights. How did you feel as compared to the first time?

Ted: I wasn't worried at all. I thought it was just another fight. In fact, I substituted for that fight. I took somebody else's place.

Mike: You were a substitute?

Ted: Yes. And I can tell you this. If I had known that Rocky would have been going as far as he had, it would have been a different type of fight, that second fight. I think I was in it for the money, the second fight. I think that Marciano's trainer finally figured out my style because before that Rocky was mesmerized. I could tell by the expression on his face. In the first fight he just kept coming at me throwing punches wild from all over and he wasn't able to hit me. But he fought differently the second time. He started moving around, and was even trying to jab.

Mike: How come nobody could beat Marciano?

Ted: [*A long silence for about 20 seconds*] I thought that I had the style to beat him. I got to give him credit. He was tough and he was a good puncher; he had a lot of heart and was well conditioned. And that's hard to beat a person like that, especially if they've got a lot of heart. And that's what you've got to have to be a fighter. You've got to have heart. If you don't have that you're not going nowhere at all. And he had confidence in himself and that's very important—confidence. He just felt like "If I hit you you've got to go." That was always on his mind—"If I hit him he's going to go" and if he doesn't go, then that upsets him. That's why he was mesmerized with me.

Mike: What was your biggest payday?

Ted: Oh, I wish I came along now [*laughs*]. You see the kind of money they're making? I had 148 professional fights and I don't think in all those fights I made a million dollars. The highest purse I ever got was $5,000. Fought Rocky twice I got $2,500 each time. From then I got $700 . . . $400 . . . $600.

23

CURTIS COKES

(Interviewed on August 20, 2014)

urtis Cokes held the welterweight title from 1966 to 1969. He was
born and raised in Dallas, Texas, where he still resides. Curtis was
a gifted all-around athlete in high school, excelling in baseball and
basketball. He earned all-state honors in both sports and briefly played
basketball for the Harlem Stars, a professional touring team. Curtis first
laced on the gloves at a local YMCA and was undefeated in 22 amateur
bouts before turning pro in 1958. This was at a time when there were
eight weight divisions and eight undisputed champions. (How quaint!)
By the mid-1960s Curtis had become a top-rated welterweight contender.
Like all of his contemporaries, he acquired contender status the old-
fashioned way—he *earned* it. (Also quaint by today's standards.) During
his climb to the title he sharpened his considerable boxing skills against
the likes of Stefan Redl, Joe Miceli, Kenny Lane, Manny Alvarez, Jose
Stable, Stan Harrington, Stanley "Kitten" Hayward, Billy Collins, and in
three memorable bouts with the great Luis Rodriguez.

The boxing world first took notice of Curtis Cokes when he upset
future welterweight champion Luis Rodriguez in 1961. Rodriguez outpointed Curtis in their rematch four months later. The rubber match took
place on July 6, 1966, in New Orleans. The bout was the semifinal of a
tournament to determine a new welterweight champion. Curtis stopped
Rodriguez in the 15th round, thus becoming the only fighter to stop the
great Cuban welterweight in his prime. Less than two months later, in the

final bout of the tournament, Curtis outpointed Manny Gonzales to win the crown vacated by Emile Griffith.

Curtis Cokes had an elegant and refined boxing style of a type that is all but extinct today. He was adept at both offense and defense but was primarily a counterpuncher—skills that were admired and appreciated by knowledgeable boxing fans. (Films of several of his fights are available on YouTube.) After five successful defenses, including impressive KOs over Charlie Shipes and Willie Ludick, he lost the title to the great José Napoles on April 4, 1969. With both of Cokes's eyes nearly swollen shut, his manager told the referee to stop the fight before the start of the 13th round. The rematch, two months later, ended similarly with Cokes unable to continue beyond the tenth round. Curtis fought for three more years before hanging up his gloves. He compiled a 62–14–4 record, including 30 knockouts. Napoles and Hayward were the only fighters to stop him. In 1972, Curtis gave a credible acting performance in *Fat City*, a boxing movie directed by John Huston.

After he retired from boxing, Curtis was involved in various business ventures, but he always remained close to the sport he loved. In 1980 he wrote, with coauthor Hugh Kayser, *The Complete Book of Boxing for Fighters and Fight Fans.*[1] I consider it one of the best boxing instruction books ever written. The book has reportedly sold more than 77,000 copies. He currently owns and operates Curtis Cokes' Home of Champions Boxing Gym in Dallas where the emphasis is on serving his community through an amateur boxing program geared to keeping young people off the streets.

Today, at the age of 76, Curtis Cokes is healthy and mentally sharp, with an amazing memory for the details of his career. Fortunately, he exhibits no ill effects from his 80 professional bouts—a testament to his superb defensive skills, physical conditioning, and knowing when to hang up his gloves. Aside from being an old-school fighter, Curtis is also an old-school gentleman. He is gracious, engaging, and warm. Interviewing this Hall of Fame boxer was a delightful experience.[2]

Welterweight champion Curtis Cokes earned his Ph.D. in boxing the old fashioned way. *Author's collection*

Interview

Mike Silver: Champ, the purists loved your smooth delivery and emphasis on basic fundamentals such as the left jab, footwork, counterpunching, and defense. I count myself lucky to have seen you fight on television. When I told a few older fans who also saw you fight that I was going to interview you, their first words were, "He was a good boxer." That is how you are remembered—that and your tremendous victories over the great Luis Rodriguez. How do you go about conveying your storehouse of knowledge to the young students at your gym?

Curtis Cokes: Before we start teaching fundamentals that involve throwing and blocking punches, or how to get away from punches, I get their legs in shape. We work on walking and running forward and backward. Footwork is such an important part of the sport. When I played baseball and basketball I knew I had to get my legs in shape because the legs are what carry the body. I think today's fighters forget about footwork. I worked every day on my footwork, turning left and right, backing up, going forward. I turned to my left to be outside of my opponent's right hand, and then I'd swing to my right to be outside of his left jab. Learning how to box is a slow process but you try to learn something every day.

Mike: Speaking of footwork, in my book, *The Arc of Boxing*, I asked the great ballet dancer Edward Villella, who was a champion amateur boxer before he became a ballet star, to explain the similarities between the two disciplines. You cover the same topic in *The Complete Book of Boxing*. Quoting from your book: "The balance and rhythm of a dancer are also important, for a boxer must be able to move quickly and change his tempo and direction at will . . . maneuverability is of extreme importance. An almost ballet type of body coordination gives a fighter a distinct edge."[3]

Curtis: The balance of a dancer is tremendous, and like a dancer a boxer has to be able to move and dance while maintaining his balance. You have to be able to have good balance to throw your punches. When I played with the Harlem Stars basketball team I used to watch Goose Tatum, how he would get in position and block people out. It was amazing to see him do that so smoothly. Goose Tatum's coordination and balance was outstanding.

Mike: Aside from footwork, what do you see as the main difference between the boxers of your generation and today's practitioners?

Curtis: Today it's all about hitting and that's all it is . . . just go out and hit, hit, hit. They don't learn the fundamentals of boxing. They don't get a Ph.D. in boxing—how to block, roll, duck, slip, and get away from punches—to hit and not get hit. You have to learn the smart part of boxing, because you want to come out of it the same as you went in. Most guys just fight, fight, fight, but "fighting" isn't "boxing." It's an intelligent sport and you have to be smart to be able to succeed in it. If you just go toe to toe it becomes a toughman contest and the toughman wins. It's not a science anymore. You don't have to be smart to box anymore. There is no sport called "fighting," it's called professional boxing. A big part of the problem is we don't have the trainers that we used to have. There are not too many people that know how to train fighters.

Mike: Who was your trainer?

Curtis: I had two trainers: Robert Thomas was my first coach and Robert "Cornbread" Smith was the coach with all the experience. He was back in

Joe Louis's day and he was a good trainer. My manager was Doug Lord. Doug was a good manager and he took care of me. He was not only my manager, he was my friend. I knew the boxing game and Doug, who owned an insurance company, knew about business.

Mike: You became welterweight champion in your 53rd professional fight. Two months ago a fighter with only 19 pro fights won a welterweight title belt. The fighter he dethroned had all of 24 pro bouts.

Curtis: I don't think there are as many fighters available as in my day. Most become champions before they are ready to be champions. To be a champion you've got to have fought some of the best fighters in the world. Even if you lose to some of the great guys it's not a shame to lose to a great fighter. You can learn from the experience. You have to take it step by step. You go from first grade to the tenth grade and then you graduate. Instead of learning the game they want to fight for a title too early even before they learn to tie their gloves on. You've got ten fights and you're fighting for a title. Back in the day you had to have at least 30 or 40 fights to get the experience before you challenged for a title. Baseball players don't go to the major leagues until they prove themselves in the minor leagues; then they go to the major leagues. It's a step-by-step process. Just because you can hit a guy and knock him out doesn't mean you can get up there and fight.

Mike: As a young boxer did you have any role models that you wanted to imitate?

Curtis: I learned from two of the best—Joe Brown and Sugar Ray Robinson. I watched those guys when they were fighting. I tried to copy their style. I tried to copy Ray's style but I worked with Joe Brown. I trained with him when I was a kid and he was lightweight champion of the world. I went to Houston and sparred with him and he told me that I was going to be a champion. Brown would show me how he would throw punches and miss them on purpose to make a guy move his head in the range of his right hand. And I started doing it—I would purposely miss a jab on the outside so my opponent would move his head to the inside where he was in my right hand range. I was a good right-hand puncher. I don't see anybody doing that today. I saw "Kitten" Hayward do it. So did Luis

Rodriguez. Emile Griffith did some of that. Those fighters, they were smarter than these guys today who just go out there and hit.

Mike: Did anyone else influence your style of boxing?

Curtis: I sparred with [former middleweight champion] Carl "Bobo" Olson in Honolulu, Hawaii, when I went over there to box one time. [*Author's note*: Cokes outpointed Stan Harrington on May 21, 1963, in Honolulu.] They all told me I was going to be champion of the world one day and they helped me quite a bit. I got Olson's jab and I got Joe Brown's movement and his right hand, and I picked up all this stuff from these guys. You have to learn how to box and you have to learn it well. You go to school to learn your ABCs and you have to learn boxing the same way.

Mike: Were feints part of your repertoire?

Curtis: Oh yes! One of my favorite feints was a silent right hand. I would feint the jab and throw the right hand. My trainer called it a silent right hand because you didn't know I was going to throw it. You thought I was going to throw the jab, but I'd feint the jab and throw the right hand. Sometimes I would throw a double right hand.

Mike: What about body punches?

Curtis: When I wanted to get your hands down I'd go to the body. I'd hook to the body and hook to the head, or throw a right hand to the body and a right hand to the head. But I wasn't a vicious body puncher. I went to the head mostly. I was a counterpuncher and I would hit guys when they weren't ready to be hit. I was always in good shape and I could move and take a fairly good punch.

Mike: Did you have a favorite combination?

Curtis: I had a good right uppercut, left hook, right-hand combination. I used it to good effect when I knocked out [Luis] Rodriguez. That was one of my favorite punches.

Mike: You spoke of learning the finer points of boxing technique from role models early in your career. Two of today's best fighters are Floyd Mayweather Jr. and Manny Pacquiao, both of whom fight in your weight class. Would you consider them good role models for young boxers to emulate in terms of their boxing styles?

Curtis: No, I would not. It would be difficult to learn anything from them. Both are unorthodox boxers with natural styles that work for them. But what works for them would not work for most other boxers. It would be difficult to imitate. They don't have anything that they can put on paper because they don't know what they are going to do next. They don't have a plan. They just go out there and fight and whatever comes to their mind happens automatically. You have to have a plan and you have to have a style. I had a style you could learn from because it was based on solid fundamentals. I threw the one-two-threes and I threw them correctly. And if you throw punches correctly you will score. And if you do it correctly you will succeed in boxing. Pacquiao and Mayweather are doing something that nobody else can do and you don't have any trainers today that can show people how to offset what they are doing. There are very few fighters today with the type of skills I would want my kids to watch and imitate. There are some guys I'm impressed with but they are mostly fighting—not boxing. Some of my guys would come to the gym excited after watching a fight on TV and say, "Did you see that?" I'd say, "Don't watch that particular fighter." I'd tell them to watch tapes of Ali or Sugar Ray Leonard and see how they use the jab and footwork—certain things that I wanted them to pick up on.

Mike: Floyd Mayweather Jr. has done very well with his unorthodox style and extraordinary speed and reflexes. How would he have done if we time-travel him back to the 1960s to face the best fighters of your era?

Curtis: I think he would have done pretty well, but he would have had way more trouble in my day than today because the fighters were much better. They were more knowledgeable. They had a Ph.D. in boxing. These guys today just go in there and fight off the top of their heads. They don't have a plan and they don't know what they are doing. They haven't gone to school.

Mike: Could fighters such as Emile Griffith, Luis Rodriguez, Jose Napoles, Carlos Ortiz, and Curtis Cokes—all of whom were outstanding orthodox boxers—defeat Mayweather and Pacquaio?

Curtis: I definitely think that. Today's champions would have a much harder time to get to a title because they would have to come through fighters of my ability and I think the top guys back in my day learned everything you could learn about boxing.

Mike: How would you have fought Floyd? How would you cope with his tremendous speed?

Curtis: His speed is nothing I hadn't seen before. You can throw punches and have speed but if there's nothing there you will hit air. His speed won't bother me. Luis Rodriguez had tremendous speed and I slowed him down. I would fight Floyd the same way I fought everybody else. I would work with my jab—make him move away from my jab. While worrying about getting away from my jab I would hit with my good right hand and left hook and I'd go home early.

Mike: Your first victory over Luis Rodriguez in 1961 was considered quite an upset. At the time he had only one loss in 40 fights.

Curtis: Rodriguez beat everyone but he had a problem with me. Angelo Dundee [Rodriguez's manager and trainer] didn't want the fight. But Luis, to his credit, wanted to fight me. He wanted to fight the best. I don't blame him. I wanted to fight the best also. In our first fight I out-boxed and outmaneuvered him. He was throwing wide punches and I was throwing straight short punches so I got inside of him and beat him to the punch. That first fight in Dallas [August 1961] was easy. I had him down and won a decision. I had a style that bothered him. Angelo tried to change his style to fight me. He wanted him to be more of a puncher with me instead of being a boxer, like he was. But that only made it easier for me to cope with. I was always good at luring guys into my style of boxing, and that's what good fighters do. You make the guy fight your fight. In our third fight, a month before I won the title, I stopped him in the 15th round. He got hit with a couple of shots and couldn't come back. Luis had a good chin but I had a good right hand.

Mike: You lost the welterweight title to the great Jose Napoles in 1969 and failed to regain the title two months later. What happened in those fights?

Curtis: Napoles was on his way up and I was on my way out. It was time for me to sit down because I'd been there for a while. In the second fight

I broke his ribs. I went to his body real good but it was time for me to go. I'd had my day. I took a few fights I should not have taken. It was time for me to retire. In both of our fights his punches caused my eyes to become very swollen. I couldn't see. [*Author's note*: Cokes's corner would not let him come out for the 13th round of their first fight.] He damaged my right eye real bad.

Mike: What would have happened if you had fought Napoles in your prime?

Curtis: If I fought Jose in my prime we would both have to retire after that fight [*laughs*].

Mike: Luis Rodriguez and Jose Napoles were two of the greatest welterweight champions to ever wear the crown. You fought both of them. Who would have won had they met in their primes?

Curtis: I really don't know. That would have been a good fight. Rodriguez didn't hit as hard as Napoles, but he threw more punches.

Mike: The other big superstar of today's boxing scene is Manny Pacquiao. Would his unorthodox style have given you problems?

Curtis: He probably would, but if he ran into my good right hand then he would straighten up too. You know, the shortest distance between two points is a straight line and that's what I would do. I'd throw straight punches and he'd run into my good right hand and my jab. It would be a good fight because I'm not a wild swinger like he is. I throw punches straight and it would probably take me some time to hit him on the chin but when I did we could go home.

Mike: Boxing has changed in many ways from the time when you were champion of the world. For example, many fighters have incorporated weight lifting into their training routines. What do you think of that trend?

Curtis: I used little hand weights of not more than two pounds. I would shadowbox with them. I never used the big weights to make muscles. Just two-pound weights. I would walk around the house with them. Big muscles slow you down. You don't want your muscles to be tight and pumped up because you can't use your arms if they're pumped like that. Weight lifting is not for boxing. It's for football players who need the muscles to tackle an opposing player or throw him down. You have to have smooth muscles like a basketball player if you are to throw your punches correctly. The heavy bag is an important tool for creating punching power, not lifting heavy weights.

Mike: Speaking of strong punchers, let's discuss two of the best—Tommy Hearns and Roberto Duran.

Curtis: Tommy Hearns was a good puncher but he didn't have a real good chin. He needed to work on his defense more than he needed to work on his offense. He was easy to hit. I would have hit him. Duran had to come to you in order to score. He couldn't stand on the outside and outbox anybody. I'm boxing. I could have beaten both Ray Leonard and Roberto Duran at welterweight.

Mike: Let's discuss some of your other opponents. Before you entered your prime fighting years you lost to Stanley "Kitten" Hayward and Jose Stable. Both fights were televised nationally.

Curtis: They said Kitten was a welterweight but when I fought him he looked more like a middleweight or small light heavy. He was the strongest boxer I ever fought. I could hit him all day long but he was so big and strong. He caught me with a good shot and had me down three times before they stopped the fight. But I had him down also. Jose Stable was a very good bob-and-weave pressure fighter. It was my first time fighting on national TV. I started strong but just didn't fight enough during the last few rounds. Even so, it was a very close decision.

Mike: The Hayward fight was a real barn burner and can be seen on You-Tube. He does indeed look much bigger than you. In fact, Don Dunphy, who was announcing the fight at ringside, comments about the disparity in size. The fight took place in Hayward's hometown of Philadelphia. Do you think there was some funny business with the scale?

Curtis: Well, it could have been. We were not allowed to weigh in at the same time. I complained about that because he got on the scale and was gone when I arrived. We never did get the chance to watch him get on the scale. I know good and well he was no 147 pounds. But I'm not using that as an excuse. It had nothing to do with him winning the fight because I had beaten big guys like that. He just caught me with a good shot that got me out of there.

Mike: You knocked Hayward down with three solid punches just before the bell ended the second round. If you had caught him with those punches a minute earlier do you think the result might been different?

Curtis: It's possible. I don't know if he could have gotten up and recovered in time.

Mike: What do you think of the current rule that has fighters weigh in a day before the fight?

Curtis: I think it's better to have a weigh-in on the day of the fight because you'd know for sure you have a 147-pounder against a 147-pounder. If you weigh in the day before the fight you know you're not going to get in that ring at 147—probably more like 157.

Mike: In 1972 you had a significant role in *Fat City*, a major Hollywood movie about boxing. How did that come about?

Curtis: John Huston, the director, knew about me as a boxer and asked me to audition for the part. It was hard work. You had to remember your lines. If somebody else remembered their lines and did it well and you missed yours they had to reshoot and the actors would get mad. I didn't have to threaten any of them but they knew not to mess with me because I would shadowbox while waiting for the next scene [*laughs*]. It was a nice experience and I had a good time with Stacy Keach, Susan Tyrrell, and Jeff Bridges. Those guys helped me quite a bit with my lines. They were tremendous with helping me. I got called for another part but I was in Paris with one of my fighters so I missed it. They wanted me to go to acting school but I was so busy doing my boxing thing with my guys.

Mike: Do you have any regrets about your boxing career?

Curtis: Not at all. I did well in boxing. I started out wanting to be world champion and I accomplished that. I'm in the Hall of Fame. I retired from boxing because it was time for me to go. Nobody took advantage of me. Before I became a pro I attended college for two years. I had a good education. I knew how to take care of myself. I knew how to count my money too. I didn't need a manager to count my money to me. I counted out my money to him.

Part IV
BONUS ROUNDS

24

"I COULDA BEEN A CONTENDER": ROGER DONOGHUE, THE MAN WHO TAUGHT BRANDO HOW TO BOX

(August 1994)

O *n the Waterfront* is not a boxing movie per se, but I think of it as such because of the main character's struggle to find his place in the world after the cheering has stopped. The renowned film critic Pauline Kael wrote this about Marlon Brando's Academy Award–winning performance in the 1954 film *On the Waterfront:* "It is one of the most powerful American movies of the 50s, and few movies caused so much talk, excitement and dissension—largely because of Marlon Brando's performance as the inarticulate, instinctively alienated bum, Terry Malloy."[1]

On the Waterfront, a gritty, no-holds-barred drama of corruption and mayhem on the New Jersey docks, won eight Academy Awards. The film, scripted by Budd Schulberg and directed by Elia Kazan, included an outstanding supporting cast. But most of all it had Brando. His Terry Malloy is perhaps the most authentically realized characterization of a down-and-out pug ever portrayed on film.

What an actor cannot draw on from personal experience and imagination, he gleans from research, observation, and instruction. It was Schulberg who suggested to Kazan that he hire a 24-year-old ex-middleweight named Roger Donoghue to coach Brando in the combination-punching and mannerisms of a professional fighter.

Schulberg knew Donoghue both as a fighter and a friend. He had followed the young man's boxing career with great interest. Fighting out of Yonkers, New York, Donoghue turned pro at the age of 18 in 1948 and remained undefeated through his first 20 fights. The six-foot, 153-pound converted southpaw was armed with a dangerous left hook and a fighting heart. He could box at long range or mix it up in close. In addition, he had looks, charm, and wit to go along with his boxing ability. Fighting regularly on the televised club circuit in and around New York City, he quickly developed a following. After all, good Irish club fighters were becoming a rare commodity on the postwar New York fight scene.

By the summer of 1951, Donoghue had won 25 of 27 fights, including 14 by KO. His only losses were to Luis Valles, a battle-scarred veteran, and a hometown decision to Connecticut's Sammy Guiliani. Donoghue rebounded from those minor setbacks and was on the verge of contender status when fate intervened. In August, before 6,000 fans at White Plains Stadium, he stopped tough local middleweight Georgie Flores in the eighth round. A rematch was scheduled for only two weeks

Roger Donoghue in his apartment, 1994. The ex-fighter inspired one of the most famous movie quotes of all time. *Author's collection*

later at Madison Square Garden. It was the semifinal to the Kid Gavilan–Billy Graham world welterweight title fight.

Donoghue again won by knockout in the eighth round. Flores never regained consciousness and died five days later.

Two months after the tragedy, Donoghue was back in the ring, but his heart was not in the fight. He won one more time, then in January 1952 lost an eight-round decision to Red DeFazio in another Garden semifinal. It was a lackluster and disappointing effort. He was knocked down several times and took a bad beating. His manager, Bobby Melnick, advised retirement. Donoghue knew Melnick was right. He no longer had the interest or desire to continue hitting people for a living. The next day he announced his retirement. His final record: 28–4 (16 KOs).

"I guess my decision to retire was probably caused by what happened in the Flores fight," Donoghue said, responding to the question somewhat reluctantly. "After the accident with Flores, my concentration was affected, maybe subconsciously. I started thinking about the day *after* the fight."[2]

The year was 1954. Donoghue was working for Rheingold beer as a wholesale distributor. He was a good salesman and was leading a normal nine-to-five existence when he got the call that was to take him from hops to Hollywood. Forty years later, he recalls how it all began.

"Budd Schulberg, whom I had met years earlier at Toots Shor's restaurant, called and asked if I would come over to the Actor's Studio. He said he and Elia Kazan were doing a picture with Marlon Brando, and they wanted me to meet him. So I went over and was introduced to Brando, Lee J. Cobb, and Karl Malden. Kazan explained that Marlon was playing an ex-fighter and they wanted me to spend some time with him."

Over the next two weeks, Donoghue took Brando to Stillman's Gym for boxing lessons, did roadwork with him around the Central Park reservoir, and spoke at length about his experiences in the ring.

"I had heard that Marlon did some sparring in the ring at Stillman's while he was doing *A Streetcar Named Desire* on Broadway," said Donoghue. "But the producers of *Waterfront* didn't want him sparring, so I moved with him upstairs to the punching bag area of Stillman's."

When the training sessions began to attract too much attention, Donoghue shifted the workouts to Brando's apartment. "Brando lived in the back of Carnegie Hall, where he had a nice small apartment," he recalled. "Nobody bothered us—outside of the chicks coming up to see him.

"I spent so many days with him and he just captured everything," continued Donoghue. "He was such a good student. Everything I showed him he repeated. He threw nice short, straight right hands, and I taught him how to throw combinations."

Donoghue remembers being impressed with the actor's concentration and dedication. "I hadn't seen him in the two weeks before we started shooting on location in Hoboken, New Jersey," he said. "We started rehearsing the rooftop scene, and were going over the combinations I had shown him when he says, 'Rog . . .' I said, 'What's the matter, Bud?' [Brando's nickname]. And he says, 'Back home you finished with a left hook, and not a right uppercut.' He was right! He had done it exactly as I had done it two weeks earlier at his apartment."

Donoghue's contribution went beyond his teaching Marlon the basics of the sweet science. An offhand comment to screenwriter Budd Schulberg inspired one of the most famous movie quotes of all time. During rehearsals Schulberg asked Donoghue if he could have been a champion if he'd stayed in the ring. "Well," Donoghue answered, "I could have been a contender." The words struck a chord with Schulberg and he incorporated them into the famous taxicab scene.

When the time came to apply Brando's makeup, Donoghue suggested something different: "They wanted to put putty on his nose, like they did in all those fight movies, where they slapped putty all over the actor's face. I told Brando, 'We're going to make you look like a *real* fighter.' What I did was cut two little pieces of clear plastic hose and had Brando put them into his nose. The hose was hollow, so he could breathe, and it just widened his nose out, and no putty was necessary. And then I did his eyes with putty. Brando played a right-handed fighter, so I said, 'Let's have a little more scar tissue over his left eye because that's the eye that faces the opponent, and then let's put one scar over his right eye—just like mine.' And if you look at the movie, or stills from the movie, you'll see that one eye had more scar tissue than the other."

This was heady stuff for a 24-year-old ex-prizefighter/beer salesman. And it wasn't over yet. Donoghue was invited to Hollywood to accompany Brando and the cast while they made their obligatory rounds of publicity appearances, dinners, and award ceremonies leading up to the Oscars. He was there the night Brando won the Oscar for Best Actor and *Waterfront* took honors for Best Picture.

Not surprisingly, Donoghue decided to extend his stay in the almost-surreal fantasyland. He enjoyed socializing with other young Hollywood aspirants and often shared a meal with them at Schwab's drugstore or Googie's coffee shop on Sunset Strip. Donoghue's main interest, however, was not in becoming an actor. (Donoghue had briefly appeared in *Waterfront* as a longshoreman.)

"I was more interested in the writing and directing aspects of the business," he said. He began collaboration with Schulberg on a screenplay titled *8th Avenue*, a boxing story based on Donoghue's career. Nicholas Ray, one of Hollywood's hottest directors at the time, became interested in the project and hired Donoghue to be his assistant while he completed filming *Rebel without a Cause*. Ray told him he wanted to direct *8th Avenue* with James Dean playing Donoghue and Humphrey Bogart in the role of his manager.

"Nick invited me to have lunch with him at Romanoff's to discuss the movie," said Donoghue. "When I arrived at the restaurant, my friggin' jaw dropped. Who am I sitting with but Peter Lorre and Humphrey Bogart! That's when Nick talked to Bogart about playing the fight manager. I remember Bogie saying what he liked about it was that they were going to shoot the whole thing in New York."

Donoghue even began giving boxing lessons to James Dean. ("He was good.") The project fell apart, however, when Bogart became seriously ill and Dean was killed in a car crash.

Ray took off for Europe and Schulberg started to work on another screenplay. Donoghue remained in Hollywood, but his attempts to launch *8th Avenue* were unsuccessful. When another boxing movie, *The Harder They Fall*, went into preproduction, he let it be known that he was available as a technical adviser. But there was politics involved.

"This one guy, an ex-fighter [Johnny Indrisano, a welterweight contender in the '30s], had it all tied up," he explained. "He was under contract to one of the studios, and for years all the actors who portrayed boxers were trained by this one person and it was all his style. This person was very upset that I was around Hollywood. The word had gotten out that I had coached Brando, so it was like I was taking his job away."

Finally, Donoghue, always a realist, said to himself, "What am I doing here?" He packed his bags, said his goodbyes, and returned to New York.

Over the next 30-plus years, Donoghue forged a very successful career in the beer and beverage industry. Prior to his retirement last October, he was the director of draft sales for Coors and Canada Dry.

He has not, however, stifled his creativity. Donoghue recently completed a play, *White Fedora*, that tells the little-known story of the friendship between bandleader Guy Lombardo and jazz great Louis Armstrong in Al Capone's Chicago of 1928. (Lombardo had been a fan and close friend of Donoghue's.)

At the time of this interview, Donoghue was preparing to host Schulberg's 80th birthday party. He has maintained friendships with a number of people from the stage, screen, and literary worlds. One of the friendships paid a great dividend: it was Norman Mailer who introduced Donoghue to his wife of 30 years, artist Faye Moore, who is well known for her impressionist paintings depicting horse-racing scenes.

And Brando? "The last time I saw him was in 1972, on the set of *The Godfather*," Donoghue said. "I was supplying some vintage props, on loan from Rheingold, that were to be used in the wedding scene. Brando sees me and we get to talking and reminiscing about the old days when all of a sudden [director] Francis Coppola comes over and says, 'What are you doing? Who are you? Why are you bothering us? This is costing us $6,000 a minute!' And Brando says, 'Wait a minute, this is my friend Roger and we're talking Hoboken.' That was Brando's last great line with me."

And the last great question: Could Brando have been a contender?

"No," answered the man who taught Terry Malloy how to fight. "I'd say he could have been a good club fighter."

As Roger Donoghue has proved, you don't have to be a contender to have class.

25

THE BROOKLYN KID
VS. THE MARSUPIAL MAULER

(February 28, 2014)

Young Allen Konigsberg, a resident of Brooklyn, New York, was always among the first chosen when sides were taken for the after-school games of stickball, basketball, or baseball. The 125-pound teenager was wiry, fast, and clever—a natural athlete. The year was 1951. The Dodgers were still playing in Ebbets Field, Harry Truman was president, and every kid knew that Jersey Joe Walcott was heavyweight champion of the world. The proliferation of boxing over the new medium of television guaranteed the sport's continued popularity throughout the 1950s. Training in a neighborhood gym, or putting on the gloves and sparring with friends were still rites of passage for many boys, even those raised in middle-class homes. But for some that wasn't enough. They wanted to test their fighting skills by entering the New York City Golden Gloves boxing tournament. The annual tournament, sponsored by the *Daily News*, had been an institution in the city since 1927. It was open to amateur boxers from ages 16 to 25. The finals at Madison Square Garden always sold out.

So, like thousands of other young men, 16-year-old Allen Konigsberg began training in anticipation of entering the famous boxing tournament. He joined a local gym and trained for several months. Allen liked boxing, but not fighting, preferring a jab-and-move style where his speed and natural athleticism would give him an edge. He was serious in his ambition to win a Golden Gloves title. But there was a problem. All boxers under the age of 18 had to have their parents sign a consent form. When the time came to submit the application, Allen's mother refused to give permission, abruptly terminating his nascent boxing ambitions. It's probably just as well. The young man's brains were better suited for his future career as a stand-up comic and filmmaker known to the world as Woody Allen.

If Allen had been born a generation earlier, he might well have become a boxer. In those days a boy didn't need a parent's consent because of the proliferation of "bootleg" amateur bouts. The professional side of the sport was even more lax in its restrictions. Boxers as young as 14 were turning pro and earning more money in one four-round preliminary bout than a sweatshop worker earned for an entire week. Of course how far "Kid" Konigsberg would have gone as a boxer is anyone's guess. His athletic skills combined with superior intelligence might have translated successfully to boxing. And, for what it's worth, there was a resemblance, physically and facially, to the great featherweight champion Abe Attell. The only inkling we have to assess the quality of his boxing skill comes from a 1966 video of Allen boxing a kangaroo.

Okay, I know it sounds crazy, but before you dismiss this ridiculous notion out of hand I urge you to take a look at the video. Just google "Woody Allen Boxes Kangaroo."

Yes, it's a comic routine (and a very funny one at that), but Allen does appear to know how to hold his hands and, most notably, demonstrates balanced and agile footwork. Maybe it's just that I'm so fed up with the limited defensive skills and lack of basic fundamentals exhibited by most of today's boxers that Allen's moves actually look good by comparison. But so help me, I think there is genuine potential on display. The kangaroo doesn't look too bad either.

It seems that boxing and kangaroos have had a long association. Not surprisingly, the tradition began in Australia. The country's national symbol is a kangaroo wearing boxing gloves, and the image is frequently seen on flags at Australian sporting events. The boxing kangaroo made its first appearance as a cartoon in a Sydney newspaper in 1891. The idea was inspired by 19th-century outback carnival shows that featured kangaroos wearing boxing gloves fighting against men, or other kangaroos.

The novelty spread to other countries and persisted into the 20th century, most often as circus acts. At least two famous boxers, Primo Carnera (who was discovered in a circus) and "Two Ton" Tony Galento (who would have been at home in one), took part in such exhibitions. The colorful Galento also boxed a 550-pound bear and wrestled an octopus in a tank of salt water.

During the tussle with the octopus, the creature squirted the contents of its ink sack into Tony's face. Shouting "I'll moida da bum," Galento, amidst much flailing and splashing, finally subdued his fishy opponent. Sadly, the octopus, perhaps out of stress or simply embarrassment, died shortly after the contest.

26

SO YOU WANNA BE A BOXER?

(July 6, 2014)

A published survey of sports films from the 1890s to 1987 revealed that 446 box-ing-themed films had been made. That is over 100 more than baseball, football, and basketball combined.[1] In the 30 years since then, the trend has continued with boxing films still outpacing other sports films. (Can Rocky 10 *be far off?)*

Boxing is a sport of drama, excitement, romance, and physical-ity—qualities that filmmakers have mined to the fullest ever since the beginning of the motion picture industry. The hundreds of boxing-themed films even include musicals, westerns, and cartoons. Most of the time the sport is central to the story, but occasionally it is used as an important subtext (as in the classic *On the Waterfront*) or simply used to spice up the narrative. In the right hands it can also be the source for comedy. I was reminded of this fact while trolling the internet for hidden gems on YouTube.

I first saw *Bugsy Malone* when it was released in 1976. I considered it then, as I do now, a work of supreme creativity and much more than just a novelty. But what made it special for me was the film's boxing sequence. *Bugsy Malone*—a gangster-themed musical comedy—is set in 1920s New York during Prohibition. Here's the novelty: its entire cast featured only child actors dressed as adults and acting as adults. The movie marked the directorial debut of Alan Parker (*Evita*, *Fame*, *Midnight Express*). The musical score is by the brilliant songwriter (and sometimes actor) Paul Williams, whose other works include "Just an Old Fashioned Love Song" (lyrics), "You and Me against the World," "We've Only Just Begun," and "Evergreen" (lyrics).

The rival mobsters are armed with what look like tommy guns (called "splurge guns" in the movie) that fire custard pies in rapid succession. Once a gangster is "splurged" (doused with custard) he is "all washed up" and his career in crime is over. The vintage cars the child actors drive are slightly downsized and look real, but they have no motor and are driven by pedaling. This is really ingenious stuff. The music is tuneful and the story fun and engaging. The words to the song "So You Wanna Be a Boxer?" are right on target and, combined with the choreography, make for a very memorable segment. *Bugsy Malone* was nominated for an Academy Award for Best Original Music Score (Paul Williams).

Another of my favorite comedic cinema boxing scenes appears in the 1980 musical comedy *Popeye*. The film is directed by Robert Altman and stars Robin Williams as the spinach-eating hero who, in a key scene, enters the ring to battle a gigantic opponent. The cartoon set that depicts Popeye's fishing village ("where the streets run at crazy angles up the hillsides, and the rooming houses and saloons lean together dangerously") is a revelation, as is this entire film. I believe the movie has a cult following—and rightfully so. I have never seen a cartoon come to life as perfectly as it does in this masterpiece. Robin Williams, in the title role, gives an astonishing performance. He actually becomes a living, breathing Popeye! Shelley Duvall is also perfect as Popeye's "goilfriend," Olive Oyl. Both actors were born to play these parts. In fact, everyone in the cast is "poifect!"

But of all the comic boxing scenes ever filmed (and there have been many), the one I believe deserves top billing appears in Charlie Chaplin's masterpiece *City Lights*, released in 1931 as a silent film. (Although sound had been around since 1927, Chaplin preferred to work with silent productions.)

City Lights is quite possibly Chaplin's best work (it was his personal favorite). The Little Tramp attempts to earn enough money so that he can pay for an operation to restore the eyesight of a poor blind flower girl (Virginia Cherrill) he has fallen in love with. Chaplin's character meets a boxer who tells him they can split $50 if he participates in a fake fight. But that night the fighter receives a telegram that says the police are after him, so he skips out. The Tramp has to take a replacement opponent who will fight for real. What happens next demonstrates the Chaplin genius in

Chaplin meets a boxer who tells him they can split $50 if he participates in a fake fight. *Author's collection*

full bloom. He creates a hilarious choreography as his character attempts to survive the boxing match.

I think comedic boxing scenes, as those described above, are actually more difficult to stage (if they are to have the desired effect) and require more creativity and imagination than attempting to stage a fight scene as depicted in a straight boxing drama such as *Rocky* or *Raging Bull*.

In 1992, the Library of Congress selected *City Lights* for preservation in the United States National Film Registry as being "culturally, historically, or aesthetically significant." In 2007, the American Film Institute's "100 Years . . . 100 Movies" ranked *City Lights* as the 11th greatest American film of all time.

27

TEDDY'S MASTER CLASS

(November 10, 2015)

A boxing teacher–trainer is part parent, psychologist, coach, and role model. He can often make the difference between success and failure for his student. Fortunate is the boxer who finds the right one.

In September 2015, Teddy Atlas took over the training of Timothy Bradley, preparing him for a welterweight title showdown on November 7, 2015, with highly regarded Brandon Rios. Looking better than ever, Bradley stopped Rios in the ninth round. It was the first time in 37 professional fights that Rios had failed to go the distance. Bradley told reporters, "I finally have a real trainer!" Indeed, his victory had "old school" written all over it. Bradley stated that Atlas's schooling taught him more about technique and strategy than ever before. Good for him—and good for boxing.

Atlas's job was not easy. He had a willing student in Bradley but also a fighter who had been worn out in fights where the strategy was simply to outwork the opponent. Bradley had also made the mistake in the past of exercising with heavy weights to increase his strength and punching power. Of course this misguided approach did just the opposite by making him muscle bound and robbing him of his punching power. Bradley's overdeveloped pecs and lats were very impressive if he was entered into a bodybuilding contest, but he could barely dent an egg with his featherlike punches. Nevertheless, Atlas recognized a desire by Bradley to do whatever was necessary to turn his boxing career around and was willing to work with him and achieve the desired results.

Trainers take note: Watch the tape of the Bradley vs. Rios fight, especially the instruction given to Bradley between rounds. What a delight to watch a boxer actually attempt to think and avoid punishment by using tried-and-true methods of the type that had been effective for almost a century but are virtually forgotten today.

Rios could have tried to counter Bradley's hit and move strategy, but he simply had no answers—and neither did his clueless corner men. Rios kept coming straight ahead and made no attempt at all to cut off the ring, or duck Bradley's counterpunches, or throw more jabs in an attempt to disrupt his rhythm. The pitiful instructions (or lack thereof) he received was typical. In between rounds the microphone (one was placed in each boxer's corner) picked up Rios's trainers telling him to "throw more punches . . . throw faster punches" and of course the oft-heard expletive-

Teddy Atlas instructs Tim Bradley on the heavy bag. *Courtesy Dr. Theodore A. Atlas Foundation*

laced "What the f–k are you waiting for! . . . C'mon, go for it!" That's it. No strategic advice was given at any time. Not even at the basest level. Why are such people even allowed into the corner? Why isn't there some sort of licensing procedure to make sure trainers have at least a minimum of boxing knowledge? It is so disheartening to see how dumbed down this sport has become.

Compare the above to a sampling of Atlas's instructions to Bradley between rounds: "Control the outside and don't stay in one place too long . . . use your jab and move to your left and then move to the right and set something up . . . catch him as he comes in and don't drop your hands . . . move off to the side after landing your jab." Atlas kept reminding Bradley to "control the geography of the ring" (meaning use footwork). Obviously these basic boxing moves had been practiced over and over throughout their training sessions. Another move involved Bradley stepping to his left after landing a jab and quickly landing a left uppercut to Rios's midsection. His incessant body punching eventually brought Rios to his knees in the ninth round and he was counted out. (If Bradley had more power, this fight would have ended much earlier.) It is worth noting that over 50 percent of Bradley's punches were aimed at Rios's midsection. This was a common practice among the top fighters of decades past but is virtually unheard of today.

Over the past 20 years, for a variety of reasons (see the author's book *The Arc of Boxing: The Rise and Decline of the Sweet Science* for a full explanation), boxing technique has fallen to its lowest level in over 100 years. Defense has become a lost art along with so much else that is missing at virtually every level. That is why Bradley's new evasive style, mobile footwork, body punches, and his effective and intelligent use of the left jab was like a dose of fresh air—at least to those who can recognize and appreciate such things.

Perhaps I am being overly optimistic, but are we seeing a trend developing here? In October 2015, we saw two rare demonstrations of some old-school boxing skills. First flyweight champion Roman "Chocolatito" Gonzalez gave a wonderful display of effective aggression while chalking up his 44th straight victory. On the same night Gennady Golovkin, the true middleweight champion, showed how effective a left jab can be when used properly to set up power punches and eventually wear down a tough and determined opponent.

Years ago these talented boxers would be considered excellent prospects because they would be competing in a much tougher environment, but today their use of solid but basic boxing techniques makes them stand head and shoulders above a very mediocre field of contenders.

Let's hope that other boxers and trainers begin to understand that boxing is an art—the art of self-defense. This will not only result in more interesting matches but will make a dangerous sport safer. Two boxers moving toward each other like two trucks in a mindless demolition derby is not boxing.

28
BOXING'S FIVE-DECADE MEN
(October 24, 2018)

The human body is capable of amazing feats of athleticism. But how can a body sustain the rigors and abuse of a professional boxing career over five consecutive decades?! In this article, I looked at three boxers who did just that. File this one under "Believe It or Not!"

In September 2018, I had the good fortune to meet up with the great Roberto Duran. The legendary four-division world champion was the guest of honor at the annual Ring 10 Veteran Boxers Association benefit. It was a rare public appearance for the now 67-year-old warrior. Yes, 67! As expected, Duran's presence electrified the 400-plus fans in attendance.

The fighter nicknamed "Manos de Piedra" (Hands of Stone) engaged in 119 bouts and knocked out 70 opponents. While those stats are indeed impressive (especially the number of knockouts), they are not unique. Boxers who accumulated 100 or more bouts were quite common during the first half of the 20th century. In addition, 55 other pro boxers have knocked out 70 or more opponents. But, in spite of that, Roberto Duran's record stands out for another reason that very few can match: he is one of only three boxers in the entire history of the sport who fought in five consecutive decades.

What qualities did these boxers possess that allowed them to survive for so many years in their brutal profession? I came to the conclusion that the first ingredient had to be a deep understanding of their craft. All three were well schooled in the finer points of boxing technique. That quality was further enhanced by the seasoning they gradually acquired during their first decade of competition. On top of that they had to be flexible and resourceful enough to make the necessary adjustments as they aged. It also helped that all three had great chins.

These boxers weren't just great athletes—they were very *smart* athletes. They were able to compensate for deteriorating speed and reflexes by combining experience with superior athletic intelligence and excellent defensive strategies. Even near the end of their careers they were rarely knocked out or subject to a sustained beating. It was a method utilized to great success by two former champions who stretched their careers to the maximum and are among the dozen master boxers who just missed the five-decade mark: welterweight champion Jack Britton (1904–1930) and light heavyweight champion Archie Moore (1935–1963). Both used an amalgam of those four skill sets—athletic intelligence, flexibility, superior defensive strategies, and vast experience— to keep them in the game long after their contemporaries had retired.

I could have added another master boxer to the list, the former heavyweight champion Jack Johnson. But despite his having fought in five consecutive decades (1897–1930), there were several gaps in his record. Johnson remained active up to his winning the title in 1908. But from 1911 to 1930 there were seven years in which he did not engage in a single prizefight. I felt this was too much inactivity, even for a five-decade man, so I decided that only a fighter with not more than three separate years without a fight could qualify. Those ground rules would have applied to George Foreman as well. Big George fought in four separate decades (1964–1997) but was idle from 1978 to 1986, so even if he had fought into a fifth decade that lengthy stretch of inactivity would disqualify him.

In chronological order, here are the three members of the exclusive "Five Decade" club:

Kid Azteca (real name Luis Villanueva Paramo, a.k.a. Kid Chino): Professional career 1929 to 1961. Won-lost-draw record: 192–47–11, including 114 wins by knockout. A legend in Mexico, and one of that country's greatest fighters, the 5'8", 147-pound welterweight had his first pro bout when Herbert Hoover was president, Babe Ruth was still belting out home runs for the Yankees, and Gene Tunney was heavyweight champion. When, 32 years later, he entered the ring at age 47 for his last pro bout, Mickey Mantle and Roger Maris were the home run

Legendary Mexican welterweight Kid Azteca fought from 1929 to 1961.
Steve Lott/Boxing Hall of Fame Las Vegas

kings for the Yankees, Floyd Patterson was heavyweight champion, and John F. Kennedy was president. But longevity is not the only item that distinguishes Azteca's boxing career. He was a top ten title contender for seven years. Between October 1933 and May 1941 (40 months) Azteca was ranked as high as the number one world welterweight contender by *The Ring* magazine.

Kid Azteca earned his rating with wins over contenders Joe Glick, Young Peter Jackson, Eddie Kid Wolfe, Baby Joe Gans, the Cocoa Kid, Izzy Jannazzo, Morrie Sherman, and future middleweight champion Ceferino Garcia (two out of three). In 1939 he lost a close decision to future welterweight champion Fritzie Zivic. After losing twice to Zivic in return matches, Azteca finally gained a victory in 1947. Other notable opponents were Jackie Wilson, Baby Casanova, Bep van Klaveren, Leon Zorrita, and former lightweight champion Sammy Angott. Most of his fights took place in Mexico City, but he also appeared in Los Angeles, Texas, and

South American rings. There are no gaps in his record—he engaged in at least one or more fights every year from 1929 to 1961.

Throughout his life Kid Azteca remained hugely popular among his countrymen and even appeared in several movies produced in Mexico. Unfortunately there are no films of him in action. Nevertheless, I don't think it would be a stretch, considering his career and high rating, to say that Azteca possessed an outstanding defense. Fighters who are "catchers" or who engage in too many wars are worn out quickly and cannot sustain a career anywhere near that length of time.

Roberto Duran: Professional career 1968 to 2001. Won-lost record: 103–16, including 70 wins by knockout.

The street urchin who emerged from the slums of Panama to become one of the sport's greatest and most charismatic champions turned pro at the age of 16. Five decades later, on July 14, 2001, in the final fight of his career, the 50-year-old legend lost a unanimous 12-round decision to 39-year-old Hector Camacho.

The Roberto Duran who lost to Camacho was many years past his prime. He was not the same fighter who took down Ken Buchanan, Esteban De Jesus, Sugar Ray Leonard, Ray Lampkin, Pepino Cuevas, and Iran Barkley. Nevertheless, he could still display the subtle boxing moves and ring smarts that kept him from being dominated by much younger opponents.

Roberto Duran was one of the greatest punchers in the history of the lightweight division. But, as sometimes happens with exciting punchers who can also box, their cleverness often goes unrecognized or underappreciated. Duran had a world of natural ability, but he also was intelligent enough to understand that there was far more to this sport than throwing punches at an opponent. There is a telling quote in Kelly Nicholson's excellent article on Duran: "As to the motivation for his career, Duran would say shortly before the first fight with Leonard, 'I got into boxing to learn it. . . . I didn't enter the ring to get out of the gutter. Those are stories. I got into it because I like it.'"[1]

Duran's nascent career benefited tremendously from the expert teaching of his two old-school master trainers Freddie Brown and Ray Arcel. These two professors of pugilism had nearly 100 years of combined experience. They answered his desire to learn as much as possible about his craft, smoothed out the rough edges, and made him even more dangerous.

They taught him the tricks of his trade, and the result was that Duran eventually developed into the type of throwback fighter that is virtually extinct today.

Watch a video of any Duran fight after 1982 and you will see that even in his dotage he never gets trapped on the ropes, often rides with and slips punches aimed at his head, and performs subtle feints to lure his opponents into making mistakes that are paid for with damaging and accurate counterpunches (especially to the body). As he moved up in weight and as he aged, Duran's punch was not as devastating as it had been during his eight-year tenure as lightweight champion. As a result, he had to rely more on his strategic boxing skills. To watch Roberto Duran fight is to experience a textbook lesson in the lost art of boxing. He is one of the few genuine ring greats who still walks among us.

Saoul Mamby: Professional career 1969 to 2008. Won-lost-draw record: 45–34–6, including 18 wins by knockout.

It is virtually impossible to go through an entire professional boxing career and expect to come out relatively unscathed. But if anyone came close to achieving such a goal, that person would be Saoul Mamby, which is all the more remarkable since he had his last professional fight at the age of 60!

Just as there are born punchers, I believe there are also born boxers. What I mean is that some neophyte boxers seem to grasp the concepts of on-balance defensive boxing more readily than most. Perhaps it's a genetic disposition that tells them it is better to give than to receive.

Saoul Mamby never thought it a good idea to receive a punch in exchange for the opportunity to land one of his own. He did not seek a knockout victory, although if presented with the opportunity his solid right cross was capable of dropping an opponent. His basic strategy involved keeping his hands up to protect his chin, using a busy left jab to keep an opponent off balance, and always keep moving. He never threw a right-hand punch unless he deemed it safe to do so. It was a style that didn't win fans, but it kept him from taking a sustained beating.

Mamby's defensive prowess was put to the test when he faced a prime Roberto Duran on May 4, 1976, in a nontitle ten-round bout. The lightweight champion tried mightily to make Mamby his 49th knockout victim. Duran won the unanimous decision, but he did not come close to scoring a knockout. Six months later Mamby faced another test when he crossed gloves with the formidable former champion Antonio Cervantes, who had knocked out nine of his previous ten opponents. Like Duran, Cervantes could not find his elusive opponent's chin and had to settle for a unanimous decision.

His first attempt to win a title occurred in 1977 and resulted in a controversial split-decision loss to the WBC super lightweight champion Saensak Muangsurin. The fight took place in Thailand, the champion's home turf. Mamby believed he was the victim of a hometown decision.

Three years later, in his second try for the 140-pound title, he challenged Sang Hyun Kim of Korea. Once again he found himself fighting in his opponent's backyard. Not willing to take any chances on a hometown decision, the 32-year-old challenger displayed a more aggressive style and was intent on ending the fight before it went to a decision. In the 14th round, Mamby saw an opening and landed a powerful right cross on Kim's jaw that dropped him for the full count.

Winning a world title seemed to energize Mamby, and in his first defense he stopped former lightweight champion Esteban De Jesus in the 13th round. Four more successful defenses followed before he lost a controversial 15-round split decision to Leroy Haley. After outpointing Monroe Brooks, he was given a chance to regain the title from Haley but lost another close decision. In 1984, in his final title challenge, he fought Billy Costello for the super lightweight championship and lost a 12-round unanimous decision.

By the 1990s Mamby was losing more often (he won only five of his last 17 bouts) but, win or lose, he continued to frustrate opponents. Mamby finally announced his retirement on May 19, 2000, in Greensboro, North Carolina, after losing an eight-round decision to Kent Hardee. He was 52 years old.

Eight years later Mamby attempted a comeback. After being told that no boxing commission would dare license a 60-year-old prizefighter, Mamby found a place that would—the Cayman Islands. On March 8, 2008, he lost a ten-round decision to a 31-year-old boxer with a dismal 6–26 won-lost record. As usual Saoul emerged unscathed.

NOTES

Preface

1. Pete Hamill, "Blood on Their Hands," *Esquire*, June 1996, 93.

2. Mike Silver, *The Arc of Boxing: The Rise and Decline of the Sweet Science* (Jefferson, N.C., McFarland, 2008), 202–4.

3. Jim Brady, *Boxing Confidential: Power, Corruption and the Biggest Prize in Sport* (Lytham Lancashire, UK: Milo Books, 2002), 16.

4. Budd Schulberg, "In Defense of Boxing," *Newsday*, April 21, 1985, 10, 11, 34.

5. John V. Grombach, *The Saga of the Fist: The 9,000 Year Story of Boxing in Text and Pictures* (South Brunswick, N.J.: A.S. Barnes, 1977), 128.

6. Harvey Marc Zucker and Lawrence J. Babich, *Sports Films: A Complete Reference* (Jefferson, N.C.: McFarland, 1987), 53–144.

Chapter One

1. Michael B. Katz and Mark J. Stern, "Poverty in Twentieth-Century America," Working Paper No. 7, November 2007, 6.

2. Mike Silver, *Stars in the Ring: Jewish Champions in the Golden Age of Boxing* (Guilford, Conn.: Lyons, 2016), 6.

3. Steven A. Riess, *City Games: The Evolution of American Urban Society and the Rise of Sports* (Urbana: University of Illinois Press, 1989), 116.

4. Mike Silver, *The Arc of Boxing: The Rise and Decline of the Sweet Science* (Jefferson, N.C.: McFarland, 2008).

5. Silver, *The Arc of Boxing*, 35.

6. Ronald K. Fried, *Corner Men: Great Boxing Trainers* (New York: Four Walls Eight Windows, 1991), 43.

7. Lawrence K. Ritter, *East Side West Side: Tales of New York Sporting Life, 1910–1960* (Kansas City, Mo.: Total Sports, 1998), 183.

8. Murray Rose, "Farewell to Stillman's," *Boxing Illustrated & Wrestling News*, October 1961, 21.

9. Ritter, *East Side West Side*, 183.

10. Ritter, *East Side West Side*, 182.

11. Rose, "Farewell to Stillman's," 20.

12. Fried, *Corner Men*, 52.

13. Fried, *Corner Men*, 32.

Chapter Two

1. Sammy Luftspring with Brian Swarbrick, *Call Me Sammy* (Scarborough, ON: Prentice Hall of Canada, 1975), 180–82.

Chapter Three

1. See chapter 11.

Chapter Six

1. Interview with the author February 23, 1978.

2. "Johnny Kilbane Outpointed by Benny Valger in Their Eight-Round Bout at Newark," *New York Times*, February 26, 1920, 19.

3. "Terris Is Winner over Benny Valger," *New York Times*, August 20, 1924, 9.

4. "Goodrich Is Victor on Foul in 6th/Seeman Put Out of Tourney by Valger," *New York Times*, May 19, 1925, 16.

5. James P. Dawson, "Valger Outpointed by Jimmy Goodrich," *New York Times*, February 26, 1920, 18.

6. "Benny Valger contre le Lyonnais Julien," *L'Auto*, January 15, 1929, 1.

7. John Jarrett, *Champ in the Corner: The Ray Arcel Story* (Gloucestershire, UK: Stadia, 2007), 76.

Chapter Seven

1. Gilbert Rogin, "Like a Little Lost Puppet," *Sports Illustrated*, May 29, 1961, 58.
2. Rogin, "Like a Little Lost Puppet," 58.
3. Rogin, "Like a Little Lost Puppet," 58.
4. "Yemini Accused of Storming Cockpit," *San Francisco Chronicle*, May 10, 2011.

Chapter Eight

1. Michael T. Isenberg, *John L. Sullivan and His America* (Urbana: University of Illinois Press, 1988), 67.
2. Sarah Kurchak, "The Strenuous Life: Theodore Roosevelt Mixed Martial Arts," Vice.com, May 4, 2015, www.vice.com/en.../the-strenuous -life-theodore -roosevelts-mixed-martial-arts (accessed November 10, 2015).
3. "On Boxing," *This Rugged Life* (blog), February 5, 2010, thisruggedlife .blogspot.com (accessed November 12, 2015).
4. Isenberg, *John L. Sullivan and His America*, 346.

Chapter Nine

1. Mike Silver, "Fight Manager Irving Cohen; An Honest Man in a Crooked Sport," *The Ring*, February 1995, 63.
2. Silver, "Fight Manager Irving Cohen," 63.
3. Silver, "Fight Manager Irving Cohen," 63.
4. Teddy Brenner, as told to Barney Nagler, *Only the Ring Was Square* (Englewood Cliffs, N.J.: Prentice Hall, 1981), 19–20.
5. Silver, "Fight Manager Irving Cohen," 64.
6. Author interview with Eddie Foy III, January 27, 2016.
7. Jack Cavanaugh, *Tunney: Boxing's Brainiest Champ and His Upset of the Great Jack Dempsey* (New York: Random House, 2006), quote on opening page, unnumbered.

Chapter Ten

1. Joseph R. Svinth, "Death under the Spotlight: Analyzing the Data; The Manuel Velazquez Boxing Fatality Collection," *Journal of Combative Sport*, No-

vember 2007, https://ejmas.com/jcs/jcsart_svinth_a_0700.htm (accessed July 29, 2019).

2. Ron Ross, *Nine, Ten, and Out! The Two Worlds of Emile Griffith* (New York: DiBella Entertainment, 2008), 60.

Chapter Eleven

1. "Jimmy Cannon Says," *New York Post*, June 28, 1951, 58.

2. Mike Casey, "Red of Tooth and Claw: Frazier's Anger Still Burns," *East Side Boxing*, May 30, 2009.

Chapter Thirteen

1. Everett M. Skehan, *Rocky Marciano: Biography of a First Son* (Boston: Houghton Mifflin, 1977), 207.

2. James Curl, *Jersey Joe Walcott: A Boxing Biography* (Jefferson, N.C.: McFarland, 2012), 44.

3. Skehan, *Rocky Marciano*, 209.

4. Skehan, *Rocky Marciano*, 208.

5. Jack Cashill, *Sucker Punch: The Hard Left Hook That Dazed Ali and Killed King's Dream* (Nashville, Tenn.: Nelson Current, 2006), 67.

6. "Sonny Liston vs. Cassius Clay (1st Meeting), BoxRec.com, last modified December 8, 2016, http://boxrec.com/media/index.php/Sonny_Liston_vs._Cassius_Clay_(1st_meeting).

7. David Remnick, *King of the World* (New York: Random House, 1998), 195.

Chapter Fourteen

1. Colleen Aycock and Mark Scott, *Joe Gans: A Biography of the First African American Boxing Champion* (Jefferson N.C.: McFarland, 2008), 156–57.

2. Aycock and Scott, *Joe Gans*, 162.

3. Aycock and Scott, *Joe Gans*, 204.

4. Aycock and Scott, *Joe Gans*, 174.

5. Aycock and Scott, *Joe Gans*, 177.

Chapter Fifteen

1. Interviews excerpted from Mike Silver, *The Arc of Boxing: The Rise and Decline of the Sweet Science* (Jefferson, N.C.: McFarland, 2008), 157–63.

2. In the September 12, 2015, fight, Mayweather was too fast for Berto and won an easy 12-round decision. After his victory, Mayweather announced his retirement.

Chapter Sixteen

1. David Margolick, *Beyond Glory: Joe Louis vs. Max Schmeling, and a World on the Brink* (New York: Random House, 2006), 20.
2. Author interview with Budd Schulberg, May 19, 1994.

Chapter Seventeen

1. Joe Frazier and William Detloff, *Box like the Pros* (New York: HarperCollins, 2006), xii.
2. Mike Silver, *The Arc of Boxing: The Rise and Decline of the Sweet Science* (Jefferson, N.C.: McFarland, 2008), 186.
3. Silver, *The Arc of Boxing*, 194–95.

Chapter Nineteen

1. Joyce Carol Oates, *On Boxing*, expanded ed. (Hopewell, N.J.: Ecco, 2002), 138 (originally published in 1987 by Dolphin/Doubleday).
2. Joseph C. Nichols, "Marciano Floored in Second Round, Stops Moore in Ninth to Keep Title," *New York Times*, September 22, 1955, 37.

Chapter Twenty

1. Gary Smith, "The Shadow Boxer," *Sports Illustrated*, April 18, 2005, 66.

Chapter Twenty-Two

1. Everett M. Skehan, *Rocky Marciano: Biography of a First Son* (Boston: Houghton Mifflin, 1977), 145.
2. Robert Mladinich, "Tiger Ted Lowry by the Tale," The Sweet Science, January 15, 2006, thesweetscience.com (accessed July 18, 2019).
3. "Tiger" Ted Lowry, *God's in My Corner: A Portrait of an American Boxer* (self-pub., PublishAmerica, 2007).

4. Jesse A. Linthicum, "Archie Moore Wins Decision," *Baltimore Sun*, August 3, 1948, 13.

Chapter Twenty-Three

1.   Curtis Cokes with Hugh Kayser, *The Complete Book of Boxing for Fighters and Fight Fans* (Palm Springs, Calif.: ETC, 1980).

2. My thanks to mutual friend Ken Burke for providing contact information for Curtis.

3. Cokes, *Complete Book of Boxing*, 21–22.

Chapter Twenty-Four

1. Pauline Kael, *5001 Nights at the Movies*, rev. ed. (New York: Henry Holt, 1991), 546.

2. This quote, and the quotes that follow, are from my interview with Roger Donoghue on May 18, 1994 (published in *The Ring* magazine, August 1994).

Chapter Twenty-Six

1. Harvey Marc Zucker and Lawrence J. Babich, *Sports Films: A Complete Reference* (Jefferson, N.C.: McFarland, 1987), 53–144.

Chapter Twenty-Eight

1. Kelly Nicholson, "The Panamanian Devil," *International Boxing Research Journal*, September 2018.

SOURCES

1. Boxing in Olde New York: Unforgettable Stillman's Gym
   (Stephen H. Norwood, ed., *New York Sports: Glamour and Grit in the Empire City* [Fayetteville: University of Arkansas Press, 2018])

2. The Night the Referee Hit Back
   (June 11, 2014, www.Boxing.com)

3. Ali vs Shavers: The Morning After
   (September 30, 1977, *News World* newspaper)

4. No Heart-Shaped Boxes on This Valentine's Day
   (February 14, 2003, www.ESPNClassic.com)

5. Where Were You on March 8, 1971?
   (March 8, 2003, www.ESPNClassic.com)

6. Benny Valgar: Forgotten Boxing Master
   (September 2008, *Journal of the International Boxing Research Organization*)

7. Boxers 2, Strongmen 0
   (April 18, 2013, www.Boxing.com)

8. The President Boxer
   (November 17, 2015, www.BoxingOverBroadway.com)

9. The Other Billy Graham
   (March 2, 2016, www.Boxing.com)

10. Don't Blame Ruby: A Boxing Tragedy Revisited
    (July 30, 2012, www.Boxing.com)

11. The Myth of "The Thrilla in Manila"
    (September 30, 2012, www.Boxing.com)

12. Get in Line Pacquiao–Marquez IV: Boxing's Top Ten One-Punch KOs
    (January 2, 2013, www.Boxing.com)

13. Foul Play in Philly
    (April 30, 2014, www.Boxing.com)

14. Fights of the Century: Then . . . and Now
    (May 17, 2015, www.Boxing.com)

15. Is Floyd Mayweather Jr. an All-Time Great Boxer? The Experts Weigh In
    (September 7, 2015, www.BoxingOverBroadway.com)

16. Boxing's Ten Greatest Quotes
    (October 25, 2015, www.BoxingOverBroadway.com)

17. Dempsey's Arm and the State of Modern Boxing
    (December 23, 2015, www.Boxing.com)

18. A World of Professional Amateurs
    (September 1, 2018, www.BoxingOverBroadway.com)

19. Archie Moore
    (May 3, 2018, www.BoxingOverBroadway.com; interview conducted February 26, 1983)

20. Emile Griffith
    (Unpublished interview, January 10, 1998)

21. Carlos Ortiz
    (Unpublished interview, February 11, 1998)

22. Ted Lowry
    (Unpublished interview, March 12, 2003)

23. Curtis Cokes
    (August 27, 2014, www.BoxingOverBroadway.com; interviewed August 20, 2014)

24. "I Coulda Been a Contender": Roger Donoghue, the Man Who Taught Brando How to Box (August 1994, *The Ring* magazine)

25. The Brooklyn Kid vs. the Marsupial Mauler
    (February 28, 2014, www.Boxing.com)

26. So You Wanna Be a Boxer?
    (July 6, 2014, www.Boxing.com)

27. Teddy's Master Class
    (November 10, 2015, wwwBoxingOverBroadway.com)

28. Boxing's Five-Decade Men
    (October 24, 2018, www.BoxingOverBroadway.com)

INDEX

ABOUT THE AUTHOR

Mike Silver is an internationally known boxing expert and commentator. He received the Bert Sugar Award for boxing journalism presented by the New York Veteran Boxers Association (Ring 10), and the Rocky Marciano Media Award given by the American Association for the Improvement of Boxing. Silver has also been honored with the Boston Veteran Boxers Association's Champion of the Year Award (2010). His articles have appeared in the *New York Times*, *The Ring* magazine, ESPN.com, Boxing OverBroadway.com, and Boxing.com. He is the author of two previous books: *The Arc of Boxing: The Rise and Decline of the Sweet Science* and *Stars in the Ring: Jewish Champions in the Golden Age of Boxing*.